# Gandhi Revisited

# Gandhi Revisited

*Edited by*

Dr. A.B.S.V. Ranga Rao
Prof. M. Lakshmipathi Raju

GANDHIAN STUDIES CENTRE
Andhra University
Visakhapatnam

AKANSHA PUBLISHING HOUSE
NEW DELHI • GUWAHATI • VISAKHAPATNAM

**AKANSHA PUBLISHING HOUSE**
4649-B/21, Ansari Road
Daryaganj, New Delhi-110002
Phones: 23268193, 09435116718
Email: ektabooks@yahoo.com
visit us: www.akanshapublishinghouse.com

*Gandhi Revisited*



First Published 2011

ISBN 978-81-8370-296-6



**PRINTED IN INDIA**

Published by Akansha Publishing House, New Delhi-110002 and printed at Harmain Offset Printers, Delhi.

# Contents

**SECTION – III**
**Gandhi's Constructive Programme**

# Foreword

It gives me immense pleasure to write foreword to the volume entitled, 'Gandhi Revisited', edited by Dr. A.B.S.V. Ranga Rao and Prof. M. Lakshmipathi Raju. I am glad that the Gandhian Studies Centre is bringing out into book form, the seminar proceedings and the collection of papers authored by experienced faculty members and scholars of various universities on Gandhi at a time when there is decadence of ethical and human values. The authors attempted to discuss the relevance of Gandhian ideology to remedy the present day evils and manifold crises that have confronted the contemporary world.

Gandhi challenges the deep inequalities he finds in India and offers a powerful defense of autonomy and, alongside a comprehensive critique of western modernity and modernization. He attacks colonialism as well as 'Untouchability because each subordinates the individual. Gandhi challenges modernity and modernization because, he sees each disabling men and women, and he confronts violence because, it treats people as a means to be used for the benefit of the powerful.

Gandhiji initiated constructive social welfare programmes designed to remove the evils that had crept into society. His constructive programme found ready acceptance among people. His concept of constructive work is not merely for producing things; it is the means of educating and spiritualizing man. It means developing self-discipline and self control. Gandhi gave to the world new and revolutionary concepts such as satyagraha (truth force), sarvodaya (welfare of all) and santhi sena (peace - brigade). These Gandhian concepts are found to gain greater relevance in the coming years.

There is, in fact, an endless array of problems that have engulfed the whole world, many of them are man-made and need to be tackled in the interest of peace, progress and sustainable development of the entire world. The UNESCO has proclaimed the decade 2001-2010 as the 'International decade of Culture of Peace and Non-violence to explore the possibilities of implementing Gandhian techniques for managing the problems of the world. The former president of South Africa and the ardent follower of Mahatma Gandhi, Nelson Mandela in 1999 aptly pointed out that the 21st century would be the Gandhian century. Truth and Non-violence are eternal and universal. The philosophy of Gandhi is mainly based on these principles.

Mahatma Gandhi stood for the higher values of peace and non-violence. He strived and sacrificed all his life for spreading the message of non-violence and it is no exaggeration to say that Gandhi is the embodiment and personification of non-violence. The name of Gandhi has become almost a synonym for non-violence. The United Nations has rightly declared October 2nd as the International Day of Non-violence. For perpetuation of human race and for the very existence of life on earth, there is no other alternative except to follow to the Gandhian way of life. We have to choose between Atom and Ahimsa, Sarvodaya and Sarvanasha (total annihilation of mankind), non-violence and non-existence.

Mahatma Gandhi, an apostle of peace and non-violence waged war without violence against the mighty British empire to win freedom for the country. He also waged war- a war of good vs evil, a war of virtues vs vices, a war of material prosperity vs peace of mind.

The paper writers dealt with wide range of issues relating to Gandhian ideology from historical perspectives to social justice, democracy, ethical values, non-violence, truth, soul force, global peace, social transformation and social reconstruction. I appreciate the judicious combination of the papers belonging to various disciplines compiled in this book, reflecting the Gandhian philosophy. The issues discussed in this volume are of transverse use for social scientists, policy makers, human rights activists and particularly for those who are working for social, transformation, social reconstruction, peace and justice.

I congratulate Dr. A.B.S.V. Ranga Rao, Programme Co-ordinator, Gandhian Studies Centre and Prof. M. Lakshmipathiraju, Co-ordinator, Department of Social Work, MR College, Vizianagaram for bringing out the edited volume on Gandhian Ideology. I am looking forward to see many more such activities by this Gandhian Studies Centre under the admirable and able guidance of Dr. A.B.S.V. Ranga Rao to spread the message of the Mahatma for the younger generation.

**Prof. Beela Satyanarayana**
Vice-Chancellor
Andhra University
Visakhapatnam

# Preface

The present volume is a collection of papers from eminent professors belonging to various disciplines, covering wide range of issues over which Gandhi bestowed his thought. He devoted his time and energy for realizing the virtues and values which he cherished and practiced as part of his mission for political independence, social reconstruction and spiritual realization. There is no human issue or aspect of life that is left untouched by Gandhi. He gave us the priceless gift of self-respect and sense of dignity as a nation along with the higher level of idealism of social, ethical and spiritual values of truth, non-violence , self-less service and sacrifice.

In view of the inter-disciplinary nature of the Gandhian thought and ideology, the papers have been arranged to make the volume more coherent and comprehensive in its scope, covering various aspects , by giving it a touch of sequence, logic, rationale, cohesion and above all an integration of the whole subject matter.

For the convenience of the treatment of the subject, the book is divided into four parts. The first part discusses Gandhi's Resistance to Hegemony. Prof. R.V.R.Chandra Sekhar Rao in his paper critically observes Gandhi's varieties of resistance to hegemony. Gandhi resisted the hegemony of the western paradigm which he saw as the dominant one engulfing Indian ethos. His Hind Swaraj contained the quintessence of this rejection. He regarded creeping westernization as the bane of Indian society. For the orthodox Hindu, criticism of Gandhi from the start rested on its conviction that Gandhi was destroyer of Hindu value system. The world at large regarded him as a saintly reformer than a bigoted Hindu chauvinist. His critics were at a loss to label him as a revivalist to reach out to Indian populace, he opted to adopt the strategy of appealing to many of the norms and forms of popular Hindu ideals yet at the same time with righteous indignation. Gandhi's ambivalence over confronting the native Hindu hegemonic legacy forever confuses what priority he accorded to his opposition to the western paradigm and to his critique of the indigenous hegemonic corpus. Gandhi believed that the spiritual heritage of Hinduism is universal in scope and essentially non-parochial. This, above all, made him spot light the positive aspects of Hinduism, sometimes exaggerating them, as in the case of non-violence and non-possession. His attack against the western tradition in similar strain identified westernization with secularization, even with atheism, again with exaggeration.

Prof. M.Lakshmipathi Raju and Dr. ABSV Ranga Rao discussed Gandhian concept of hegemony. Gandhi has deep commitment to the autonomy of everyone, since he has expansive view of power which he finds in the state, economy and society. He shows resistance to hegemony – political, economic and social. He wants victims to show resistance to their victimizers. He demands courageous, non-violent action in the face of injustice. Gandhi both resisted hegemony and the one that he himself created. Gandhi resisted the western paradigm which is dominant and engulfing Indian ethos. He regarded westernization as the bane of Indian society. Gandhi found many aspects of western civilization as unworthy legacy.

Ashutosh Pandey holds the view that Gandhi does not make any distinction between morality and politics and ethics and economics. He does not want only to raise the standard of democracy but the quality of democracy and the quality of living in such a system. Gandhi said that true democracy must be the ruler of the people in its real sense. The transfer of power from Britishers was not the end but the means for improving the condition of all men and women. He said, " the congress does not believe in the domination of any group or any community. It believes in democracy which includes in its orbit Muslims, Hindus and Christians – every one of the communities inhabiting this vast country".

To Gandhi, truth is the ultimate reality, " It is his conception of truth that is central to his life and work". He considered 'satyagraha' to be the best weapon for the evolutionary process of social change. Satyagraha is the natural outcome of his love for truth. Gandhi said that satyagraha was the inherent birthright of a person and it implied the exercise of the purest soul-force against injustice, oppression and exploitation.

Dr. D.V.R. Murthy and G. Anitha state in their paper that

Marxist scholars argue that the society is divided into different economic classes and that the economically dominant class is also the class that rules in views and ideas. Marx argued that the ruling class could impose their values and ideas on the rest of the population because of their privileged economic and political position. The author also observes that the rise of global media impacts people of the less developed countries in terms of their culture and their life styles. With the rapid flow of information, the western media dominate the international communication and they are culturally influencing the people of the Third World nations.

Dr. S. Subba Rao, while discussing about hegemony, observed that Gandhi challenged the conventional notions of authority, law and obligation by appealing to his conceptions of natural law or Dharma and self-suffering. There is no external authority that can claim a higher status than Satya either in the religious or in the political spheres. He was certain that it would be impossible for him to face the British rulers with any unethical and immoral method. Therefore, he chose to confront them by attracting the attention of their conscience and reason to their own misdeeds. He wanted to challenge the rulers on moral ground.

Dr. V.B.T. Sundari, in her paper delineated the resistance movement before Gandhi. She observed that the movements before Gandhi can be divided into three sections, pre-Mutiny (1757-1856), Mutiny(1857), and post-Mutiny (1857-1905). The cause for resistance movements were: financial policies of the Government, excessive land revenue demands, insults and humiliation, loss of independence, racial discrimination and social and religious grievances. Most of the resistance movements before Gandhi were crushed with brute force. Indians were not a match to the British in weapons. So Gandhi advocated non-violence and Satyagrah as weapons against them and obtained Independence.

Dr. G. Lakshmi discusses Gandhian approach to resistance and described it as non-violent defenses or non-violent direct action – a novel way to resist encroachments upon human freedom. Non-violent resistance is a strategy for countering the power of violent force with the power of an integrated system. She further holds that Gandhi's strategy aimed at making the unjust system unable to function by using non-violent measures and at the same time offering a constructive alternative. Gandhi employed a careful balance between the negative and positive-between campaigns of civil resistance and constructive programme. Gandhi thought, women were much better placed at the movements cultural and ideological levels to attempt the method of non-violent passive resistance. His approach led to the juxtaposition and demands of domestic obligation and public participation of women in India.

Sona Kanti Barua discussed the methods and forms of resistance to fight British imperialism, namely civil disobedience based on truth and non-violence, mass participation, non-cooperation, satyagraha, salt tax movement and swaraj(Home Rule). Gandhi helped to introduce to India and the world a completely a new set of weapons to fight foreign rule.

The second section deals with Gandhian approach to conflict resolution. Dr. A.N. Panda holds that Gandhiji outlined his own theory of conflict resolution. Gandhi put forward his method of dealing with a dispute and an adversary. Because of his own experience and pragmatic mind, he was able to provide alternative way to tackle a crisis situation. Gandhi believed that an unethical means never brought a good result and to him, violence was unethical. Hence he did not prefer the means of violence for challenging the bad governance of the rulers. He felt that instead of adopting the principles of 'blood for blood', it was easier to win over the enemy with the help of non-violent means. He wanted to challenge the rulers on moral ground. He preferred to awaken their conscience by his rational approach. Gandhi was convinced that violence would be a failure in the long run and only a peaceful means would bring an everlasting result and independence to India. To him, the eastern culture strongly supported the notions of peace and non-violence. Gandhi believed, " To use violence for securing rights may seem an easy path, but it proves to be thorny in the long run, those who live by sword also die by sword". He felt that violence bred violence and it would not bring a good result.

Dr. Nagaraju, Battu, states that the Harvard School of Business Management has hailed Mahatma Gandhi as management guru of the 20th century. His management was born out of non-violence, care, compassion and modern values of liberty, equality and fraternity. Adoption of the principles and

practices of decentralization in the Management domain is another example to Gandhi's relevance as Management Guru. In the context of Trusteeship theory of Gandhi the employee-employer relations are characterized as 'co-equals' or 'co-owners'. Gandhi believed that under the philosophy of trusteeship, there is no room for conflict of interests between workers and management. According to Gandhian philosophy, where conflicts exist, they should be resolved by 'satyagraha' i.e non-violent, non-cooperation. He pleaded that strike is the last weapon in the armoury of industrial workers and should not be resorted to unless all peaceful and constitutional methods of negotiations, conciliation and arbitration are exhausted. If we examine writings of Mahatma Gandhi from his collected works, we find that he gave importance to the workers and labourers in a factory as a major stakeholders. He further emphasized that "workmen should be regarded as equals with the shareholders

The Third section describes Gandhi's constructive programme. Ms. B.Lilly Grace Eunice and Mande Ramesh bring out the relevance of Gandhian Economic ideas to the modern society. Gandhi developed doctrine of trusteeship which alone can be the solution for the present day mal-distribution of wealth. Gandhi's economic ideas basically emanated from a strong argument to remove poverty, distress and reduce the gap between poverty and prosperity. He repeatedly emphasized that the people were exploited by the rich and accumulated wealth from the blood of the poor.

Gandhi worried about unemployment, underemployment and disguised employment in agricultural sector. So as to tackle this problem, he laid emphasis on the development of village industries, cottage industries as an effective remedy to solve the problem of unemployment. According to Gandhi; the usage of machines should be minimum when they are inevitable only but must not be allowed to displace human labour. The core contents of Gandhian Economics related to village self-sufficiency, removal of income inequality, poverty and employment generation. Gandhi clearly visualized the development of country was not possible without growing rural economy. As emphasized by Gandhi, we should wage war in the form of non-violent revolution for the eradication of poverty, by means of land distribution. Economists like E.F.

Schumacher considered Gandhi as the "greatest innovative and original economic thinker of the 20th century".

Prof. P. Srinivasa Subba Rao, Suseela Rani and G.V.L.Srikant observed that Gandhiji was against the use of machinery. He held that machinery displaced labour and hence concentrated wealth in the hands of the few. Gandhiji believed that the key to the country's progress lay in the strengthening of the decentralized, self sufficient, village economics and ethics. Economics that hurts the moral well-being of an individual or a nation is immoral, and therefore sinful. He opined that supreme consideration is to be given to man than the money. Gandhi laid special emphasis on 'plain living which helps in cutting down your wants and being self-reliant.

Prof. K. Visweswra Rao and Miss. P. Sailaja discuss in their paper Gandhi's perception of women. Gandhi was completely opposed to many social customs and traditions which had been oppressive of women in India. He also advocated equal rights for women. Gandhi was more concerned about the status of women. "His attitude to women's rights was uncompromising under all conditions". "He could visualize women only as man's companion, gifted with equal mental capacities, possessing 'the right to participate in every minute detail in the activities of man" and an equal right of freedom and liberty. Although, he had great reverence for the traditions of the country, he also realized that certain customs and traditions of the Indian society were antithetical to the spirit of development of the women of the nation. He defined dowry marriages as "Heartless". The custom of child marriage became a target of his criticisms. Gandhi was extremely perturbed by the plight of widows, particularly child widows According to Gandhi, education for women was the need of the time that would ensure their moral development and make them capable of occupying the same platform as that of men.

K.M. Kumar, P.M. Kumari and Prof. B.S. Rao observe in their paper, that there are certain unprivileged classes in the society. The lower class people (Harijans) and the female folk in all classes of society were considered as unprivileged. As the females are almost fifty percent of the population and if they remained powerless and downtrodden in the society, one cannot think of the

development of the economy. Hence empowerment of women has to be the ultimate goal to improve the quality of the society and development of the economy. Gandhiji really emphasized the empowerment of village women. In the agricultural operations, the women folk are equally engaged in the field with men apart from their household work. Gandhi wanted the mass education to both men and women and emphasis was given to the female folk as he believed that the female is to mould the family and the society. Once she is empowered with education, she can fight for her rights in the family and in the society and can obtain equal status in the social life.

Prof. M. Lakshmipathi Raju and Dr.V.Venkateswarlu hold that constructive programme is like preventive approach or preventive social work. According to Gandhiji's concept of village swaraj, every village has to think that he is the maker of his own destiny. He is his own legislator. Gandhi felt that the constructive programme is to enable masses to emerge out of unfreedom into freedom and out of economic and social deprivation into self-reliance and out of state alienation into cooperative living. The objective of constructive programme was to bring about socio-economic changes and reconstruction of social older based on freedom, equality and respect for individual personality. The ultimate purpose was to build a non-violent, non-exploitative social and economic order for a society based on the ideas of sarvodaya. The present and future crisis can be reduced by adopting fully constructive programme as evolved by Gandhi. Constructive work should become both a lamp and a mirror; it will show us what we are.

M. Gopi, T. Srinu and Prof. D. Shyamala Devi in their paper on "Gandhi and rural development", state that Gandhiji's approach to India's rural development was holistic and people centered. Gandhiji emphasized that people under decentralized economic and political system will be quite competent to run and manage their panchayats and other social self-governing institutions. He strongly pledged for decentralization through the organization of village panchayats. Gandhiji observed that in our villages there are inexhaustible resources not for commercial purposes in every case but certainly for local purposes in almost every case. Gandhiji believed, "If the village perishes, India will perish too". So there is greater need to improve the condition of people in rural areas.

Mande Ramesh and B.Lilly Grace Eumice held that Gandhian approach of rural development may be divided into three parts (1) city civilization and rationale for separate attention to the village; (2) model of an ideal village community, and (3) the measure for revitalization of the existing villages. According to Gandhiji, the basis of rural and urban relationship was conspiracy and exploitation of the former by the latter. Villages have to fend for themselves by becoming self-sufficient and self sustaining.

K. Hari Babu and A.S. Acharyulu explain in their paper Gandhi's views on Rural Development. According to them, Gandhi in his various speeches and articles written throughout the freedom struggle spoke highly of democratic decentralization and rural development. The rural character of the economy and the need for regeneration of rural life was stressed by Gandhi: He wrote in Harijan(Gandhi, 1936), "India is to be found not in few cities but in its 70,000 villages. But we town dwellers have believed that India is to be found in its towns and the villages were created to minister to our needs. We have hardly paused to inquire if those poor get sufficient to eat and clothe themselves with and whether they have a roof to shelter themselves from sun and rain".

Dr. N. Sreerama Murthy in his paper explains Gandhi's concept of rural development. Gandhi conceptualizes rural development in its totality, consistent with the Indian situation....His concept of rural development was not mere economic prosperity for few at the cost of many; it was the participation of the entire population in production as well as consumption "unto the least of all". The pathetic conditions of villages pained him. He maintained that Indian Villages were not originally like this and that the deplorable condition was brought by foreign rule and continuous neglect. He stressed the great importance of the village in the Indian social system; Gandhi declared that, "if the villages perish, India will perish too". (Harijan, 1936)

Prof. D. Syamala Devi, Prof. K.A.P. Laxmi and Ms. Sandhya stated in their paper that Gandhiji concentrated his entire attention on the development of rural areas. His ideas of rural reconstruction had two main aims to make the Indian villages self-sufficient and to make them independent of government to the possible extent. As part of a larger non-cooperation movement to reject British control over India, Gandhi launched the Khadi movement (alternatively called the Swadeshi movement) in 1915. Gandhi encouraged all Indians to wear Khadi to abolish mill cloth. In his 1908 book Hind Swaraj, Gandhi described the handloom and the spinning wheel as "The panacea for the growing pauperism in India. Gandhi encouraged women to make khadi, and fellow Indians to wear it. As Gandhi wrote, "My idea is to get these (Semi- starved, semi-employed) women to spin yarn and to clothe the people of India with Khadi woven out of it. The authors observed that one of the most vivid elements of Gandhi's struggle for people's self-reliance can be seen in the Khadi movement.

Dr. D. Pulla Rao discusses in his paper Gandhian approach for empowerment of the rural poor. Gandhiji, as a great participatory rural appraiser has made two basic observations. Firstly Indian agriculture cannot provide enough employment and income for all the rural population. Secondly the largest universally accepted handicraft shall be promoted among the rural masses for a better living. Gandhiji suggested the spinning wheel for the poverty stricken rural masses to provide them a better living. Gandhian prescription of empowerment of rural masses through creation of extra employment outside agriculture is highly valid than before.

Dr. Y. Ashok Kumar presents in his paper Gandhan vision for Harijan Upliftment. According to Gandhi, Harijans should not look upon themselves as lowly, weak or crippled. The disease of untouchability is fairly old in our society. Gandhi called these so-called religious sanctions as a serious stigma on the fair name of a society which have a deep rooted culture and historical tradition to support its identity. Caste Hindu had a personal obligation to fulfill towards the Harijans which they must do unconditionally and it was to be their atonement. He stated that rest of the world apart, in India who could be more friendless, helpless or weaker than the forty millions or more of Hindus of India who were classified as untouchables. Gandhi believed Hinduism will die if untouchability lives and untouchability has to die if Hindusim is to live (Yogesh Chandra,1947). Gandhi always preached to the Harijans, cleanliness, abstention from carrion eating and intoxicating drinks and drugs, necessity of taking education themselves. Gandhi always wished to give the Harijions a place of honor and respect in our society which was denied to him since centuries. Gandhi used to spend some time with the Harijan by living himself with them. He taught them the sense of cleanliness and advised them to raise their economic and social standard of hard work and honest means. He raised their colonies and advised them to raise their economic conditions to devise schemes of their Upliftment.

M. Gopi and Dr. T. Srinu delineated in their paper Gandhi's contribution to the eradication of Untouchability. Gandhi publicly treated the abolition of untouchability along with Hindu- Muslim unity as pre-requisites for India's true independence. He also made the name of 'Harijan' (Children of God) for the untouchables. Gandhi selected the Bhangi, a scavenger caste of north India, to represent the problem of untouchability. Gandhi opined that the colour prejudice in South Africa was nothing but a form of untouchability. Gandhi wrote in 1931, untouchability cannot last long. Some years ago we obstinately clung to it, today we are indifferent.

A. Srinivasacharyulu and K.Haribabu in their paper, emphasized the importance of Panchayat for achieving Swaraj. Mahatma Gandhi for the first time made mention of the Panchayats on February 14, 1946, in a Madras Missionary Conference, "Following the Swadeshi; I observe, the indigenous institutions and village panchayats hold me. The plea for greater autonomy to rural local bodies received conceptual strength with the advent of Mahatma Gandhi on national scene. Mahatma Gandhi was careful to state that his concept of "Ram Rajya" of which Panchayat autonomy was an integral component, was not derived from any specific historical period but it was an ideal construct based on the best features of different periods of ancient Indian history (Iqbal Narain, et, al, 1970) Gandhi believed in the supremacy of the people, and insisted on the people's democracy and sovereignty at the grass roots level, which he called Panchayat Raj. For Gandhiji, Panchayat Raj was a kind of commonwealth of reformed and reconstructed village communities.

Dr. Rajeswari Gullipilli and Dr. Rama Rao, Dharmana attempt to explain in their paper, the Gandhian approach to tribal development. Gandhiji mentioned that we should 'respect the tribals as humans and show sympathy towards them and bring them on par with other communities.'. Gandhiji repeatedly emphasized the need of social service to the poor and downtrodden communities including the advasis. Gandhi's principle of non-exploitation definitely protects the tribals from outside agencies which have the way for their Upliftment. The influence of Gandhiji on Pandit Jawaharlal Nehru was considered as origin of 'Panchsheel' approach of tribal development. Gandhiji urged the Upliftment of adivasis which was also considered by the Indian government after independence , in formulation of polices and programmes for tribal development.

Dr. P. Kishore kumar and Dr. A.B.S.V. Ranga Rao delineate the views of Gandhiji about youth. Gandhi did not consider youth as passive receivers; he sees youth involved in social movements for global change for peace, social justice, equity and creating peace for the mankind to live with dignity in diversity. Besides political movements, Gandhi called the youth to participate in various works like community development, swadishi, health and sanitation. He accepted many draw backs which inherited in the community and tried to remove them with the help of participation of youth. Gandhi persuaded many youth to live a simple life in ashramas and work constructively for the community around them.

The fourth section of the book discusses Gandhi's concept of swaraj' and Home Rule. Dr. Vijayam states that Hind swaraj is in the form of dialogue between Gandhi and the Indian extremists, who, in 1905, came to prominence in London. Gandhi's moral and principled argument with Savarkar was that violence was intrinsically evil and opposed to human values. Gandhi wanted an India where terrorism and violence were not an option to resolve conflicts. Gandhi pleaded for life-long for non-violence, love and understanding of opponent. Gandhi highlighted the need for ethical dimension in political and economic relations. Swaraj would not result in dependency. Gandhi's main concern was change in the value system of the people. Gandhi was convinced that it would be a doom for India, if it forgets strong points in the centuries of tradition and apes the west. Even though he did not use the term decentralization in the book, in effect, he was arguing for

Gram Swaraj or democratic decentralization. Dr. Vijayam points out that some of the ideas expressed by Gandhi in Hind Swaraj as sign-posts to the future generation to ward of themselves from impending dangers and pit-falls. He appeals to the humanity to follow a path to peace and human prosperity.

Dr. Ch. Mutyala Naidu, in his paper traced the historical background of the events leading to congress demand for Swaraj in 1906. But Swaraj was not meant clear, whether it was complete independence or continuation of British rule. Since India had got rich civilization and culture and attracted all over the world with her Vedas, Upanishad, Sanskrit language etc, she must have a government of her own based on her culture but not in continuation of English arms. Gandhiji's ideas of Hind Swaraj were in a process of evolution towards the ultimate goal of complete independence. He started with self government, later demanded outright withdrawal of the British and finally Purna Swaraj in 1929 at Lahore Congress.

Dr. N. Srinivas Rao expresses the views of Gandhi on hospitals and medical profession. Mahatma expressed that hospitals are institutions for propagating sin for the sake of mistaken care of human body, they kill thousand of animals. It is not necessary to take so many lives for the sake of our bodies. Mahatma also said that we become doctors so that we may obtain honors and riches. The author holds the view that there is gradual degeneration or morals in the society as a whole and it is reflecting on the medical profession also. The people should raise their voices, revolt against existing system.

Dr.T. Sobhasri and Dr. G. Sanjeevayya explain Gandhian concept of Home Rule and its relevance in the 21$^{st}$ century. Indian Home Rule (Hind Swaraj) is the dream project of Mahatma Gandhi. In their opinion, it teaches the gospel of love in place of hatred. It replaces violence with self sacrifice and soul force (satyagraha) against brute force. He was against to see swaraj being born because of dependency. Swaraj must ensure all Indians irrespective of their religion, caste, class, or education and provide equal opportunities in every sphere of life. He wished that one's moral values would underpin every activity. Gandhi draws attention to three major revolutions that we need today (1) revolution against unbridled consumerism (2) revolution against technology beyond human control; and (3) revolution to provide human motivations in our dealings with fellowmen. A nation that is desirous of securing Home rule cannot afford to despise its ancestors. According to Gandhi, "civilization in the real sense of the term, consists not in the multiplication but in the deliberate and voluntary reduction of wants.

Dr. Dasarathi Bhuyam explained in his paper, the concept of Swaraj and social democracy Gandhi did not consider swaraj to be a mere political concept. For him it had a wider connotation. His approach integrated swaraj at three levels, i.e, at the level of the individuals; swaraj to him means- controlling oneself or swaraj of the self. At the levels of the state, it meant national independence and at the levels of community, his dream was to establish gram swaraj and social democracy. His concept of true swaraj; is 'self rule' or self government by the people. The ideal basic unit of a democratic government was the Indian village where people lived as a face- to- face community.

K. Bhima Kumar in his paper explains the concept of swaraj as it appeared in Gandhi's writings. The concept of swaraj for the first time was expressed by Gandhi in his Hind swaraj. Swaraj for Gandhi had both a negative and a positive implication. Negatively speaking swaraj meant freedom from alien rule and its influence on civilization. Positively swaraj meant freedom for the whole people, the peasants, the workers, and the women, everyone included. Gandhiji's call for swaraj represents a genuine attempt to regain control of the "self" - our self-respect, self-responsibility and capacities for self-relization from institutions of dehumanization. The author observes that Swaraj was a great leveler that could actually inspire the common people of vast country who were not bound by the common ties of language, religion and culture. For Gandhi, Swaraj was never conceptualized in its narrow meaning of political independence; it was a holistic concept for him which included social, economic and moral dimensions apart from the political one.

*Editors*

# Acknowledgements

At the outset, we deem it a privilege to express our deep sense of gratitude to Prof. Beela Satyanarayana, former Vice-Chancellor, Andhra University for inspiring and guiding us in running the Centre for the last three years.

We thank him for his help and appreciation of the efforts of the Gandhian Studies Centre.

We are indebted to Prof. S.V. Sudhakar, Vice-Chancellor, Dr. B.R. Ambedkar University, Etcherla, and In-Charge Vice-Chancellor of Andhra University for writing forward for this book entitled; Gandhi Revisited and who is instrumental in making the Centre a reality.

It is also our bounden duty to acknowledge our respectful thanks to Prof. G. Hara Gopal, Central University, Hyderabad who has been a source of inspiration and for his encouragement and guidance and offering his valuable insights in the development of Gandhi literature from our Centre.

We owe a great debt of thanks to Sri K.S. Sastry, Secretary, Gandhi Centre, Visakhapatnam for his kind help and encouragement.

We express my thanks to Prof. K. Sreeranjani Subba Rao, Head of the department of Politics & Public administration, Prof. G. Veerraju, Head of the department of Philosophy and Prof. K. Visweswara Rao, Dean of Examinations, Andhra University for their constant support and valuable suggestions as members of the Advisory Committee of the Gandhian Studies Centre in running the Centre.

We immensely thank our dynamic former Vice-Chancellors of Andhra University, Prof. Y.C. Simhadri and Prof. L. Venugopal Reddy for their encouragement and also to the Registrar, P.V.G.D. Prasada Reddy for providing timely suggestions.

We must express my gratitude and appreciation to all the learned contributors who contributed their analytical articles to this volume.

We heartfully acknowledge the help of University Grants Commission, New Delhi for their generous financial help to the centre.

Our thanks are due to Dr. P. Kishore Kumar, Research Associate, Gandhian Studies Centre, for his support for facilitating the preparation and editing of the book.

We thank .our publishers, Akansha Publishing House, New Delhi for their promptness in bringing of out this book in so short a time.

We thank all others who in some way or the other, directly or indirectly contributed for the publication of the present volume.

*Prof. A.B.S.V. Ranga Rao*

*Prof. M. Lakshmipathi Raju*

# Our Contributors

**R.V.R. Chandara Sekar Rao,** Former Vice- Chancellor, Andhra Pradesh Open University, Hyderabad

**Professor M.Lakshmipathi Raju,** Department of Social work, M.R. PG College, Viziangaram

**Dr. A.B.S.V. Ranga Rao,** Associate Professor, Dept. of Social Work, Andhra University, Programme Co-ordinator, Gandhian Studies Centre, Visakhapatnam.

**Ashutosh Pandey,** Senior Lecturer, Department of Political Science A.S. (PG) College, Lakhaoti, Bulandarshahr, Uttar Pradesh.

**Dr. D.V.R. Murthy,** Associate Professor, Dept. of journalism and Mass Communication, Andhra University.

**Dr. G. Anita,** Assistant Professor, Department of Journalism and Mass Communication, Acharya Nagarjuna University, Guntur.

**Mr. S. Subba Rao,** Teaching Associate, Department of Social work, MR College, Vizianagaram.

**Mrs. V. B.T. Sundari,** Reader & Head, Department of History St. Joseph's College for Women, Visakhapatnam.

**Ms. G. Lakshmi,** Assistant Professor, Department of Dr. Ambedkar Open University, Hyderabad.

**Prof. A.N. Panda**, Associate Professor, P.G. Department Political Science, Panchayat (Govt. Lead College), Bargarh, Orissa.

**Dr. Naga Raju,** Assistant Professor, Bommidala, Dept. of HRM Acharya Nagarjuna University, Guntur, Andhra Pradesh.

**Dr. Lilly Grace Eunice**, Assistant Professor, Department of Economics, Dr. B.R. Ambedkar University, Etcherla, Srikakulam.

**Professor P. Srinivasa Subba Rao,** Head, Dept. of Management Studies, Commerce & HRM, M.R.P.G. College, Vizianagaram.

**Dr. P. Suseela,** Asst. Professor, Dept. of MBA. TRR College of Engineering, Hyderabad.

**Dr. G.V.L. Srikant,** Asst. Professor, Department of Management Studies, M.R.P.G. College, Vizianagaram.

**Professor K. Visweswara Rao,** Department of Social Work, Andhra University, Visakhapatnam

**Ms. P. Sailaja,** Guest Faculty, Dept. of Social work, Andhra University.

**Mr. K.M. Kumar,** Research Scholar, Department of Economics and Applied Economics, Acharya Nagarjuna University, Guntur.

**P.M. Kumari,** Research Scholar, Department of Economics and Applied Economics, Acharya Nagarjuna University, Guntur.

**Professor B.S. Rao,** Department of Economics and Applied Economics, Acharya Nagarjuna University, Guntur.

**Dr. V.Venkateswaralu,** Assistant Professor & Coordinator, Department of Sociology & Social Work, Acharya Nagarjuna University, Guntur.

**Mr. M. Gopi,** Research Scholar, Department of Politics & Public Administration, Andhra University, Visakhapatnam.

**Mr. T. Srinu,** Research Scholar, Department of Politics & Public Administration, Andhra University, Visakhapatnam.

**Professor D. Syamala Devi,** Department of Politics & Public Administration, Andhra University, Visakhapatnam.

**Dr. Mande Ramesh,** Post Doctoral Fellow, Department of Rural Development, Dr. B.R. Ambedkar University, Etcherla, Srikakulam.

**Mr. K. Hari Babu,** Research Scholar, Department of Political Science and Public Administration, Acharya Nagarjuna University, Guntur, AP.

**A. Srinivasacharyulu**, Research Scholar, Department of Politics & Public Administration, Acharya Nagarjuna University, Guntur.

**Dr. N. Srirama Murty,** Reader, P.G, Department of Social workD.N.R. College, Bhimavaram, Andhra Pradesh

**Prof. K.A.P.Lakshmi,** Department of Politics & Public Administration, Andhra University, Visakhapatnam.

**Ms. M. Sandya,** Research Scholar, Department of Politics & Public Administration, Andhra University, Visakhapatnam

**Professor D. Pulla Rao,** Dept. of Cooperation and Applied Economics, Andhra University, Visakhapatnam.

**Dr. Y. Ashok Kumar,** Assistant Professor, Department of Sociology & Social work, Acharya Nagarjuna University, Guntur, AP.

**Dr. G. Vijayam,** Athest Centre, Vijayawada, Andhra Pradesh.

**Professor Ch. Mutyalayya Naidu**, Dept. of History, Andhra University, Visakhapatnam

**Professor N. Srinivasa Rao,** HOD of Medicine, (Rtd.), Andhra Medical College), Visakhapatnam.

**Dr. T. Sobhasri,** Associate Professor, Dept. of Social Work, Andhra University, Visakahpatnam.

**Dr. G. Sanjeevayya,** Assistant Professor, Department of Social Work, Dr. B.R. Ambedkar University, Srikakulam, Etcherla 532410 (AP).

**Dr. Dasarathi Bhuyan,** Department of Political Science, Bellallaguntha Science College, Bellaguntha PO, Ganjam Dist., Orissa

**Dr. K. Bhima Kumar,** Lecturer, Department of Philosophy, University of Allahabad, Allahabad – 211002.

# Introduction

The eternal teachings of Gandhi – the great and benign lamp of wisdom and humanity are for posterity. He gave the priceless gift of self-respect and sense of dignity as a nation. His success rested upon the moral grandeur of his soul. He was a fighter who pushed back the mightiest empire on earth without the use of force. He was a spirit of profound wisdom and captivating humility. He was a frail man who confronted the brutality of military strength with the dignity of simple human being.

Gandhiji said, "We must go back to the spirit and ideas of those halcyon days when we practiced the philosophy of nation first and foremost; when we spoke of the language of the heart, when we breathed the air of idealism, when we walked hand-in-hand on the path of selfless service and sacrifice; when all sons and daughters of the motherland prided themselves in being, "Indian first, Indian last and Indian always." The need of the hour is that leaders and people should get inspired by Gandhi's teachings.

Mahatma Gandhi made significant contribution to social development by constructive work and programmes, aiming at removing of disabilities, of the people at the social, political, economic and spiritual levels. His work in South Africa for elimination of racial discrimination was remarkable. He has given us a new school of thought leading to social development.

Gandhiji's constructive programme is a comprehensive instrument of reconstruction which specially included the needs of non-persons, the outcastes, the half persons, the castaways and the lowliest and the poorest section of human population. Gandhi believed that "No social order, be it international or national or any lesser unity of human organization, can be considered 'normal' unless the creative energies of these 'Non-persons' and "half persons" are not harnessed fully by making them participate in socio-economic life on the basis of freedom, honour, dignity and equality." Gandhiji's constructive programmes included abolition of untouchability, promoting communal amity, prohibition, development of rural industries, basic education, emancipation of women, organization of peasantry, village sanitation, uplift of the adivasis, improvement of cattle, charka and khadi. He initiated constructive social welfare programmes designed to remove the evils that had crept into society. His constructive programmes found ready acceptance among people.

Gandhi's work, teachings and his thought have greater relevance. Gandhi's constructive programme is the key to the construction of poorna swaraj or complete independence by truthful and honest means and it has greater relevance today. We have to remember the relevance of his thought in our life today. The relevance of Gandhian thought is as old as the constructive programme. There are some concepts of Mahatma Gandhi; they are truth, non-violence (Ahimsa), ends and means, non-possession, trusteeship, vows, and gram swaraj. All these concepts are found to gain greater relevance and currency. Based on the two basic principles of truth and non-violence, Gandhi developed the concept of constructive programme. Mahatma Gandhi helped in setting up the Harijan Sevak Sangh in Delhi, and the All-Inda Village Industries Association etc. at Sevagram, Wardha, as part of constructive work; it was a movement for economic betterment and improvement in the social life of the people.

Religion for Gandhi means truth and Ahimsa. Religion means truth alone since truth includes ahimsa. The students should cultivate the habits of understanding the doctrines of great religions of the world. Preservation of one's own culture does not mean contempt for others. What is required is assimilation of the best in all cultures. The same should be the case with religion. His religious ideas were not revolutionary. He was quite traditional on certain matters. By religion he means religion of humanity and it includes the best of all the religions. He described religion as religion of truth. Instead of saying "god is truth", he was saying "truth is god". To be true to such religion one should be dedicated to continuing service of all life. One should be merged and identified with this limitless ocean of life. One cannot escape from social service. His views are at times too philosophical. He said "if I stop believing in god, I would die at once. For him god is love and truth. God is character and morality. God is fearlessness. God is light and source of life. God is above all and beyond all. God is conscience. Gandhi declined material world and material achievements. He was against consumerism because he wanted to promote the ideals of selfdenial, control of palate and control of animal passions.

Gandhi has developed ideas and concepts of Sarvodaya originally for the task of social construction. These ideas were manifestation of the transformation of Indian values, norms in the early $19^{th}$ century. The term Sarvodaya means "the rise or welfare of all." It consists of two Sanskrit words, Sarva and Udaya which mean "all and rise" respectively. Gandhiji borrowed this term from Jain writer Acharya Samanthabhadra. He used this term first as the title of the booklet in Gujarat of John Ruskin's famous book, "Unto the Last." The word Sarvodaya denotes way of life or ideology based on truth and non-violence as propounded by Gandhiji. Sarvodaya stands for philosophy of life and programmes of action which embrace many aspects of life. It means that the good of all resides in the good of every one and vice-versa. The goal of Sarvodaya Movement is to create a stateless and classless society through non-violent means; in such a society, there will not be exploitation of man by man. Every individual will have freedom of expression. There will not be any kind of hatred among the peoples of different religions. Every person will work according to his capacity both for himself and society.

The essential features of ideology of Sarvodaya may be stated as follows: Man is essentially good. Goodness is natural or god given. The search for truth, non-violence, altruism, courage, sacrifice etc., are the chief attributes of the goodness. Followers of the Sarvodaya believe that it is possible to promote the inherent goodness of man through proper education. Sarvodaya looks upon society as "union of spirits." They believe that through proper education, we can persuade people to remove violence and inequalities in society. Sarvodaya was the foundation of the alternative society to the present one which is based on competition and exploitation. Gandhiji's idea of Sarvodaya (the welfare of all) envisaged a reconstructed Indian village with people engaged in production for local use rather than profit. It was a society of equals, a kind of communication, wherein each individual would place the common welfare above their own self-interests and the principle of "from each according to their ability, to each according to their need", would be paramount.

This vision of society of small, largely self-sufficient village communities, a just and non-violent, political, social and economic order, was far removed from the modern industrial society. It aims at a complete transformation of the present social structure through quiet, constructive, social work carried on primarily at the village level with a view to initiating a non-violent revolution and establishing a more just social order. It looks upon service to society as the raison d'etre of man's life on earth.

Gandhiji said that, real Swaraj will come not by the acquisition of the authority by a few but by the acquisition of the capacity by all to resist authority when it is abused. In other words, Swaraj is to be obtained by educating the masses to a sense of their capacity to regulate and control authority. "The Swaraj of my dream recognizes no race or religious distinctions. Nor is to be the monopoly of the lettered persons nor yet of moneyed men. Swaraj is to be for all, including the farmer, but emphatically including the maimed, the blind, the starving toiling millions. It is complete independence of alien control and complete economic independence. So at one end you have political independence and at the other the economic. It has two other ends. One of them is moral and social; the corresponding end is Dharma, i.e., religion in the highest sense of the term. It includes Hinduism, Islam, Christianity, etc. but is superior to them all.

In Swaraj based on Ahimsa people need not know their rights, but it is necessary for them to know their duties. Those only are true rights which flow from a due performance of one's duties. To him who observes truth and non-violence comes prestige, and prestige brings rights. And people, who obtain rights as a result of performance of duty, exercise them only for the service of society, never for themselves. "I shall work for an India, in which the poorest shall feel that it is their country in whose making they have an effective voice, and India in which there shall be no high class and low class of people; an India in which all communities shall live in perfect harmony. There can be no harm in such an India for the curse of untouchability or the curse of intoxicating drinks and drugs. Women will enjoy same rights as men. Since we shall be at peace with all the rest of the world, neither exploiting, nor being exploited, we should have the smallest army imaginable. All interests not in conflict with the interests of the dumb millions will be scrupulously respected, whether foreign or indigenous. This is the India of my dreams.... I shall be satisfied with nothing less.

Gandhiji disliked modern civilization based on industrial growth and development. In 1940 he wrote that evils are inherent in industrialism. His idea of social development was different from industrial and economic growth and development. Industrialism is going to be a curse for mankind. Industrialism depends entirely on our capacity to exploit. Gandhiji objected to the craze for machinery, not machinery as such. He was against labour saving machinery which throw thousands of workers out of employment.

Industrialization on a mass scale will necessarily lead to passive or active exploitation of the villagers. "I do not believe that industrialization is necessary in any case for any country. It is much less so far India. Indeed I believe that Independent India can only discharge her duty towards a grooming world by adopting a simple but ennobled life by developing her thousands of cottages and living at peace with the world. High thinking is inconsistent with complicated material life based on high speed imposed on us by Mammon Worship. All the graces of life are possible only when we learn the art of living nobly.

Economics that hurt the moral well-being of an individual or a nation are immoral and, therefore, sinful. Thus, the economics that permit one country to prey upon another are immoral. It is sinful to buy and use articles made by sweated labour. According to Gandhi, the economic constitution of India and for that matter, of that of the world, should be such that no one under it should suffer from want of food and clothing. In other words, everybody should be able to get sufficient work to enable him to make the two ends meet. And this ideal can be universally utilized only if the means of production of the elementary necessaries of life remain in the control of the masses. An economics that inculcates Mammon worship, and enables the strong to amass wealth at the expense of the weak, is a false and dismal science. It spells death. True economics, on the other hand, stands for social justice; it promotes the good of all equally including the weakest, and is indispensable for decent life. Economic equality is the master key to non-violent independence. Working for economic equality means abolishing the eternal conflict between capital and labour. It means the leveling down of the few rich in whose hands is concentrated the bulk of the nation's wealth on the one hand, and a leveling up of the semi-starved naked millions on the other. A non-violent system of government is clearly an impossibility so long as the wide gulf between the rich and the hungry millions persists.

The contract between the palaces of New Delhi and the miserable hovels of the poor, labouring class cannot last one day in a free India in which the poor will enjoy the same power as the richest in the land. Simple home from which there is nothing to take away require no policing; the palaces of the rich must have strong guards to protect them against dacoity. So must huge factories. Rurally organized India will run less risk of foreign invasion than urbanized India.

As soon as man looks upon himself as a servant of society, earns for its sake, spends for it benefit, then purity enters into his earnings and there is Ahimsa in his venture. Moreover, if men's minds turn towards this way of life, there will come about a peaceful revolution in society, and that without any bitterness.

Civilization in the real sense of the term consists not in the multiplication but in the deliberate and voluntary reduction of wants, which promotes real happiness and contentment and increases the capacity for service. One can reduce one's wants by perseverance, and the reduction of wants makes for happiness – a healthy body and a peaceful life.

> "I never said that there should be cooperation between exploiter and the exploited so long as exploitation and the will to exploit persists. Only I do not believe that the capitalists and the landlords are all exploiters by an inherent necessity, or that there is a basic or irreconcilable antagonism between their interests and those of the masses. All exploitation is based on cooperation, willing or forced, of the exploited. However much we may desist admitting it the fact remains that there would be no exploitation if people refuse to obey the exploiter. What is needed is not the extinction of landlords and capitalists, but a transformation of the existing relationship between them and the masses into something healthier and purer."

Gandhi said, "I have found that the town-dweller has generally exploited the villager, in fact he has lived on the poor villager's subsistence. No one has, to my knowledge, said that the Indian villager has enough to keep body and soul together. On the contrary, they have admitted that the bulk of population lives on the verge of starvation and ten percent are semi-starved, and that millions have to rest content with a pinch of dirty salt and chillies and polished rice or parched grain". The cities are capable of taking care of themselves. It is the village we have to turn to. We have to disabuse them of their prejudice, their superstitions, their narrow outlook and we can do so in no other manner than that of staying amongst them and sharing their joys and sorrows and spreading education and intelligent information among them. The task before every lover of the country is how to reconstruct the villages of India so that it may be as easy for anyone to live in them as it is supposed to be in the cities. The village movement is as much an education of the city people as of the villagers. Workers drawn from cities have to develop village mentality and learn the art of living after the manner of villagers. This does not mean that they have to starve like the villagers. But it does mean that there must be radical change in the style of life.

The village communities should be revived. Indian villages produced and supplied to the Indian town and cities all their wants. India became impoverished when our cities became foreign markets and began to drain the villages dry by dumping cheap and shoddy goods from foreign lands. It is only when cities realize the duty of making an adequate return to the villages for the strength and substance which they derive from them, instead of selfishly exploiting them, that a healthy and moral relationship between the two will spring up. The villagers should develop such a high degree of skill that articles prepared by them should command a ready market outside.

Mechanization is good when the hands are too few for the work intended to be accomplished. It is an evil when there are more hands than required for the work, as is the case in India. The problem with us is not how to find leisure for the teeming millions inhabiting our villages. The problem is how to utilize their idle hours, which are equal to the working days six months in the year. Every mill generally is a menace to the villagers. Thus spinning and weaving mills have deprived the villagers of a substantial means of livelihood. "I would say that if the village perishes, India will perish too. India will be no more India. Her own mission in the world will get lost. The revival of the village is possible only when it is no more exploited. Industrialization on a mass scale will necessarily lead to passive or active exploitation of the villagers. Therefore, we have to concentrate on the village being self-contained, manufacturing mainly for use. Provided this character of the village industry is maintained, there would be no objection to villagers using even the modern machines and tools that they can make and can afford to use. Only they should not be used as means of exploitation of others.

Gandhi expressed that Swadeshi is not merely identified with the use of Khadi or what is produced in one's own country. Swadeshi means reliance on one's own strength. He took a vow that he would not use cloth made by foreign companies. He also associated self-reliance with Swaraj(independence). He has also not encouraged international trade saying that one should not tolerate economic drain. He also said that trade within the country should also not to be encouraged. People should use whatever things are available nearby. He was in favour of cottage industries, not heavy industries. He advocated maximum decentralization of political power, economic resources and judicial system.

Much of the deep poverty of the masses is due to the ruinous departure from Swadeshi in the economic and industrial life. If one article of commerce had been brought from outside India, she would be today a land flowing with milk and honey. "I think of Swadeshi not as a boycott movement undertaken by way of revenge. India can live for herself only if she produces and is helped to produce everything for her requirements within her own borders. A true votary of Swadeshi will not harbour ill will towards a foreigner and not be actuated by antagonism towards anybody on the earth. Swadeshi is not a cult of hatred. It is a doctrine of selfless service that has roots in the purest Ahimsa, i.e., love.

Drink is more a disease than a vice. The state does not cater to the vices of its people. We must not live in order to eat and drink and be merry, but eat and drink in order to make our bodies temples of god and use them for service of man. Gandhi holds drink to be more damnable than thieving and perhaps even prostitution. The drink habit destroys the soul of man and tends to turn him into a beast, incapable of distinguishing between wife, mother and sister. The drink and the drug evil is in many respects infinitely worse than the evil caused by malaria and the like; for, whilst the latter only injure the body, the former saps both body and soul. "I would rather have India reduced to a state of pauperism than have thousands of drunkards in our midst. I would rather have India without education if that is the price to be paid for making it dry. Nothing but ruin stares a nation in the face that is a prey to the drink habit. History records that empires have been destroyed through that habit.

Gandhi said, "I have a horror of smoking, as of wines. Smoking is considered to be a vice. It deadens one's conscience and is often worse than drink, in that it acts imperceptibly. It is a habit which is difficult to get rid of when once it seizes hold of a person. It is an expensive vice. It fouls the breath, discolors teeth and sometimes even causes cancer. It is an unclean habit". Smoking is in a way greater curse than drink, in as much as the victim does not realize the evil in time. It is not regarded as a sign of barbarism; it is even acclaimed by the civilized people. Tobacco has simply worked havoc among mankind. Once caught in its tangle, it is rare to find any one get out again. Tolstoy has called it the worst of all intoxicants. In India people use tobacco for smoking, snuffing and also for chewing. Several people are addicted to one, two or all the three of these habits. They do not appear loathsome to them. All the three are most dirty habits.

The correspondence that should exist between the school training and the character imbibed with the mother's milk and the training received through her sweet speech is absent when the school training is given through a foreign tongue. We are traitors to our mothers by remaining under such a system. A gulf has been created between the educated classes and the uneducated masses. The educated class experience the difficulty of contact with the masses. Owing to the barrier thus created, the flow of national life suffers impediment. The belief in the necessity of English training has enslaved us. It has unfitted us for true national service. By reason of English being the medium of instruction, our intellect has been segregated; we have been isolated from the masses; of all the superstitions that affect India, none is so great as that a knowledge of the English language is necessary for imbibing ideas of liberty and developing accuracy of thought.

Gandhi remarked "I would have our young men and young women with literacy tastes to learn much English and other world languages as they like, and then expect them to give the benefits of their learning to India, and to the world. The foreign medium has caused brain fag, put an undue strain upon the nerves of our children, made them crammers and imitators, unfitted them for original work".

The notion of education through handicraft rose from the contemplation of truth and love permeating life's activities. Love required that true education should be easily accessible to all and should be of use to every villager in his daily life. Such education was not derived from nor did it depend upon books. It was learnt from book of life which cost nothing and which could not be taken away from one by any force on earth.

Gandhi opines, "I hold that true education of the intellect can only come through a proper exercise and training of the bodily organs, e.g. hands, feet, eyes, ears, nose etc. In other words an intelligent use of the bodily organs in a child provides the best and quickest way of developing his intellect. But unless the development of the mind and body goes hand in hand with a corresponding awakening of the soul, the former alone would prove to be a poor lop-sided affair. By spiritual training I mean education of the heart. A proper and all-round development of the mind, therefore, can take place only when it proceeds with the education of the physical and spiritual faculties of the child. They constitute an indivisible whole.

On the other hand what goes by the name of education in our schools and colleges in the cities today is in reality only intellectual dissipation. Intellectual training is there looked upon as something altogether unrelated to manual or physical work. The young man who emerges from this system can in no way complete in physical endurance with an ordinary labourer. The slightest physical exertion gives him a headache. As for the faculties of the heart, they are simply allowed to run to seed or to grow anyhow in a wild undisciplined manner. The result is moral and spiritual anarchy. And it is regarded as something laudable. Man is neither mere intellect, nor the gross animal body, nor the heart or soul alone. A proper and harmonious combination of all the three is required for the making of the whole man and constitutes the true economics of education.

We have upto now concentrated on stuffing children's minds with all kinds of information, without ever thinking of stimulating and developing them. Let us now cry a halt and concentrate on educating the child properly through manual work, not as a side activity, but as the prime means of intellectual training. "My plan to impart primary education through the medium of village handicrafts like spinning and carding etc. is thus conceived as the spear head of a silent social revolution fraught with the most far-reaching consequences. It will provide a healthy and moral basis of relationship between the city and the village and thus go a long way toward eradicating some of the worst evils of the present social insecurity and poisoned relationship between the classes. It will check the progressive decay of our villages and lay the foundation of a juster social order in which there is no unnatural division between the 'haves' and 'have-nots' and everybody is assured of a living wage and the right to freedom. What we need is educationists with originality, fired with true zeal, who will think out from day to day what they are going to teach their pupils. The teacher cannot get this knowledge from musty volumes. He has to use his own faculties of observation and thinking and impart his knowledge to the children through his lips, with the help of a craft. This means a revolution in the method of teaching, a revolution in teacher's outlook.

This education is meant to transform village children into model villagers. It is principally designed for them. The inspiration for it has come from the villages; primary education is a force designed without regard to the wants of the India of the villages, and for that matter even of the cities. Basic education links the children, whether of the cities or the villages, to all that is best and lasting in India. It develops both the body and the mind, and keeps the child rooted to the soil with a glorious vision of the future in the realization of which he or she begins to take his or her share from the very commencement of his or her career in school.

Those who harbour feelings of fear will always be potential enemies. Fear is a deep-seated emotion that is hard to fight. The false impression of fearlessness is easily seen through by others and therefore what must be aimed at for internalized non-violence is the removal of fear and its replacement with trusts. As Naess observes, personal relationships are an area where this substitution can be commenced as a first step towards integrating it as a life-style.

To prevent structural violence, Gandhi proposed the theories with ideals of Satyagraha, Sarvodaya, Swaraj, Swadeshi, Decentralization of power and wealth, trusteeship, social harmony and communal unity, economic equality, democracy of enlightened majority etc. Gandhi's approach had always been holistic as human life is synthetic whole, which cannot be divided into watertight compartments of social, religious, political life etc.

*Mangala Prabhat* (from Yervada Mandir) is a small treatise on the foundations of human living, eqully applicable for the reconstruction of a new social order. In those pages we find the eleven vratas (vows) of life. They are: Ahimsa (non-violence); Satya (truth); Asteya (non-stealing); Brahmacharya (chastity); Asangraha (non-possession); Sareerasrama (bodily labour); Aswada( control of the palate); Sarvatra bhayavarjana (fearlessness); Sarvadharma samanata (respect for all religions); Swadeshi (neighbourliness); Sparsa bhavana (Untouchability).

Gandhi was impressed by socialism. But he wanted to develop a union of capitalism and socialism. He disliked the wide gap between the rich and the poor. Socialism advocates that wealth should be snatched from the rich and it should be equally distributed. He has written that one can get real happiness by voluntary surrender of the wealth. The rich should be persuaded to surrender their wealth voluntarily in the interests of the public. Like Marx, Gandhiji was also against capitalism. He was in favour of abolishing it. But it was not the end which was important. The means must be such as to justify the end. The means were equally or even more important. Trusteeship means that owners of the means of production would still own them but will not use for their profit. They will act as trustees and the profit will be used for the public. With the help of persuasion, capitalism would be replaced by the system of trusteeship. Gandhi assumed that rich people are so good that they will be persuaded easily and not resist to this great sacrifice. Vinobha Bhave and jai Prakash Narayan experimented in the form of Bhoodan and Gramdan, but it could not be implemented successfully.

According to Gandhi Rama Rajya is a moral based social system. It is a rule of justice and social justice. It would be a democratic state. There will not be too much consumption and large scale production. In the words of R.N. Mukherjee, Rama Rajya would care for duties in place of rights, service in place of selfishness, sacrifice in place of rights and sacrifice in place of possession.

Gandhi said that the real meaning of swaraj is to remain free from government control. According to him the state is an organized and centralized form of violence. He took the idea of stateless democracy from Tolstoy. Self-reliance is the gist of independence. He thought that a loose type of state structure would be required for the time being to fight against criminal elements. There is no stateless democracy in the whole world. If it is possibly built, it may start from India. Gandhi knew that stateless democracy is impracticable. He thought that state would have as small role as possible. To him state was a necessary evil.

The concept of environmental conservation and survival of human beings was inherent in the ideology of Mahatma Gandhi. Gandhi was ahead of his time and a precursor of environmentalism. As early as 1927, he warned the world that large scale industrialism would create problems of the type we are confronted with today.

Nature is becoming the victim of human greed. Indiscriminate misuse of natural resources in the name of economic development and disregard of the ecological implications has brought mankind to the present impasse. Gandhi stated that "the earth provides enough to satisfy every man's need but not every man's greed." He was of the view that as long as greed prevailed and the fruits of economic development were not shared equitably among the masses, poverty and hunger would exist. The present ecological crisis demands a different world view. Giving up the present life style and a reduction in consumerism would directly support the Gandhian ideology of simple living and high thinking.

Man must realize that he does not own nature. He is only one of its many offsprings. Nature is not due to man, man is due to nature. He is among its components. More importantly, the wisest animal on earth should play the role of "trustee" of nature's enormous wealth. Exploiting nature ruthlessly amounts to genocide and hence is a crime. Every living component of nature has a right to a dignified existence. Being the most evolved, man should be the "custodian" and protector of the dignity of all (M.K.Gandhi).

The important elements of Gandhian environmentalism can be summed up as follows: (1) human beings should act as though they are part of nature rather than apart from nature. (2) Materials available on earth should not be used with an element of greed, (3) human beings should practice non-violence not only towards fellow humans but also towards other living organism and inanimate materials because overuse of such materials also amounts to violence. (4) a conservationist and sustainable life-saving approach should prevail over a consumerist self destructive approach; (5) humans rarely think about how much is enough for a simple, need-based, austere and comfortable life-style ; (6) ethics and self-discipline in resource use us an overriding criterion of development.

A.P.J. Abdul Kalam, while addressing the three-day international conference on the occasion of golden jubilee of Indian Parliament on 23-1-2003 said, "That poverty, illiteracy and unemployment were sowing seeds of terrorism worldwide. He exhorted the delegates that global sharing of resources to address these issues for world peace and development is essential. In other words, when there is "a will" in the leaders, there is a way and the way as shown by Gandhiji." In everything that he did therefore the "common man" was before his eyes. The common man has lost his self-respect and his soul. It is unfortunate that Gandhiji's ideas and words not commanded attention from the leaders in the contemporary society.

The Gandhian model envisaged that development and governance should be bottom-up and not be top-down; goal should be self defined and not stranger-defined; production should be aimed at basic goods to fulfil basic values with useful value and not at non-basic and greed-oriented luxury goods; the process of production should be by the masses and not through mass production and the whole approach should be holistic and not sectoral. The Gandhian model in the words of J.C.Kumrappa, leads to decentralized economic planning and actually. Economics of permanence, while in the model of industrial economy there is the danger that the rich becomes the richer. The need of the hour is that leaders and people of the country be inspired by the ideals and teachings of Mahatma Gandhi.

The Gandhian model of development requires active involvement and participation of man building his own destiny. This is possible if some of us belong to so called rich and middle class voluntarily instead of drifting towards consumerism are willing to sacrifice and share our pleasures in the interest of down-trodden of our society.

Gandhi was a great communicator. Realizing the impact of communication on the people that Gandhi had wielded, Sir J.H.Holmes wrote, in 1920s: "This man holds absolutely in his hands today the destinies of his people. When Gandhi speaks, India speaks. When Gandhi acts, it is India that acts. When Gandhi is arrested, it is the India that is outraged and humiliated. More truly, I believe than any other man who has ever lived, this great Indian is the incarnation of a people's soul." He further holds today the centre of world's attention. His position of primary is now occupied by a little oriented who has never held any official position who seeks neither glory nor power." The best quality of the communicator must possess is to practice what he preaches. He practiced whatever he preached. His thoughts and actions always went together. He used to say that one ounce of action is better than tonnes of thought without any action.

The thought of Gandhi is the thought of the future. The coming century may be described as a century of Gandhi, and the world today has accepted Gandhi as a model to solve the problems of the present century. Gandhi gave to the world new and revolutionary concepts such as Satyagraha (truth force), Sarvodaya (welfare of all), and Shanti Sena (peace-brigade). In the coming years particularly in the twenty-first century, these Gandhian concepts are found to gain greater relevance. In fact, Gandhi is more relevant today than ever before. We have to choose between ahimsa and atom, Non-violence and non-existence, and between Sarvodaya and Sarvanasa (total annihilation).

SECTION - 1

GANDHI'S RESISTANCE TO HEGEMONY

# 1

# Vagaries and Varieties of Resistance to Hegemony

*R.V.R. Chandrasekhar Rao**

I am delighted to be here with you and thank you for your very kind invitation. To be in the midst of former colleagues, students and friends is pleasure. This University provided me with the privilege of sharing an environment of seeking knowledge and imparting it to young students to the best of my ability. Its eminent teachers made me realize that in such company one remains a disciple. For this opportunity I gratefully acknowledge my life-long indebtedness.

The Seminar is well conceived. The topic is of perennial relevance. More so because more than sixty years have elapsed since the Mahatma had been laid to rest. But the trouble with him is that he left a legacy that does us not allow us to rest in peace! It is as if he left a written legal testament not only to India but to the world at large to litigate about on all fronts. Some allege it as mala fide, ab initio'; some find lack of clarity in intention; others hold that the listing of the inheritors contains 'spelling' mistakes; most curious of all, every one seems to insist that the testament has written and unwritten codicils.

Another merit of the Seminar is its Hegemony rubric. The Hegemony perspective is a very appropriate one far from being a

* Keynote address delivered in the National seminar on Hegemony, Resistance and Gandhi held by Gandhian Studies Centre, Andhra University, Visakhapatnam
Former Vice-Chancellor, Dr. B.R. Ambedkar Open University, Hyderabad.

pejorative concept, Hegemony, thanks to Gramsci, acquires a positive connotation ideal to examine Gandhi's complete ideas and activities.

## Hegemony

Hegemony is a hold—all word acquiring in contemporary times a specialized meaning in the social sciences. In the broadest sense it means the influence that ideas wield over people and shape their thinking and actions. This may be the result of either their persuasive nature or they being physically enforced by a dominant group which may be a minority group. Understood thus, one can say that all thinking and formulation of ideas in language is hegemonic in nature. There is an Egyptian fable that a Pharaoh questioned the use of learning and invention as both disturbing to governing people and a convenient device to manipulate them in ruling. There is also the common usage about 'bugbear of literacy'. The point is that all systematic thought leads to influencing people. Obliviously, this cannot be the purport of the term Hegemony. Only where a well-knit set of ideas come to be used, consciously or otherwise, as instruments of an overpowering nature operate, can we refer to a hegemonic situation.

Hence a brief etymological tracing is useful to our present context. The Greek root-word – 'egemon'—just meant leader, ruler. It stood for a predominant, or 'master principle'. Here it was not limited to matters of direct political control as we understand it today. In modern social theory, it is traceable to Marx and Engels who introduced the idea of Ideology as a manipulating device by ruling classes to rule over the 'masses'. However, to Marx and his collaborator, dialectical materialism will smash the ideological verbiage as a classless society ushered in by proletarian revolution establishes a scientifically based truth about societal governance. It was Lenin who sought to use the overall import of Hegemony as a strategy for revolution, a strategy under which the working class should adopt to win the support of the majority through alliances. The word 'hegemony' itself was first used by Russian Marxists before Lenin used its implication as a strategy. George Plekhanov used the term to denote the need for working classes (industrial working classes), such as they were, forge an alliance with the peasantry for the overthrow of Tsarism. Lenin built on it in advocating a broader national approach to alliances to include even the bourgeois, and thus capitalize on the revolution that the bourgeois already initiated in Russia. In this way the working class, then a small minority of the population, would be able to win the support of the great majority of the people.

Gramsci transformed the content of the concept of hegemony from being a mere strategic tool to a full-blown concept, theory and practice. First, he went beyond Lenin to advocate the incorporation the ideas and practices (praxis) of even the capitalist class in mobilizing the proletarian revolutionary cause both in gaining state power, and in maintaining that power once it has been achieved. It was in this context that he accorded a higher niche to the intellectual and moral forces behind ideas that make people believe and act according to codes of conduct even though they are crafted by and used by upper classes for manipulative purposes. Cultural matrices are so overpowering that it is both unwise and futile to dismiss them as mere superstructures and can be wished away even by a proletariat of any society. Marxists have a tendency to see Gramsci as a modifier of orthodox Marxism. He was in fact more than that. The influence of cultural mores was strong on him. He remained a votary of some of the seminal ideas of the Italian idealist Benidito Croce. Gramsci's summarization of how and why social groups sustain hegemony through ideas was given in the first of his 29 Prison Notebooks:

> "A social group must, already exercise 'leadership' before winning governmental power ( this is indeed one of the principle conditions for the winning of such power), it subsequently becomes dominant when it exercises power, but even if it holds it firmly in its grasp, it must continue to lead as well."

We can further explicate the notion by quoting an authority on Gramsci who said that "the crucial aspect of the notion of hegemony is not that it operates by forcing people against their conscious will or better judgement to concede power to the already-powerful, but that it describes a situation whereby our consent is actively sought for those ways of making sense of the world which 'happen' to fit in with the hegemonic alliance of classes or power bloc."

Where then does the need for resistance to hegemony arise?

The resistance consists in a sort of dialectical struggle to eliminate both the dominating (coercive) nature of the former social structures and of the regimen of the former dominant classes. The jettisoning of the entire corpus of hegemonic thought does not follow.

Hegemony strictly speaking is different from Ideology though they are causally related. Hegemonicl idea-structures are far more deeply and informally enveloping a social fabric than Ideology which is more narrowly focused and rather consciously canvassed as control mechanisms.

When we use hegemony in non-Marxian contexts, we are denoting in the broader sense that Gramsci's exegesis left as a legacy for discourse on social theory. Therefore, in discussing Gandhi and his critics like Ambedkar we adopt this theoretical background. What is the hegemony that Gandhi resisted and the one that he himself has created. For, there is no doubt he did both.

Hegemonies in a loose sense of the term can be many. Because any set of ideas having a deleterious influence on a society can constitute targets. But we highlight those of a more comprehensive hold, or potential hold, can more properly be regarded as truly hegemonical to resist and struggle against with determination. Understood thus Gandhi resisted two distinct categories of hegemonies, though with different intensity of negation. The first and foremost is the hegemony of the Western paradigm which he saw as the dominant one engulfing Indian ethos. His *Hind Swaraj* contained the quintessence of this rejection. This resistance of his was of the 'lock stock and barrel' category. Rightly or not, he regarded creeping westernization as the bane of Indian society and gave no place in India if Swaraj is to be won and sustained. Gandhiji himself summarized the baneful hold of this hegemony 1929 long after *Hind Swaraj's* publication in these words:

> "The Western civilization which passes for civilization is disgusting to me. I have given a rough picture of it in Hind Swarj. Time has brought no change in it". Though he admired many aspects of this civilization, on the whole he found it to be an unworthy legacy. In contrast with this, he was unabashed about the innate superiority of Hinduism vis-à-vis the contemporary Western counterpart. Professor Bhikhu Parekh puts the basis for the claim well: "The clear distinction between the impersonal

and personal conceptions of God, the emphasis on non-attachment to the world while remaining active within it, the principle of unity of all life and the doctrine of non-violence were unique to Hinduism."His whole agenda of his economic, social and political ideology consisted of the rejection of western economic ideas which need not be detailed here.

But then how about his response to the indigenous hegemony of the Hindu ethos? It is to be acknowledged that here lies a problem. How intensive and extensive was his resistance to this ethos? Prima facie, he after all expressed a visceral attachment to Hinduism almost as a fetish. Even his admirers were nonplussed at this curious attachment to many of its beliefs and practices, including the repeated endorsement of the caste system. And his critics, like Dr. Ambedkar, poured scorn questioning either his sanity or his authenticity. In fact the Ambedkar-Gandhi confrontation itself revealed Gandhi in a rather ironical situation of demanding Ambedkar to own up to being a Hindu. This episode related to the most critical phase of their confrontation – that over the Macdonald Award granting separate electorates to the Scheduled Castes. Gandhi's fast unto death over this is part of his saga. Ambedkar was unrelenting for some time. It was one of his close Dalit colleagues, M.C. Rajah of Madras that persuaded Ambedkar to meet with Gandhi in prison on fast. The event is narrated in a magisterial work: Gandhi and Churchill: The Epic Rivalry That Destroyed an Empire and Forged Our Age, by Arthur Herman, that came out as recently as last year. On this episode, the author: Analysing and Fighting Caste (2006). The following extensive quotation is from Herman's book:

> Note that Ambedkar's first words to Gandhi for agreeing to any compromise were: 'I want my compensation'. Gandhi's response to Ambedkar settling for the Poona Pact were: 'In accepting the Poona Pact you accept that you are a Hindu.' The Mahatma's insistence that Ambedkar confess to being a Hindu could easily be interpreted as clinching testimony to his commitment to Hindu hegemonic ideals far from challenging it.

But this is not sufficient evidence. For, Gandhi's resistance to the orthodox Hindu doctrine is indeed overwhelming. While protesting vehemently that the core of that doctrine is sublime and everlasting he rejected, with equal vehemence, the entire ritualistic credo. Thus, it is only by an over-extension of linguistic usage that he could be classed as Hindu. As you judge a person from knowing who his friends are, it is even more significant too know who his enemies are. The orthodox Hindu criticism of Gandhi from the start rested on its conviction that Gandhi was destroyer of Hindu value system. Indeed he found his final nemesis in them. The world at large regarded him as a saintly reformer than a bigoted Hindu chauvinist. More importantly his critics on the left, both Ambedkar and the radical left were at a loss to label him even remotely as a revivalist. The gravamen of their charge was that his use of the religious idiom in politics had the great danger of being misconstrued by the masses already wallowing in illiteracy and poverty. Even Ambedkar was extremely reluctant to categorise him as Hindu of the genre he very legitimately excoriated. He found in him a very inconvenient, even a mischievous, adversary, thwarting his own leadership-base. In short, to Ambedkar, Gandhi was a Prachchnna Hindu critical of Hinduism and yet a supremely successful mobiliser of the masses. A 'devious' foe to contend with.

But the tragic irony was that Gandhi himself added to this confusion. To reach out to the Indian populace he opted to adopt the strategy of appealing to many of the norms and forms of popular Hindu ideals yet at the same time with righteous indignation, like Jesus chasing out the money-changers from the Temple, he denounced everything that was inhuman in his native belief and action. To relate Gandhi to the Gramscian doctrine, it would seem that Gandhi was purposefully adapting the Hindu symbolism of a spiritual tradition for revolutionary politics of his vintage.

## Ambedkar's Hegemony-target

Let us now turn to Ambedkar's own struggle against hegemony. His target was the Hindu creed. In its intensity the struggle was exactly similar to Gandhi's against the modern Westernization paradigm. Both were the 'lock, stock and barrel' rejectors and resistors of their respective betenoires of hegemonical systems. Arguably, probably Gandhi knew he was exaggerating the identification of Western civilization with worship of the mammon, Ambedkar had never any reservations in not giving a benefit of the doubt to even some parts of the pernicious Hindu doctrine. His resistance to the Western ethos was less than marginal. Except in so far as some of the Western nations turned to Imperialism and held down their colonial subjects with racialist arrogance, Ambedkar welcomed Westernization. Patriotism and even Nationalism was a strong bond but not the one based on his native civilisational pride as the majority of Hindu nationalists reflected. His adoration of Abraham Lincoln and appreciation of the United States that inherited Lincoln's legacy were immense. And, of course, his admiration of the great advances the US made in extending the benefits of science and technology were further evidence of his commitment to most of the aspects of modern Western tradition. The Lincoln ideological connection had of course the tie-up with the Emancipation Proclamation and the abolition of Slavery which synchronized admirably well with Ambedkar's own vision of the emancipation of the Dalits in India from Hindu hegemony.

Here, it is apposite to ask why Ambedkar did not extend the same admiration, not even concede a modicum of credit, to Gandhi's work on behalf of the 'harijan's'. Probably because Gandhi was poaching on his (Ambedkar's) own turf? Or was Ambedkar firmly believed that none else than the Dalits can take up the cause, as the present day Dalit sensibility insists? Mark Juergensmeyer in his admirable brief study of Gandhi, in his, *Gandhi's Way: A Handbook of Conflict Resolution*, resorts to creative device of an imaginary conversation between 'Gandhiji' and his alter-ego Mohandas, in which the Ambedkar-Gandhi stand-off over Macdonald Award and Gandhi's fast forms one item. The imaginary dialogue between the two Gandhi personas reflecting the doubts that gnaw the conscience of the Mahatma. One persona, 'Gandhi, says:

> Your opposition—the Untouchables, at least those led by Dr. Ambedkar—also hopes for a better role for the outcastes. It is true that some Untouchables regard Hinduism as oppressive, and want to disassociate themselves from it. But no one has suggested that they secede from the nation. Have you really waged a careful search for the truth in this matter. Perhaps you should talk again with Dr. Ambedkar."

To this the other Gandhi persona, Mohandas replies:

"With due respect, my real opposition is not Ambedkar but the prejudices of the upper castes. I understand why the Untouchable leaders distrust me, since I am a member of a superior class, as it is miscalled. But even though "touchable" by birth, I am an Untouchable by choice, and I think I qualify to represent them, even their lowest strata, as well as Dr.Ambedkar does. I would, however, be delighted to talk with him and any other friends. But let the fast continue."

Even though the above is only a clever authorial device, Juergensmeyer brings out the conflict hidden behind Gandhiji's conviction and actions. Gandhi was aware that his 'outsider' status partly compromises his authenticity over the Scheduled Castes issue.

To summarise the respective anti-Hindu hegemony agendas of Gandhi and Ambedkar, the latter's was far more clear and focused than Gandhi's. His (Gandhi's) ambivalence over confronting the native Hindu hegemonic legacy for ever confuses what priority he accorded to his opposition to the Western paradigm and to his critique of the indigenous hegemonic corpus.

The problem can be attributed to the unique hold that religion, or more precisely spiritualism, has in any hegemonic discourse. Many a radical reformer ready to attack any other control mechanism that seeks to control society gets shy of convincing themselves that spiritual matters are simply artificial constructs crafted by vested interests to manipulate the majority. Particular spiritual regimens may still be challenged but the spiritual dimension as a broad category seems a hard nut to crack as it were.

Gandhiji's ambivalence in attacking the entire corpus of the Hindu praxis rests 'lock, stock and barrel' rested on his conviction that the spiritual heritage of Hinduism is universal in scope and essentially non-parochial. This, above all, made him spotlight the positive aspects of Hinduism, sometimes exaggerating them, as in the case of non-violence and non-possession. His attack against the Western tradition in similar strain identified Westernization with Secularization, even with atheism, again with exaggeration.

It should be noted that Ambekar was not also exempt from this reluctance to reject or resist the spiritual dimension. His conversion to Buddhism was itself revealing in its implications.

First, it acknowledges his spiritual sensibility. Yet again it leaves the doubt whether he opted because of the agnostic face of Buddhism or of its transcendental aspect.

Even more interesting is the fact that he did not choose either Islam or Christianity even though he was time and time again wooed by the protagonists of those religions. For more than two and a half millennia Hinduism, Buddhism and Jainism remained closely allied belief systems, far more than Judaism's relationship with Christianity and Islam. No wonder, many modern scholars have pointed out to the fact that the borders between Buddhism, Jainism and their parent, Hinduism have remained most porous. When most of the cultural and literary discourse on the revival of the spiritual dimension in contemporary decades alludes to the Buddha, there is the sub-text of reference to the ancient Indian and subliminal Hindu spiritual sensibility. It is not far off the mark to regard that Ambedkar himself did not choose to remove himself from the fold of the indigenous spiritual moorings. Is there in this proof of the unique hold of the 'spiritual' factor in confronting hegemonical systems.

Now, I wish to turn to talk about whether Gandhiji's anti-hegemonic thesis produced its own hegemonical anti-thesis. Gandhian thought has without doubt generated its own 'incubus' of a vast corpus of ideas and practices which, pose to many thinkers, the problem that Gandhism has itself become a hegemone of ideology (my apoligies for the loose use of idealogy and hegemony). Many thinkers do think so. It has become a pell-mell collection of ideas and 'ritualistic' routines. It is by now common to club together anything related to the counter-culture fashion with the Gandhian paradigm. Right from the Seventies of the last century at the present, the 'protesting progenies' are willy nilly associated with Gandhism.

Now that the spirit of secularization appears to be global in its sweep in spite of the outward manifestation of religiuosity,the Gandhian norms have become more like shibboleths than pristine tenets to emulate. The party (or parties) that still hope to derive mileage from the Gandhian past swear by loyalty cynically to some other Gandhi's. Many a political operator may even be feeling that Gandhism has become an albatross round their necks much like the Ancient Mariner as depicted by Coleridge. I know the analogy itself is cynical in temper, but remember high idealism can become so burden some that pragmatic times may wish to was it down. Yet, either because of an iota of piety or because of considerations of profit, people to walk wearily with albatrosses. Is this the predicament are in?

So much so, even the credibility of the Gandhian commitment, especially to the uplift of the under-classes, is challenged and that noble task now is now almost appropriated by the leadership of the sections of the populace that belong to the under-classes. The Ambedkar agenda thus is more compelling. But is this in the danger of becoming hegemony in itself?

# 2

# Gandhi and His Resistance to Hegemony

*M. Lakshmipathi Raju & A.B.S.V. Ranga Rao*

"Hegemony' was most likely derived from the Greek *egemonia*, whose root is egemon, meaning, "leader or ruler (Williams, Keywords). Since 19th century 'hegemony' has been commonly used to indicate, "political predominance, usually of one state over another", (Williams, Keyword). According to Lenin, hegemony refers to the leadership exercised by the proletariat over the other exploited classes.

Italian communist thinker, activist and political leader, Antonio Gramsci(1819-1937) defines hegemony as form of control exercised by a dominant class, in the Marxist sense of a group controlling the means of production. The Bourgeoisie are the class of modern capitalists – owners of the means of social production and employers of wage labour. The subordinate class was the proletariat who are the class of modern wage labourers; They have no means of production of their own; they are reduced to selling their labour-power in order to live. Hegemony means the influence that ideas wield over people and shape their thinking and actions. Our thinking and ideas in language is hegemonic in so far as they influence people. When ideas are used as instruments of an overpowering nature, we refers to a hegemonic situation.

Resistance is a sort of a dialectical struggle to eliminate the dominating nature of the former social structures and former dominant classes. Hegemony is different from ideology. Hegemonic ideas and structures are far more deeply enveloping a social fabric than ideology. Gandhi both resisted hegemony and the one that he himself created. Gandhi resisted the western paradigm which is dominant and engulfing Indian ethos. He regarded westernization as the bane of Indian society. Gandhi found many aspects of western civilization as unworthy legacy. Though Gandhi adopted many beliefs and practices of Hindu ideas, he expressed his righteous indignation to some of the practices like untouchability.

Gandhiji applied the concept of hegemony in explaining the domination of superstructure of Indian society, the indegenous patterns of domination, modernity and modernization, which are affecting antonomy and freedom of the individual. He dreams about an equalitarian society to curtail the domination of the above factors in India. He defends tradition as foundation for autonomy, but he challenges its defects in order to reform it.

Gandhi challenges the deep inequalities in India and offers a powerful defence of autonomy. He attacks colonialism and untouchability, because they subordinate the individual. He shows resistance to modernity and modernization, because he thinks that they disable men and there are hidden costs to community and individual freedom. He confronts violence because; he thinks that people are used as means for the benefit of the powerful. Gandhi has deep commitment to the autonomy of everyone, since he has expansive view of power which he finds in the state, economy and society. He shows resistance to hegemony—political, economic and social. He treats power as a form of dominance and he holds that everyone should take charge of his or her own life. He asks Indians to get their country freed from the indigenous patterns of domination.

Marks and Engels used ideology as a device by ruling classes to rule over masses. For ideology Lenin Hegemony is a strategy for revolution; it is a strategy which the working class adopt to win the support of the majority. Gramsci expanded the concept of hegemony as a full-blown concept. A social group exercises 'leadership' before assuming governmental power.

### *(1) State and Civil Society*

For Gramsci, hegemony refers to the control exercised through society's superstructure. Raymond Williams identifies three ways in which 'superstructure' is used by Karl Marx.

(1) The legal and political forms which express real relations of production.

(2) Forms of consciousness in which a particular class view is expressed.

(3) Men becoming conscious of a fundamental economic conflict and then try to fight it out.

Gramsci divides the superstructure into two major levels – called 'civil society', and the 'political society' or the 'state'. Civil society includes organizations such as churches and trade unions. According to Gramsci, civil society corresponds to hegemony; political society or 'state' corresponds to 'direct domination'. Gramsci describes these two forms of control as follows.

Social hegemony is 'spontaneous' consent given by the masses to the dominant fundamental group(i.e. the ruling class– in Gramsci's Western Europe, the Bourgeoisie). This consent is given by the masses because of the prestige which the dominant group enjoys because of its position in the world of production.

Political Government devises "apparatus of the state coercive power for enforcing legal discipline on the groups which do not consent, when spontaneous consent failed. Gramsci does not treat 'social hegemony' and 'political government' as distinct categories. He brings them together under the "Integral State". Integral state includes both the functions of social hegemony and political government.

State is "dictatorship + hegemony".

"State = political Society + Civil Society, in other words hegemony protected by the armour of coercion. State represents both the practical and theoretical activities by which it maintains its dominance and manages to win the active consent of those over whom it rules over.

Gramsci emphasizes the importance of civil society by suggesting that it is stronger than the state in acting as coercive apparatus. Political struggle for Gramsci involves a struggle of hegemony, a class's struggle to become a state and take up the role of state as educator.

### *(2) Hegemony as Education*

For Gramsci, one of the important functions of the state is to educate the masses, to raise the masses to a particular cultural and moral level – a level that corresponds to the needs of productive forces – that is to say – to promote the interests of the ruling class. The ruling class in Gramsci's Italy was the bourgeoisie.

According to Gramsci, the State is equivalent to the 'fundamental economic group' or ruling class (bourgeoisie). The state implements its educative project through various channels; the school performs the positive educative function while the court acts as negative educative agencies. Hegemony is a process by which, the individual's consent is obtained by applying educative pressure, by exploiting their necessity; the ruling class thus moulds the free subject to the needs of economic system.

Educative practices, particularly literary studies have been used to establish hegemony in a colonial setting. The English studies in colonial settings –served to strengthen western cultural hegemony in many complex ways. The study of literature by the Indian Colonial subjects was linked to the consolidation and maintenance of British rule in India (Viswanathan, G.).

### *(3) Struggle and Resistance*

Gandhi seeks a peaceful world, a stable society and a coherent, spiritual life. Gandhi sees these goals as desirable but elusive in the modern world. He argues that struggle and resistance are requirements for a self-governing life. Gandhi offers materials to struggle with both ancient and modern enemies of autonomy. Gandhi is interested in such critical issues as how, we are implicated in the politics and practices of our government and society.

When Gandhi works to abolish untouchability, he turns to Hinduism, to supply him with moral resources for his assault. Because any tradition can decay, he wants the members of defective tradition to repair it to counteract the expressions of domination, both ancient and new, that appear in any society.

Gandhi as deconstructionist questions some of the practices and ideals – our views of modernity, and necessity for violence. He challenges their worth and utility, he exposes their heavy costs in the lives of ordinary persons. The pain caused by violence makes many persons captives to fear and dependent on powerful. He wants victims to show resistance to their victimisers. He demands courageous, non-violent action in the face of injustice. He tries to reintroduce principles for the care of traditions to serve as guardians of autonomy in the struggle with domination and violence. Postmodernism, for many, is a rebuttal to modernism. Gandhi's encounters with domination and violence often bring him close to post modernism.

### *(4) Freedom*

Freedom is defined as the absence of constraints. There are many kinds of constraints such as social, political, economic, religious, and psychological and so on. There are two aspects to the problem of freedom; one is freedom from 'interference' and the other is freedom 'for action'. Outside interference with freedom of man frustrates the ethical development of man. It also destroys individual's initiative and self-reliance. The interference may be caused by church, state, or society with the freedom of man. The individual can develop his talents, skills and moral nature in a free and open society. But freedom cannot exist in isolation. Freedom can exist only in society. One can enjoy freedom only in an organized society. Men have struggled against religious tyranny, political despotism and restrictions imposed by unequal society. If economic and social privileges are confined to a minority, then the freedom of the individual well be reduced. The individual can enjoy freedom and develop his personality only when society is free form social inequalities, economic exploitation, fear of the future, hunger, poverty and so on.

Order is an essential condition of society. One cannot enjoy absolute freedom since it curtails the freedom of others. One can enjoy freedom only when it is not jeopardizing the freedom of others. When there is order, the freedom of the individual can be protected. But order many curtail the freedom of the individual. Hence we have to strike a balance between these two social aspects, 'freedom and order'. Freedom cannot consist in the complete absence of restraint. Absolute absence of restraint may lead to anarchy. As order and anarchy are contradictory, freedom and restraint are complementary. There is contrast between individualism and collectivism. Human race will enjoy collective freedom in the future society.

### *(5) Gandhi's Concept of Freedom*

Gandhi resisted the coercive character of the state. He looked upon "the state as an organ of violence in an organized form. Gandhi believed in the good nature of man. He stood for self regulation and self-control. The regulation of the state is not called for. According to Gandhi the compulsive nature of the state will take away the moral value of individual action. Gandhi developed his anarchistic views of the state. He said that though the state minimizes the exploitation of the individual, it destroys individuality which contributes to all progress.

Gandhi viewed political power as means for bettering human conditions. The sovereignty of the state will challenge the moral right of man to shape his own destiny. What he wanted is the sovereignty of the people based on pure authority. He treated the state as soulless machine; it cannot be free from violence. Gandhi preferred non-violent democratic government which governs least. If people consciously hold political power, the state interference with the freedom of the individual would be reduced to the minimum.

### *(6) Gandhi on Democracy*

Gandhi believed that democracy will harmonize the interests of the individual and the State; it can protect the weak and respect the individuality of man. He did not accept the Western capitalist democracy, since any kind of exploitation is treated as violence by Gandhi. For Gandhi centralization of power is an evil and it is conducive to violence. He pleaded for a decentralized democratic form of government. He visualized a non-violent state based on federation of self-governing autonomous village republics with equality pervading every sphere of life. The essence of democracy lies in the individual freedom. Referring to majority rule, he observed that the opinion of an individual should have greater weight than the opinion of many, provided that the opinion is sound on merits. He believed in individual liberty. If individual liberty goes, then surely all is lost. If individual is deprived of freedom, man becomes automation and society is ruined. For Gandhi both individual and society are inseparable. Unrestricted individualism is the law of the beast of the jungle. Willing submission to social restraint enriches both the individual and the society.

### (7) *Individual Freedom*

According to Gandhi, the individual freedom in capitalist society is reduced to the freedom of few and leads to exploitation of the weak. By individual freedom, Gandhi meant the freedom of the lowliest and the weak in the society. Gandhi's concern is for human dignity and individuality. The society must subserve the growth of the individual. For Gandhi political obligation denotes the reciprocal obligations of the ruler and the ruled. The state has to create favourable conditions for individual's life and growth. Freedom according to Gandhi does not descend upon people as a gift from above, but they have to raise themselves to it by their own effort. Gandhi wrote, that he will work for an India in which the poor have voice in its making there are no high and low class of people; all communities live in perfect harmony; there is no curse of untouchability. All interests are not in conflict with one another.

## REFERENCES

1. Adamson, Walter L. (1980). *Hegemony and Revolution – A Study of Antonio Gramsci's Political and Cultural Theory*, Berkely: University of California press.
2. Chandrasekhar Rao, Prof. RVR (2009). Keynote address on, "Vagaries and varieties of resistance to Hegemony, National Seminar on Hegemony, Resistance and Gandhi 30th -31st, March, 2009 Andhra University, Visakhapatnam.
3. Choudary, G.P. (1985). (ed) *Relevance of Gandhism*, Capital Publishing House, Delhi.
4. Gangrade, K.D. (2005), *Gandhian Approach to Development and Social Work*, Concept Publishing Company, New Delhi.
5. G. Gramsci, Antonio; Antonio Gramsci (1994). *Pre-prison Writings.* Cambridge UP.
6. Gramsci, Antonio, *Prison Notebooks*, I – II .Ed and trans .Joseph A Bultigieg Trans. Antonio.
7. Ray, B.N. (2008). *Reading Gandhi*, AuthorsPress, Delhi.
8. Singh R.R (1995). (ed.) *Association of Schools of Social Work in India*, Delhi School of Social Work, Delhi.
9. Viswanathan, Gauri (1989). *Masks of Conquest: Literary Study and British rule in India*, New Delhi.
10. Williams, Raymond.Keywords (1997). *Marxism and Literature.* Oxford: Oxford UP.

# 3

# Gandhian Perspective of Satyagraha and Democracy

*Ashutosh Pandey*

> My notion of Democracy is that under it the weakest should have the same opportunity as the strongest. That can never happen except through non-violence. No country in the world today shows any but the patronizing regard for the weak.
>
> *Harijan: May 18, 1940*

Gandhi does not make any distinction between morality and politics and ethics and economics. He does not want only to raise the standard of democracy but the quality of dem'ocracy and the quality of living in such a system. In the light of these issues, Gandhian alternatives have been discussed and analyzed keeping in view the contemporary problems in Indian democracy.

## Introduction

The idea of Satyagraha is the most important contribution of Mahatma Gandhi to political thought. The meaning of Satyagraha is holding on to truth, hence truth force. Gandhiji also calls it the soul force. Gandhi was a democrat. Writing in the *Harijan*, he said that true democracy must be the ruler of the people in its real sense.[1] the transfer of power from the Britishers was not the end but the means for improving the condition of all men and women. In his address to All India Congress Committee on August 8, 1942, he said. "the congress doses not believe in the domination of any group or any community. It believes in democracy which includes in its orbit Muslims, Hindus, and

Christians—every one of the communities inhabiting this vast country."[2] Democracy meant complete decentralization of political powers. It must begin from the bottom and not from above; this is why Gandhi laid emphasis on the Panchayati Raj. Such a democracy is possible only through non-violence. Democracy sustained by violence cannot protect the weak. "My notion of democracy", he said, "is that under it the weakest should have the same opportunity."[3] Democracy must provide social justice to all.

## Gandhian Perspective of Satyagraha

Satyagraha is compatible with democratic political process because it is closely analogous to other methods generally considered the essence of democracy. For, example, written and verbal communication with the public is an attempt to sway the majority to particular view.[4] the concept of Satyagraha or insistence on truth has a very comprehensive meaning. To Gandhi truth is the ultimate reality. "It is his conception of truth that is central to his life and work." [5] He considered 'Satyagraha' to be the best weapon for the evolutionary process of social change. Satyagraha is the natural outcome of his love for truth. It is necessary for the Satyagrahi to make all endeavors for the realization of truth through peaceful means. "If truth is the ultimate reality then it is imperative for a votary of it to safeguard the criteria and foundation of truth. A votary of God, who is the highest Truth and highest Reality, must be utterly selfless and gentle." [6] Gandhi said that Satyagraha was the inherent birthright of a person and it implied the exercise of the purest soul- force against injustice, oppression and exploitation, never according to Gandhi, Satyagraha for the sake of truth and justice, to be given up. But Satyagraha, although based on moral resistance to unjustified authority is also never to become a formula of social and political disintegration. A Satyagrahi must have first rendered intelligent, spontaneous and willing obedience to the laws of states.[7] He thought that a lover of truth must devote his life to experience truth and be prepared to face any kind of suffering. Resistance to evil must be done with personal suffering to awaken the conscience of the evil-doer. The Satyagrahi appeals to the soul of the evil doer. "The efficacy of satyagrahi depends upon the tenacity to resist evil which, while it abjures force, develops in the satyagrahi to faculty to fancy all risks cheerfully."[8] To Gandhi, certainly, the Satyagrahi obeys the laws of the state not because of the fear of penal sanctions but because he regards them as promoting the common good. Gandhi himself claimed have been, by nature, law-abiding and stated that the capacity for civil resistance came from the discipline undergone in process of obeying the civil and moral laws of the state, "Democracy comes naturally to him who is habituated normally to yield willing obedience to all laws, human or divine. I claim to be a democrat both by instinct and training. Let those who are ambitious to serve democracy qualify themselves by satisfying first this acid test of democracy."[9] But Gandhi was also believer in the categorical superiority of loyalty to the commands of conscience to man-made law. The dictates and commands of any government, if they conflicted with the sense of higher loyalty to conscience, had to be resisted. Thus, according to political teachings of Gandhi, Satyagraha is a perpetual law against anything repugnant to the soul. In his conception of democracy, he rejected the adoption of any form of government imported from either the western countries or the eastern countries as he found fault in them. He thought that if swaraj was to be desired it should be built upon Swadeshi. Analyzing the models of government of the west and the east he said, "The motive lying behind the western type and the eastern type is the same – the greater welfare of the whole society and the abolition of the hideous inequalities resulting in the existing millions of have- nots and a handful of haves. I believe that this end can be achieved when non-violence is accepted by the best minds of the world as the basis on which a just social order is to be constructed."[10] Similarly, Gandhi also maintained that Swaraj was not an alien concept and it could be achieved by self- reliance. He felt that Swaraj could be attained by the people of India if they realized and accepted the importance of all things what were native to India. Thus he said, "We do not realize that Swaraj is almost wholly attainable through Swadeshi. If we have no regard for our respective vernaculars, If we dislike our clothes, if our dress repels us, if we are ashamed to wear the sacred shikha, if our food is distasteful to us, our climate is not good enough, our people uncouth and unfit for company, our civilization faulty and the foreign attractive, is short, if everything native is bad and everything foreign is pleasing to us, I should not know what Swaraj can mean for us... It seems to me that before we can appreciate Swaraj we should have not only love but passion for Swadeshi."[11] Gandhi called his model of government "Ram-Rajya" after the political order which was in operation in ancient India and which used to ensure the betterment of all by providing them an ideal living condition. To Gandhi, it signified a social relationship that allowed Poorna Swaraj for each. [12] Gandhi considered that no government considered as good unless it safeguarded the interest of the poorest of the poor. According to him the government had to protect the interest of all and had to act as the servant of the people and not behave as their master. "Essentially, power had to go along with the purpose of service. The power elite had to live at the level of the masses to justify and legitimize the holding of power."[13] In Gandhian political society the individual, the minority and the rural areas, are given due importance and all are considered the integral parts of it. He thinks that if any part is overlooked then the whole suffers and there cannot be true Swaraj in such a society. Gandhi believed in the betterment of all and their involvement in political sphere. He prescribed for a social system in which all will be emancipated. To him, all the people must be uplifted to enjoy good life in the society. He propagated for a social order promoting the good of all. He called this concept 'Sarvodaya'. The goal of Gandhi's Sarvodaya was the overall transformation of the entire race of mankind at all levels of human existence. It represents ideal social order based on self-control, self-suffering, love, renunciation and social justice. T.K.N. Unnithan gave a short summary of the Sarvodaya philosophy which was founded by Mahatma Gandhi. He says, "In a world of increasing complexity he preached simplicity, in a world of increasing confusion he pointed to the simple qualities of character in which the solution might lie; in a world devoted to material goals he clearly showed their limitations, in a period of urbanization, he showed the decentralization meets other important needs that material gains can offer."[14] The Gandhian model of government was not an elite model where only selected few ruled the people unchecked by any moral precepts or any legal rules. Rather Gandhi emphasized that all are creations of God and all have equal importance and equal share in all things created by God. He did not overlook the downtrodden of society whom he called 'Harijans'. Gandhi said,

"None can be born untouchable, as all are sparks of one and the same fire. It is wrong to treat certain human beings as untouchable from birth."[15] He was of the opinion that "all the objects of the world are pleaded by God, there is none that is high and none that is low, all are absolutely equal, equal because all are the Creatures of that Creator."[16] Hence, to Gandhi democracy is not merely a form of government. It is also a gospel of the social system. It is a principle of self-reliance, equality, freedom, emancipation of all, and love for one's own things. It is a system where everybody performs his duty and gets his due. It is a social order where pure means are adopted to achieve good ending welfare for all.

## Gandhian Perspective of Democracy

Democracy in India Gandhi believed that a democracy, which served the welfare of all, would be marked by Minimum State intervention in social life. He criticized parliamentary democracy. However this system was certainly an advance over monarchy and oligarchy. He remarked, "I do not believe in any government but parliamentary government is better than capricious rule."[17] So, he accepted parliamentary Swaraj as an immediate goal and a point in the struggle for Swaraj. In 1924, he said, "Parliament is indeed barren. I do not imagine that its nature can change India I live, however, in the hope that our Parliament will only remain barren and not give birth to wicked son. I cannot abandon practical considerations. The ideal is one only, namely Ramrajya... I am suggesting many ways to ensure that the voice of parliament is really the voice of the people, and not the hired voters. With the end in view I am searching for a device which will enable us to listen to the voice of the entire people. All systems are bound to be defective. We are looking for a system, which will yield maximum benefit of India."[18] Although in the Hind- Swaraj, Gandhi was bitterly hostile to the patterns of functioning of the British Parliament, he prescribed for India a parliamentary government based on Universal Suffrage. His conception of Swaraj inculcated a government based on the consent of the people. This consent of the people was to be ascertained by the largest number of adult population. He wrote: "By Swaraj, I mean the government of India by the consent of the people as ascertained by the vote of the largest number of the adult population, male or female, native born or domiciled who have contributed by manual labour to the service of the state and who have taken the trouble of having their names registered as voters."[19] He felt that for the success of a democratic government it was essential that the representatives should be given only general instructions and should not be subjected to detailed dependence on the electorate. It would not be possible for the legislature to operate if the representatives were compelled to consult the constituencies on all issues. It can be said that he upheld the'mandate' and not the' delegate' theory for the representative. Gandhi wanted India to evolve "*True Democracy*" and laid down six conditions for its realization in India:

1. Satyagraha expressed through charkha;
2. Growth of village Industries;
3. Primary education through handicrafts;
4. Removal of untouchability;
5. Communal harmony; and
6. Non-violent organization of labour.

Gandhi also advised the Indians not to copy the western model. He remarked that one nation suited in one condition was not necessarily good enough of another differently suited. Accordingly, he suggested evolving a decentralized people's democracy on non-violent lines at the lower levels. Gandhi declared: "The end to be sought is human happiness combined with full mental and moral growth. I use the adjective moral as synonymous with spiritual. This end can be achieved under decentralization. Centralization as a system is inconsistent with a non-violent structure of society."[20] His opposition to centralization was based on a fundamental ground. He held: "Centralization cannot be sustained and defended without adequate force."[21] According to him centralization leads to the concentration of power in the hands of a few and that in its turn, robs the people of its supreme authority in the matter of determination of public issues. Not only that, in an over- centralized state man loses his human dignity and becomes a cog in the wheel of the vast and impersonal state machines. Man becomes de-personalized. That is why he stood for thorough decentralization of political power and economic production. He wanted to give a new direction to politics and for that he went to the roots. According to Gandhi, India cannot be imagined without its villages. To think of a developed India with its undeveloped villages is a ridiculous idea for him. Therefore, he championed the cause of an enriched village life. He propagated for making the village's self- sufficient and self- reliant. He maintained, "Every village of India will almost be a self- supporting, self-contained unit."[22] He stood for the improvement of villages and for the success of democracy; democracy should originate from the grass root level. He believed that power to be effective and genuine from the standpoint of the masses, must lie with the people which could only be possible in small communities of villages. "Society based on non-violence can only consist of groups settled in villages in which Voluntary Cooperation is the condition of dignified and peaceful existence."[23] He projected the state as the servant of the people; it had the duty to carry out the will of the people. He was for the prevention of exploitation of any kind of the rural people. "Exploiting of villages is itself organized violence. If we want Swaraj to be built on non- violence, we shall have to give villages their proper place."[24] Hence, he cried for village Swaraj, Panchayati Raj or democracy from below. According to him, "True democracy cannot be worked by twenty men sitting at the centre. It has to be worked from below by the people of every village."[25] He advocated that in democracy the independence must begin at the bottom. It means that at grass-root level people must be independent in making their policies and implementing them without any rigid and strict control from the above. Thus, every village, to him, could become a republic having the institution of panchayat with sufficient authority and powers. It means every village had to be self sustained and capable of managing its own affairs and even to the extent of defending itself against the whole world. Ultimately, it would be the individual who was to be the unit. He clarified that it did not exclude dependence on and willing help and cooperation from the neighbors or from the world too. It would be free and voluntary play of mutual forces.[26] Thus, he wanted India to evolve a decentralized structure of power based on the effective reconstruction of self- reliant and self- sufficient villages. The village organization was to be based on the principle of constructive social and economic efforts, sacrifice and the abnegation of illegitimate self interest. Similarly, he had also pointed out that the political structure of Independent India was to be not a pyramid with the apex sustained by the bottom. In the Panchayat Raj the toiling labourer and the rich capitalist had to be treated as equal. There was to be solidarist spirit of mutual independence and harmonious co-operation. The communal tensions which were spreading to the rural areas from the towns had to be eliminated. The self- sustained villages were to manage their own affairs. They were not to rely on the help of a central army for defence. They should morally develop themselves to the extent even of having the strength of perishing the attempt of self-defence.[27] He dreamed of village Swaraj where every village would have its own government in the form of panchayat which would be independent in all spheres of administration. "The government of the village will be conducted by a Panchayat of five persons annually elected by the adult villagers, male and female, possessing minimum prescribed qualifications. These will have all the authority and jurisdiction required. Since there will be no system of punishment in the accepted sense, this panchayat will be the legislature, judiciary and executive combined to operate for its year of office."[28] In essence, the panchayat of every village republic was a key unit for decentralization of legislative, executive and judicial powers. Every village with its characteristics of self- rule and self-sufficiency was supposed to represent the values of a true democracy, wherein authority and power were shared and exercised by different functionaries. The individual would have complete freedom to shape his destiny according to his wishes. His thoughts and actions would be pervaded by the spirit of non- violence in an atmosphere of genuine freedom. The spirit of self- sacrifice and patriotism would be the mainspring of all constructive actions in such a village republic. Gandhi argued that in such a setting it was possible to secure "perfect democracy" based upon individual freedom. The individual is the architect of his own government. The law of non-violence rules him and his government. For the law governing every village is that he will suffer death in defence of his and his village honour.[29] The only way, according to Gandhi, to emancipate the nation from its age- long torture and frustration was to make the villages of India self sufficient and self- reliant through the decentralized structure of village republics. Thus alone could the villagers also develop their intellectual powers and could acquire the social-economic consciousness necessary or contemplate non- violent society of the future. Thus, according to Gandhi, decentralization was a technique for revolutionizing the psychology of the people for building a more perfect society.[30]

This deep attachment to the concept of decentralization indicates the radical and fundamental nature of Gandhi's theory of democracy because he wants to begin the reform at bottom. According to him, the common masses have to feel the thrill of participation in the exercise of power thus alone can the universal will of the people become a reality. Gandhi not only gave his ideas through speeches and writings but he was a man who developed a model of' exemplary' life by making his own life – including its most intimate aspects – a museum of national learning. He converted large and already widely discussed dilemmas of Indian social structure into charismatic symbols: he labeled the vast masses of untouchables as Harijans (sons of God) and launched a powerful movement to ameliorate their oppression, which became a plank for the national movement. He championed the cause of women and spoke of their liberation almost in the style of feminism. He made the symbolism of Hindu-Muslim unity a general plank of social solidarity. He made the indigenous homespun cloth (Khadi) emblematic of all who would aspire to be nationalists, a symbolism that still continues to prevail among political cadres. He developed a comprehensive programme of constructive work in the villages, and among tribes and dalits. He rarefied traditional concepts of sacrifice and austere living into minimum qualifications for nationalist workers. He ordered the educated middle classes to go into villages and serve the people. He transformed the whole appeal and draw of individual prayer into a routine institution of the nation during which his solutions for problems of politics were highlighted and diffused. Gandhi turned the symbolism of a pacifist, saintly India to a militant organizational style, indeed the well-knit organizational drive of the Congress, with a programme of action and a powerful identity and discipline. This enabled him to include in the Congress all streams of ideological thought and all important social interests. It gave rise to a high tolerance of ambiguity in the concerns of the national movement, allowed dissent to become part of the overall consensual style of the Congress, and imbued the Congress with great flexibility and freedom to maneuver. By providing an overriding symbolism –

that had the sanction of tradition and had passed the test of functionality – he built bridges all over. Gandhi had the great gift of transforming dimensions of time (the bridging of several centuries) into concrete dimensions of space (bridging the gap between the city and the village) and penetrating both with an idiom of modernization that had indigenous meaning, simplicity of communication and great organizational as well as personal potency. He constantly reinterpreted traditional concepts of authority, social obligation and self-realization, and furnished them with meaning that proved functional in the development of national consensus and political identity. Above all, he wielded tremendous personal authority – the Congress high command and the vast band of Gandhian Workers – by resolving tensions and cleavages in the government through definitive solutions and formulae that could not be effectively challenged even by other popular heroes of the movement. Gandhi made prominent a certain consensual style in Indian tradition by grafting and reinterpreting this aspect in the context of modern politics and giving it an ideological colour by invoking labels such as 'non- violent struggle' and' peaceful disobedience' waged by a' servant of the people' even when he was combating a powerful enemy. As for his own rank and file in the Congress, he emphasized the great virtue of discipline in the maintenance of political potency; he accommodated men of diverse capacities and intellectual background, and always valued the cohesion and discipline of the movement above any ideological or doctrinal considerations, or even considerations of personal pride. He even symbolized and made functional the Indians tolerance of humiliation and deprivation, and turned these into programmatic plans of 'Civil disobedience' and mass imprisonment at the hands of the colonial power. All this enabled him to build distinctive structure of political organization. It was the latter that ultimately succeeded in gaining power from the alien rules and provided the nation with a framework of political authority.

The dominant model of democracy today emphasizes competitive elections and interest group pluralism. Voters choose who will represent and govern them for a period of time, and if satisfied will return the incumbents, if dissatisfied will turn to alternative candidates. Between elections, organized groups are expected to represent the interest of the members before various government agencies to influence public policy.[31]

Gandhiji's departure from this model at the institutional level is obvious. He wanted a small setting with a relatively simple economy, while the pluralists have been concerned with the problems of representation in large, highly diversified societies.

## Conclusion

Gandhiji contribution to democratic theory is not that he offers specific institutional alternatives to representative democracy and pluralism, although he does that. Rather, his importance comes from offering alternative ways of thinking about politics in general and democracy in particular.

Gandhi attempted to reintroduce political culture and political psychology as vital elements in the theory and practice of democracy. A restructured society, where no one saw responsibilities and everyone attempted to pursue his own interest, would be no great improvement for Gandhi. Those who had been at the bottom would have additional resources to enter the political conflicts of the day. The formula of politics would not change, but new winners and losers would appear. Accordingly, Gandhi emphasized structuring a community of common purpose and individual responsibility to the community.

As western democracies move towards the prospect of slower growth and increasing scarcities, the model of interest group politics may lead to phenomenal cleavages. To meet these new challenges, the need for restraint, responsibility, and community becomes more important than is easier, carefree times, and Gandhiji theory of democracy may help to understand and meet these challenges.

Gandhi himself believed that Satyagraha was not only an effective and heroic mode of emancipation of the people of a weak country, but also.....a beacon light... for Europe with all its discipline, science and organization. If Europe but realizes that, heroic as it undoubtedly is for a handful of people to offer armed resistance in the face of superior numbers, it is for more heroic to stand up against overwhelming numbers without any arms at all, it would save itself and blaze a trail for the world.[32]

## REFERENCES

1. *The Harijan*, January 18, 1948.
2. D.G. Tendulkar, *Mahatma*, Vol., VI, p. 159, New Delhi, Publications Division, Government of India, 1962.

3. M.K. Gandhi, *Non-violence in Peace and War*, Vol., I, p. 269, Ahmedabad, N.P.H. 1948.

4. Cohen, Carl, "Essence and Ethics of Civil Disobedience" in *The Nation*, March 16, 1964, No. 198, pp. 261- 62.

5. Santhanam, K., "Basic Principles of Gandhism" in Ramchandran, G. and Mahadevan, T.K. (eds.), *Gandhi: His Relevance for Our Times* (New Delhi: Gandhi Peace Foundation, 1967), p. 310.

6. Verma, V.P., *Modern Indian Political Thought* (Agra: Laxmi Narayan Aggarwal Publishers, 1996) (Eleventh edition), p. 343.

7. Gandhi, M.K., "A Himalyan Miscalculation" in Autobiography (Ahmedabad: Navajivan Publishing House, 1927), p. 392.

8. Munshi, K.M., "The Spiritual Basis of Satyagraha" in Ramchandran G. and Mahadevan, T. K. (eds.), *Gandhi: His Relevance for Our Times, op. cit.*, p. 121.

9. *Harijan*, 27-05- 1939, Vol. VII, No. 16, p. 136

10. Hingorani, A.T. (ed.), *The Village Reconstruction* (Bombay: Bhartiya Vidya Bhawan, 1966), p. 129.

11. *Ibid.*, p 115.

12. Jha, M.N., *Modern Indian Political Thought, op. cit.*, p. 197.

13. Sethi, J.D., *Gandhi Today* (New Delhi: Vikas Publishing House Pvt. Ltd., 1979) (Second Edition), p. 42.

14. Unnithan, T.K. N., *Gandhi in Free India* (Groingen: Wolters, 1965), p. 9.

15. Gandhi, M.K., *From Yervada Mandir* (Ahmedabad: Navajivan Publishing House, 1945), p. 31.

16. *Harijan*, 30-01- 1937, Vol. IV, No. 51, p. 408.

17. *Harijan*, 21-07- 1940, Vol. VIII, No. 23, p. 211.

18. CWMG, Vol. XIV( October1917- July 1918), *op. cit.*, March 1965, p. 444.

19. *Ibid.*, Vol. XXV, (August1924- January 1925), p. 34.

20. *Young India*, 29-01- 1925, Vol. VII, No. 5, p. 40.

21. *Harijan*, 18-01- 1942, Vol. IX, No. 1, p. 5. 180. *Ibid.*, 30-12- 1939, Vol. VII, No. 47, p. 391.

22. Hingorani, A.T. (ed.), *The Gospel of Swadeshi* (Bombay: Bhartiya Vidya Bhawan, 1967), p. 5.

23. *Harijan*, 30-12- 1939, Vol. VII, No. 43, p. 391.

24. Hingorani, A.T. (ed.), *the Gospel of Swadeshi, op. cit.*, p. 125.

25. *Harijan*, 18-01- 1948, Vol. XII, No. 51, p. 519.

26. *Ibid.*, 28-07- 1946, Vol. X, No. 25, p. 236.
27. *Ibid.*
28. *Ibid.*, 26-07- 1942, Vol. IX, No. 28, p. 238.
29. *Ibid.*
30. Verma, V.P., *The Political Philosophy of Mahatma Gandhi and Sarvodaya, op. cit.*, p. 213.
31. The thesis that democracies rest on competitive elections is presented by Joseph Schumpeter, *Capitalism, Socialism and Democracy* (New York: Harper, 1950), pp. 250-73. The classic position of the pluralist view is advanced by Robert Dahl in several books including Who Governs? (New Haven: Yale University Press, 1961) and after the revolution (New Haven: Yale University Press, 1970).

   *Gandhi, a Pilgrimage for Peace* (Ahmedabad: Navajivan Publishing House, 1950), p. 56. Emphasis added.

# 4

# Culture, Hegemony and Mass Media: A View

*D .V. R. Murthy & G. Anita*

Culture in today's world constitutes any act or practice that is specific to the individual or the group that exhibits or practices it. For instance, culture includes artifacts such as newspapers, television programmes, movies and popular music, but also practices like shopping, watching sports events, going to a club, or hanging out in the local hotel (Gigi Durham and Kellner, 2001: 6). Yet, this culture is the result of the extrinsic factors which permeate the society because of the constant flow of ideas and opinions from the elite or intellectuals. Marxist scholars argue that the ruling classes employ intellectuals and cultural producers practice ideas that glorify the dominant institutions and the ways of life and propagate these ideas in cultural forms such as literature, the press, or film and television. Hence, Gramsci (2001) observed that the press would play an organized role in perpetuating the superstructure. He said:

> A study of how the ideological structure of a dominant class is actually organized; namely the material organization aimed at maintaining, defending and developing the theoretical or ideological "front". It's most prominent and dynamic part is the press in general: publishing houses... The press is the most dynamic part of this ideological structure; but not the only one. Everything which influences or is able to influence public opinion, directly or indirectly, belongs to it: libraries, schools, associations and clubs of various kinds, even architecture, and the layout and names of streets...

Thus, Marxist analysis argues that the society is divided into different economic classes and that the economically dominant class is also the class that rules in views and ideas. Marx saw the economic realm of society as its 'base'. Everything else sits upon and flows from, this base; Marx called this the super structure. So, applied to media, Marx argued that the ruling class could impose their values and ideas on the rest of the population because of their privileged economic and political position (Casey *et al.*, 2002:112). In this context, scholars have analyzed the influence of the Gramsci's theory of hegemony in the media studies. In media discourse, Bagdikian (1987), and Machesney (1999) and others criticize the big media for their dominance in the markets with their contents. These scholars argue that the corporate media intend to perpetuate the neo-liberal agenda and hence the media content is aimed at making profits. In fact, neo liberalism refers to the policies that maximize the role of markets and profit making and minimize the role of non market institutions (Machesney, 1999:6). Therefore, it is not surprising that the big media promote consumerism, the market, class inequality, and individualism as virtues to be adopted or practices in life. Further, they undervalue political activity, civic values and anti market policies.

With this in view, the rise of global media impacts the people of the less developed countries in terms of their culture and their life styles. The global flow of information is classified by Appadurai (2000) into five dimensions of global cultural flows to demonstrate the various ways the culture moves across the borders and around the world. He outlined the five dimensions or scopes that need to be taken into consideration when examining the global cultural flows: ethnoscapes, mediascapes, technoscapes, finanscapes, and ideoscapes. Ethnoscapes refers to the flow of people around the world (e.g. Tourists, immigrants, or refugees). Technoscapes refers to the flow of technology (e.g. transnational business relocations or the hosting of mega-events like the Olympics that include the movement of new technologies to various countries. Finanscapes refers to the patterns of capital transfer on a global level. Mediascapes refers to the modes of mediated image distribution (e.g. Electronic or print media) and how these images allow viewers to gain access to other parts of the world. Ideoscapes refers to the images that are invested with political-ideological meaning (eg.

Propaganda images distributed to and from through mass media outlets). Because of this flow, the global media perpetuate their imperialism in the third World while trying to erode the indigenous culture.

This influence is described as cultural imperialism. McPhail (1981) who described cultural imperialism as electronic colonialism observed:

> Electronic colonialism is the dependency relationship established by the importation of communication hardware and foreign produced software which along with engineers, technicians and related information protocols vicariously establish a set of foreign norms, values, and expectations which, in varying degrees, may alter the domestic cultures and socialization process (p 20).

Tehranian (1999), for example, pointed out that the cultural imperialism would affect the Third World population in five dimensions: 1) exacerbated their conditions of social, economic, political, and cultural dependency, 2) undermined their national identity in favour of consumerism and materialized colonialism, 3) privileged the economic and cultural interests of an urban and Westernized elite against the vast majority of semi rural and rural populations, 4) encouraged conspicuous consumption through global advertising at the expense of social investments in education, health, and infrastructure, and 5) failed to create genuine development projects and perpetuated repressive and rapacious elites.

With the rapid flow of information, the Western media dominate the international communication although their contents are subjected to criticism as they are culturally influencing the people of the Third World nations. Scholars like Schiller (1981), Mankekar (1981), Blum (2007) and diplomats like Masmoudi (1979) share a common thesis that the Western media influence the culture of the less developed countries (LDCs). The Western media, it is argued, serve as a vehicle for western values, western norms, and western culture. Blum (2007) wrote:

> Western culture is carried by multiple vectors including popular music, films, television, tourism, migration. As such diffusion takes place through broadly dispersed social and technological channels which frequently circumvent state institutions and affects mass publics directly. In its most obvious forms the

> diffusion of pop culture in each city takes place in typical fashion, as young people are intimidated by global media flows and then imitate western styles of dress, music, and behavior. While it is possible to detect variations and subcultures in urban settings the general tendency is absorb superficial styles uncritically (and at times even unwillingly). Much of this is purely a matter of fashion and image as youth respondents in a focus group freely admitted (p 75).

The purpose of this imperialism is two-fold: economic and political. The West tries to capture markets by exporting their cultural and entertainment products. In the political arena, cultural imperialism plays a major role in distancing people from their cultural roots and traditions by replacing them with media created needs (Murthy, 2002: 61). Petras (1993) identified ten characteristics. Some of them are:

- Cultural imperialism is oriented towards masses, instead of elites;
- Cultural imperialism is impacting the masses all over the globe homogenously;
- In cultural imperialism, political interests are projected in the form of soft news like political biographies achievement of workers as success stories;
- Cultural imperialism seeks to destroy the identity of nations by impacting them with socio-economic content.

With the increasing viewer ship of satellite television channels, the viewers tend to be influenced with the fast moving consumer culture on the belief that the aping the west is the best. Though products advertised on StarTV and Zee TV tended to be from the MNCs, especially the Japanese such as Sony and Panasonic, there were others like Colgate-Palmolive's Lux, and P&G Pampers that preferred domestic campaigns and media (Thomas, 2006:112-113). For instance, a television commercial for the Indian jeans company, Ruf & Tuf, features a rude, impatient American who yells at an elderly farmer to move his tractor, to promote the product (Bucher, 2003:213). Furthermore, the commercials of multinational corporations targeted an urban youthful market especially were characterized by a synthesis of global/western and local/regional elements of culture (Bucher, 2003; 209-220). Cultural studies of youth have highlighted the role of consumption practices in the formation of youth cultures. These studies have focused on the ways young people deploy music and clothing styles in order to form sub-cultural youth identities which are seen as acts of resistance against a dominant culture. This body of research has opened up the possibility that consumption does not simply produce victims of capitalist hegemony, but is a site for a complicated mediation of youth identities (Lukose, 2005).

In fact, the argument to halt cultural imperialism of the West began in the early 1970s when the UNESCO set up a commission to study the mass media content at the instance of the Third World countries. Diplomats like Mustapha Masmoudi (1979) Tunisian ambassador and permanent delegate to UNESCO and journalists like D.R. Mankekar (1978, 1981) in India raised their voice through mass media programmes to make the native culture insular from the external influences. However, long back Gandhiji aptly described these consumer goods as bodily comforts which provide the well being of the individual physically while distancing her/ him from culture of the country. Gandhiji said in *Young India* on June 1, 1921,

> "I do not want my house to be walled in all sides and my windows to be stuffed. I want the cultures of all lands to be blown about my house as freely as possible. But I refuse to be blown off my feet by any. I refuse in other people's houses as an interloper, a beggar or a slave. I refuse to put the necessary strain of learning English upon my sisters for the sake of false pride or questionable social advantage."

## REFERENCES

1. Appadurai, A. (2000). *Modernity at Large: Cultural Dimensions of Globalization*. Minneapolis, MN: University of Minneapolis.
2. Bagdikian, B (1987). *Media Monopoly (Second edition)*. Boston: Beacon Press.
3. Bucher, M (2003). *Transnational Television, Cultural Identity and Change: When*
4. *STAR came to India*. New delhi: sage Publications.
5. Blum, Douglas,W ( 2007). *National Identity and Globalization: Youth, State and*
6. *Society in post-Soviet Eurasia*. Cambridge: Cambridge University Press.
7. Casey, B, Casey, N, Calvert, B, French, L, and Lewis, J. (2002).

*Television Studies: The Key Concepts,* London: Routledge.

8. Gigi Durham, Meenakshi and Kellner, Douglas (eds) *Media and Cultural Studies: Key works,*London: Blackwell
9. Gramsci, A (2001). (i) History of the subalteran classes, (ii) the concept of ideology, (iii) Cultural themes: Ideological material. In Meenakshi Gigi Durham and Douglas Kellner(eds) *Media and Cultural Studies : Key works (pp 43-47),* London: Blackwell
10. Lukose, R (2005). Consuming globalization: Youth and gender in Kerala, India. *Journal of Social History, 35* (4).
11. Mankekar, D R (1981). *Whose Freedom? Whose Order? A plea for a new international Information Order by Third World.* Delhi: Clarion Books.
12. McChesney, RW (1999). Rich media, poor democracy: Communication politics in dubious times. Chicago: University of Illinois Press.
13. McPhail, T. (1981). *Electronic Colonialism: The future of International broadcasting and communication.* London: Sage Publications.
14. Mousmadi, M (1979). The New World Information Order. *Journal of Communication,* 29 (2)
15. Murthy, D V R (2002). *Mass Communication: Concepts and Issues.* Cochin: Olive Green Publishers
16. Petras, J (1993). Cultural Imperialism in the late 20th century. *Journal of Contemporary Asia,* 23(2).
17. Schiller, H I (1981). *Who knows: Information in the Age of Fortune 500?* New Jersey: Ablex.
18. Thomas, A.O. (2006).*Transnational Media and Contoured Markets: Redefining Asian Television and Advertising.* New Delhi: Sage Publications.

# 5

# Resistance: The Weapon of A True Satyagrahi

*S. Subba Rao*

Among all the leaders, who have made extraordinary contributions towards attaining India's Independence, Mahatma Gandhi will be remembered as the most prominent leader. He became actively involved in Indian politics at a time when the country was in need of proper guidance and the national movement was on the brink of losing its direction. Displaying a remarkable leadership quality during the independence movement, Mahatma Gandhi successfully guided the nation to achieve its goal. He was the man who transformed the freedom movement from an elite movement into a mass movement and associated the common people to effectively oppose the colonial rulers. He could enthuse the common man to correlate himself to the national ethos and made him a part of the freedom struggle. Appropriately, he is called the father of the nation because he acted as the guardian of the nation at its hour of crisis. He rightly deserves that status and he will be remembered in the country as the man who shaped India's destiny.

Gandhi's concepts of satya and ahimsa are the most prominent of his entire social and political philosophy. Immediate resistance to injustice and coercion as well as long-term programme of social and political reconstruction must alike be legitimated in terms of the twin absolutes of truth and non-violence. His concept of *Satya*, with *ahimsa* as the means, determined his doctrine of satyagraha or active resistance to authority, while the concept of *ahimsa*, with *satya* as the common end, enabled him to formulate his doctrine of sarvodaya, or non-violent socialism.

The doctrine of Satyagraha was meant to show how the man of conscience could engage in heroic action in the vindication of truth and freedom against all tyranny, in his appeal to justice against every social abuse and sectional interest. Gandhi challenged the conventional notions of authority, law and obligation by appealing to his conceptions of natural law or dharma and self-suffering or tapas. Satya and ahimsa alone can secure an enduring basis for social consensus and political loyalty. There is no external authority that can claim a higher status than satya either in the religious or in the political spheres. There is also no political or social sanction that can be assigned a legitimacy superior to ahimsa.

Gandhi had to gain the confidence of the people and lead them in their opposition against the foreign rulers. However, as a champion of peace and non-violence, he could not approve the violent method of the extremists and as a man of action, he could not follow the method of appeal as preferred by the moderates and wait for things to happen; he neither wanted to make India free through bloodshed nor wished to be a mute onlooker to the misrule of the British. In his wish to bring independence to India, Gandhi also could not favour a means which was unacceptable to his conscience. He was not unscrupulous while he attempted to achieve his objective.

Though Mahatma Gandhi earnestly desired to free India from the British rulers he did not want to do it with the help of a method which was not honourable or moral. He believed that an unethical means never brought a good result and to him violence was unethical. Hence, he did not prefer the means of violence for challenging the bad governance of the rulers. He felt that instead of adopting the principle of 'blood for blood' it was easier to win over the enemy with the help of non-violent means. According to him, violence resulted in more violence and there was the possibility of inviting the severe oppressive power of the government if a violent means was opted for opposing the government. He was certain that it would be impossible for him to face the British rulers with any unethical and immoral method. Therefore, he chose to confront them by attracting the attention of their conscience and reason to their own misdeeds. He wanted to challenge the rulers on moral ground. He preferred to awaken the conscience by his rational approach. Gandhi decided on this method to attain his objective as he was convinced that violence would be a failure in the long run and only a peaceful means would bring an everlasting result and independence to India. And ultimately, he succeeded in bringing independence to India through peaceful means.

Gandhi's Satyagraha has in it, indeed, all the elements of non-violence which the pacifist demands, and has this element in its highest and most positive form. "The true rendering of the word Ahimsa in English" writes Gandhi, "is love, or charity." "For me, the only means of knowing god is non-violence, Ahimsa, Love." To refrain, not only from all ill-will and bitter thought against an opponent, and to seek continually to win him by love and self-suffering, is of the essence of satyagraha. Yet satyagraha has in it, also, a relentlessly aggressive quality. It is the exercise of the greatest measure of "soul-force" within our power in opposition to evil, and it will not rest till it has overcome it, suffering to this end, if need be, even to the point of death.

Regarding the British subjection of India as an evil thing, injurious to his country and to the British themselves, Gandhi set himself with all the might of soul-force to bring the British raj to an end. With no hatred for the foreigner, but only love and goodwill towards him, he was led, nevertheless by the very principles of his faith, to an uncompromising aggression to the foreign yoke. He did not counsel his fellow-countrymen to sit passively unresisting in fact of the moral evils of western domination. On the contrary, he set himself to break through such "slave-mentality", which he considered to be even lower in the moral scale than forcible resistance; and by his method of non-violent non-cooperation he showed to India a pathway to freedom which was at once defiant of evil and free from hate. It demanded an onslaught upon foreign rule equal in determined intensity of that of a war of violence, yet demanding in those who took part in it the highest measure of self-discipline, self-suffering and love. He advised the German Jews, who were vaporized by the million in gas chambers during the World War II, to offer non-violent resistance and challenge the Nazis to shoot them or cast them in the dungeon. And, that, suffering voluntarily undergone would bring them (Jews) an inner strength and joy. He gave similar advice to the Poles, the Czechs and the Abyssinians, and assured them that, this must ultimately melt him (aggressor) and his soldiers. In May 1940 he wrote a letter to the Viceroy from jail, offering to go to Germany to plead with Hitler for peace. He also advised Britain to lay down arms and oppose Hitler with Non-violence.

If there was anything Gandhi abhorred more than violence, it was 'cowardice'. believe, he said, 'if there is only choice between cowardice and violence I would rather advice violence.' For instance if one's mother or wife is attacked, 'I would rather have taken resort to arms in order to defend her honour rather than she should in a cowardly manner become or remain a helpless witness to her own dishonour.' He was very fond of the word 'manly' which represented to him the essence of dignity and self- esteem in man. And whether at the national or the individual level, he was not prepared to compromise it at any cost. 'If you felt humiliated and hurt' he said, 'you will be justified in slapping a bully in the face to vindicate your self-respect.' In fact in certain situations resort to violence became a duty. 'I would rather have India resort to arms in order to defend her honour than that she should, in a cowardly manner become or remain a hopeless victim to her dishonour.' In all these instances we find Gandhi moving away from his absolutist insistence on non-violence, as cowardice he could not accept at any cost.

Satyagraha was basically conceived as a non-violent instrument of conflict resolution. It was an article of faith with Gandhi that nobody is in possession of complete and infallible truth, and everybody's version of truth depended on the limb of the elephant of truth he was holding. Thus, the use of violence to enforce one's views violated this basic character of truth. The only fair and rational approach to resolve conflicts was through dialogue, failing which, by resort to such non-violent means of persuasion as satyagraha, fasts, hartals, non-cooperation and civil-disobedience. Gandhi laced these purely secular methods with religious ideas.

It is believed that the term 'civil disobedience' may have first been used by American Transcendentalist, Henry David Thoreau who refused to pay the poll tax for which he had to spend one night in jail in 1845. For him it was intended to show his refusal to support a government that he considered illegitimate because it condoned slavery and was seeking to expand slave territory through Mexican war. Actually his short prison sojourn resulted in a lecture to the Concord Lyceum in mid-February 1848 called 'The Rights and Duties of the Individual in Relation to Government'. This changed the world's view as we shall see when we look at its impact on Gandhi who once said 'I found a suitable English translation "Civil Disobedience" for the Indian word "Satyagraha" and Thoreau's ideas greatly influenced my movement in India." Gandhi refined Thoreau's concept of civil disobedience by incorporating ideas from Ruskin and Tolstoy. Gandhi integrates the concept of civil disobedience with his overall commitment to non-violence and satyagraha and dignity of labour. Gandhi, like Green accepts common good without denying a pivotal role to the individual, endowed with moral law and duty (dharma). As a bearer of moral authority, he has the right and even the duty to judge the state and its laws, by the standards of dharma, which in turn combines the essentials of satya and ahimsa. The individual can challenge and even disobey the state, for all states violate satya and ahimsa. According to Gandhi, 'Every citizen renders himself responsible for every act of his government. And loyalty to a capricious and corrupt state is a sin, disloyalty a virtue.' He declares civil disobedience 'as the birth right that cannot be surrendered without losing self-respect.' Like Locke and Jefferson he believes loyalty to a constitution and its laws needs to be reviewed and affirmed once in every generation. Satya, ahimsa and dharma are the three cardinal tenets of Gandhian philosophy.

Satyagraha as conceived by Gandhi is not a formula of social and political disintegration. A satyagrahi must have first rendered willing obedience to the laws of the state. One must have shown a willing, intelligent and spontaneous obedience to the laws of the state. Gandhi writes: 'A satyagrahi obeys the laws of society intelligently and of his own free will, because he considers it to be his sacred duty to do so. It is only when a person has thus obeyed the laws of society scrupulously that he is in a position to judge as to which particular rules are good and just, and which are unjust iniquitous. Only then does the right accrue to him of the civil disobedience of certain laws in well defined circumstances.' Mahatma Gandhi claimed to have been by nature law-abiding.

The capacity for civil resistance comes from the discipline undergone in process of obeying the civil and moral laws of the state. A satyagrahi while resisting the laws of the government should see that the social structure is not subverted.

There are different forms of Satyagraha. Non-cooperation with the evil doer is a mild form. Civil disobedience of the laws of the government is a strong and extreme form of satyagraha. Gandhi meant by civil, in the concept of civil disobedience, a sense of discrimination, discipline, civility and non-violence. There can be individual as well as mass civil disobedience. The latter means spontaneous action by masses. In the beginning masses will have to be rigorously trained for action. Gradually they will learn this art.

According to Gandhi complete civil disobedience implying a refusal to render obedience to every single state-made law can be a very powerful movement. It can become 'more dangerous than an armed rebellion', because the stupendous power of innocent suffering undergone on a great scale has great potency. But bringing the scrutinizing glare of public opinion on the evils of an autocratic state, the fall even of despotic political regime is ensured.

Gandhi was a believer in the superiority of the soul. He would never sanction any submission to any law if it conflicted with the moral stature of a man. The voice of Atman - the inner conscience—is supreme. The dictates and commands of any government, if they conflicted with the sense of higher duty of a person, have to be resisted. According to the political teachings of Gandhi, Satyagraha is a perpetual law against anything repugnant to the soul. Even if alone, a man of truth and conscience will resist the laws and commands issued by a representative legislature if they go against the higher law of the Atman. A true satyagrahi will risk all dangers for the sake of truth. Gandhi wrote: "But even so a call may come which one dare not neglect, cost it what it may. I can clearly see the time coming to me when I must effuse obedience to every single state-made law, even though there may be a certainty of bloodshed. When neglect of the call means a denial of God, civil disobedience becomes a peremptory duty."

The Gandhian philosophy and sociology of Satyagraha is a spiritualized and moralized form of the concept of resistance. In western political thought resistance has been advocated. Some of the scholastic philosophers sanctioned tyrannicide. John Calvin advocated partial resistance by 'inferior magistrates'. Thoreau was an arch-champion of civil disobedience. During the Swadeshi movement Tilak, Aurobindo and the extremist school also advocated passive resistance. Sometimes the Gandhian satyagraha is confused with the passive resistance advocated by Quakers. But there are vital differences between them. To begin with, satyagraha is a dynamic force because it contemplates action in resistance of injustice. Passive resistance is compatible with internal violence towards the enemy but Satyagraha stresses continuous cleansing of the mind. It emphasizes even inner purity. Passive resistance is mainly contemplated at a political level. Satyagraha can be practiced at all levels - domestic, social and political. Satyagraha goes beyond passive resistance in the stress on a spiritual and moral teleology because the final source of hope and consolation for the satyagrahi is God. The Gandhian theory of satyagraha is far more comprehensive than the passive resistance as advocated in India in 1906-1908. Tilak and Aurobindo would not condemn violence on moral grounds. But Gandhi accepted the absolutism of Ahimsa. The passive resistance of 1906-1908 was a political technique of limited application. Sometimes it meant only swadeshi and boycott, while sometimes it was extended to cover disobedience of unjust laws and decrees. The Gandhian theory of satyagraha is a philosophy of life and politics, and it contemplates stupendous mass action for paralyzing the total structure of a despotic government.

The disobedient willingly accepts full penalties, including the rigours of jail discipline, while resistance is respectful and restrained, for it is undertaken by law-abiding citizens. A satyagrahi cooperates not out of fear of punishment but because cooperation is essential for the common good. Gandhi resorts to civil disobedience only after exploring other efforts of constitutional political action of persuasion and petition. Gandhi prescribes non-cooperation (strikes, walkouts, resignation from offices and titles), hartal, picketing, economic boycott, dharna, fasting and non-payment of taxes as different forms of satyagraha. He advised that non-payment of taxes had to be resorted to only on rare and final occasions, for taxes constitute the life support of a government and refusal of payment meant its death. He prescribed constructive programmes as a positive method that included: communal harmony, removal of untouchability, prohibition, hand-spun cloth (khadi), encouragement of village industries, village sanitation, primary and adult education, upliftment of women, education in health and hygiene and the propagation of Hindi as a national language.

Gandhi rejected passive resistance which was first used by Bipin Chandra Pal (1858-1932), as too weak and preferred to use Satyagraha, as it did not denote violence more out of deliberate choice; and fight injustice armed with the power of truth rather than physical or brute force. Satyagraha was resistance without any acrimony or hatred or injury to the opponent. He considered disobedience to evil laws as a moral duty and described the resisters as 'real constitutionalists', for in disobeying and accepting punishment they were obeying the law. The existence of injustice justified political resistance and that political protest was basically moral. Therefore, it could take place in both democratic and non-democratic systems. Gandhi's unique contribution was to transform Thoreau's definition of civil disobedience as the pursuit of a solitary individual into a technique and programme for mass action.

For Gandhi civil disobedience is a tactic for social change, a weapon of the powerless 'and the oppressed. It is the Gandhian model that subsequent practitioners of civil disobedience employ. Moreover, Gandhi also demonstrates that the success of civil disobedience depends on whether it has a universal rather than a local appeal.

Gandhi constantly harped on the theme that the British were ruling India with our cooperation, as we did not resort to non-acceptance of repugnant laws: 'For even the most powerful cannot rule,' Gandhi said as far back as 1905, 'without the cooperation of the ruled.' In view of his thesis that a government depends on the cooperation of the ruled for its sustenance, and it would collapse if that cooperation was withdrawn, Gandhi started his first major Satyagraha with the Non-cooperation Movement. By refusing to cooperate with government institutions, and boycotting goods produced in the country of the ruler, his intention was to bring the government to its knees. The next stage was deliberate defiance of the laws through the Civil Disobedience Movement, so that the legal framework which sustained the raj was brought into disrepute. These acts of open non-cooperation and disobedience were also aimed at instilling courage and confidence in the people to stand up to the might of the ruler, as also to demonstrate the hollowness of his power.

Having all along held the state as evil owing to its reliance on violence, just a fortnight before his assassination he said, 'when power descended on him (Sardar Patel) he saw that he could no longer successfully apply the method of non-violence which he used to wield with signal success. I have made the discovery that what I and the people with me termed non-violence was not the genuine article but a weak copy known as passive resistance. Naturally, passive resistance can avail nothing to a ruler.'

The above observations of Gandhi are eminently sensible and pragmatic. But his claim to greatness does not rest on such pragmatism. He placed before the world a sublime ideal. He also repeatedly pointed out that an ideal was like the Euclidean line or point; that pure non-violence was an ideal which was not possible to achieve in practice. Yet the beauty of his crusade lay in the fact that all his life he heroically strove to enlarge the limits of the possible and establish the superiority of the non-violent method of conflict resolution over the largest possible area. But with the passage of time he was assailed by doubts about the effectiveness of his precepts and agenda, and even wondered if he has not been' living in a fool's paradise.' It is in this context that one feels stricken at seeing him throw in the sponge at his 'discovery' that his non-violence was not the genuine article. The pedestrian 'discovery' and its acceptance was unfair to his lofty calling, as also to hundreds of satyagrah is who gave their lives at his bidding.

## REFERENCES

1. Hiren Mukerjee, *Gandhi - A Study,* People's Publishing House, 1960.
2. C.F. Andrews, *Mahatma Gandhi's Ideas,* George and Allen and Unwin Ltd., 1929.
3. B.R. Nanda, *The Nerhrus,* Oxford University Press, 1989.
4. Subhash Chandra Bose, *The Indian Struggle,* Asia Publishing House, Bombay.

5. Rajni Palme Dutt, *India Today*, People's Publishing House, 1949.
6. S.C. Biswas (Ed.), *Gandhi's Theory and Practice - Social Impact and Contemporary Relevance*, Indian Institute of Advanced Studies, Simla.
7. *Congress Centenary*, Volume II.
8. *Nehru - Selected Works*, Jawaharlal Nehru Memorial Fund, Volume II.
9. Ayesha Jalal, *The Sole Spokesman*, Cambridge University Press, 1985.
10. Judith Brown, *Gandhi's Rise to Power*, Cambridge University Press, 1972.
11. Ronald J. Tercheck, *Gandhi - Struggling for Autonomy*, Vistaar Publications, 2000.
12. Raghavan N. Iyer, *The Moral and Political Thought of Mahatma Gandhi*, Oxford University Press, 2000.

# 6

# Resistance Movements Before Gandhi

*V.B.T. Sundari*

Eighteenth century India witnessed the decline of Mughal Empire, political anarchy, chaos and confusion, and the growth of English East India Company into a paramount power. The English by defeating other European rivals became strong and established its political authority over India .Then began a long period of foreign rule which ignored the welfare of the masses and worked for the vested interests of very few. Adam Smith opined that "the government of an exclusive company of merchants is perhaps the worst of all governments for any country whatever". Therefore the merciless exploitation and ruthless oppression of the people by the British led to many outbursts and resistance movements before the advent of Gandhi.

The movements can be divided into three sections pre-mutiny (1757-1856), mutiny (1857) and post-mutiny (1857-1905).

**Causes for the resistance movements:**

- financial policies of the government
- excessive land revenue demands
- insults and humiliation
- loss of independence
- racial discrimination
- social and religious grievances.

*Pre-Mutiny:* After the battle of Plassey the English company obtained a foothold in Bengal and resulted in its expansion of company's authority all over India. Due to the above mentioned causes there were number of popular revolts and mutinies against foreign rule .The sanyasis of Bengal ,the Santhals in Rajamahal Ahoms in Assam ,Kols in Chotanagpur Bhils and Kolis in Khandesh and the revolt of the raja of Vijayanagar were some of the many movements. Sepoy mutinies were not uncommon during the period.

*The Mutiny:* The revolt of the sepoys considered by some historians as first war of independence - an important landmark in the history of resistance movements and it shook the mighty English empire. The expansionist policies of the British economic exploitation and administrative innovations adversely affected all except the few English educated Indians. Inspite of the best efforts of Nanasahib, Jhansi Lakshmibai , Tantiatope ,Bahadurshaw to mention a few , the mutiny failed and Indian administration was transferred to the crown .

*Post-Mutiny:* 'Julius Ceasar dead was more powerful than when he was alive'. Like that mutiny of 1857 became a symbol of challenge to the mighty British Empire. The stories of 1857 inspired the people in the post mutiny period. The Britishers who were now masters of India used their political power to further their own interests both political and economical Indian masses were deprived of the benefits of the economy.There were popular risings here and there against the British. Among them mention should be made of Indigo riots in Bengal (1860) Kuka revolt in Punjab the Birsa movement in Chotanagpur and the Wahabi movement.

Except 'Indigo riots' all the other movements were suppressed by the British government. The former occupied a special place in history as it was the first historical instance of organized non-cooperation and passive resistance which became a mighty weapon used by Mahatma Gandhi half a century later. The peasants in Bengal suffered a lot in the hands of Indigo planters. Dinabandh Mitra's drama 'Nildarpan' reveals the atrocities of the planters. Bishnu Charan Biswas and Digambar Biswas of the village of Chaugach in the district of Nadia became real heroes in rescuing the ryots from the cruelties of the planters. They were the Dewans of indigo factories but left the service and began to think remedial measures. They made the cultivators of their village take the vow of "Never planting indigo again" and the planters used many violent actions against the ryots . Inspite of that, more cultivators joined the group and took the vow "Non cultivation of indigo even at the risk of their lives". This spread to other districts also and ultimately the government recommended reasonable rights and privilages of both cultivators and planters. It was a great popular victory. Amrit Bazar Patrika of 22nd May 1874 expressed that – "it was the indigo disturbances which first taught the natives the value of combination and political agitation...".

Riots in Poona and Ahmednagar generally known as the Deccan riots (1875) took place because of the heavy assessment of land revenue. So the peasants took money from the Mawari money lenders at high rate of interest and sometimes mortgaged their lands as security. The money lenders compelled them to compromise the honour of their females to get relief from the crushing debts. Provoked by such outrages the villagers of Kardeh declared a social and economic boycott of the Mawaris which resulted in the latter's quitting the village. This was followed by other villages also.

In Assam people particularly of hill tribes broke into open revolt. Loss of freedom, heavy assessment of land revenue, imposition of new taxes led to a series of out breaks organized by the popular assemblies under the leadership of locals. In Kamarup the people started an organized campaign for non payment of revenue at the increased rate. They were firm and shouted "we won't pay the increased revenue".

Likewise in Benaras the whole population adopted a novel device to sit dharna, a non violent protest against a house tax imposed by government. Even though they were not successful in organizing a country wide dharna, the Supreme Court repealed the tax.

The freedom movement in India began with the establishment of Indian National Congress and the first phase was known as moderate era who followed peaceful and constitutional methods. The period from 1905-1919 known as extremist era changed the methodology adopted by the moderates. Under the able leadership of Lal, Bal, Pal, they advocated economic boycott of British made goods and use of swadeshi. They infused new spirit into the freedom struggle by propagating new slogans – non cooperation, passive resistance, mass agitation, self reliance and discipline of suffering.

They called the patriots for service and suffering for the nation. Terrorist movements also began during this period to obtain freedom from foreign rule. With the advent of Mahatma Gandhi passive resistance movement became more popular.

Most of the resistance movements before Gandhi were crushed with brute force. Indians were not a match to the British in weapons. So Gandhi advocated non violence and satyagraha as weapons against them and obtained Independence. Because non violence is a force which is more positive than electricity and more powerful than even ether.

## REFERENCES

1. Shriman Narayan (ed.) (1968) –*The Selected Works of Mahatma Gandhi,* 6 vols. Navajivan trust.
2. B. L. Grover (2006) A new look at Modern Indian History, New Delhi, R.C. Majumdar (1970) *British Paramountcy And Indian Renaissance* vol. 9 , Bombay.

# 7

# Gandhi's Approach to Resistance with Particular Reference to Women in the Freedom Movement

*G. Lakshmi*

This paper outlines some of the key ideas of Gandhi's approach to resistance and comment on its value. An attempt is made to set forth the Gandhian approach to resistance which has great relevance today and for the centuries ahead of us. In our own day and age, Gandhi's lessons of nonviolent resistance are more essential than ever. Gandhi evolved a technique of direct mass action which placed unhesitating reliance on the creative political role of the common masses of the people and on the independent initiative for action.

This paper would also marginally refer to the way Gandhi adopted this approach to mobilize women on a mass scale for the cause of the country's independence. It is to the credit of Gandhi that women participated in large numbers in the nationalist struggle. The Gandhian approach has proved its worth, in general, in the freedom struggle, particularly with the participation of women in the freedom movement.

## Non-violent Defense

Gandhian approach to resistance can be described as *Non-violent Defense* or *Non-violent Direct Action* – a novel way in the history of mass actions waged to resist encroachments upon human freedom.. Gandhi called non-violent action the way "of the strong and wise", and added: "..with right which is on their side and the choice of non-violence as their only weapon, if they will make it such, a bright future is assured."[1] Non-violent resistance is a strategy for countering the power of violent force with the power of an integrative system. It is the most expeditious method known to the world of winning over the opponents. It is a mild form but can be immensely potent technique when undertaken on a mass scale.

Gandhi's approach to resistance had three basic ingredients: first, it included personal nonviolence as a way of life or personal discipline. Second, it included constructive work — a programme for transforming society, third, the use of nonviolence against direct and structural violence — a method for engaging in conflict. It was unique in the sense it was a two-pronged approach, juxtaposing non-violent civil resistance [i.e., opposition to evil and injustice] and constructive programme, targeted to the needs of the people. Gandhi's strategy aimed at making the unjust system unable to function by using non-violent measures and at the same time offering a constructive alternative. Gandhi employed a careful balance between the negative and positive between campaigns of civil resistance and constructive programme [elaborated later in this paper] His approach included a belief that means cannot be separated from ends, a belief in the unity of all life, and a willingness to suffer for one's beliefs.

## Satyagraha

*Satyagraha*, the name, Gandhi gave to this new way of resistance and overcoming injustice, means "holding on to truth" or "soul force". . It literally means holding on to truth. In Gandhi's terminology, *Satyagraha* – 'truth-force' or 'soul force' — was an outgrowth of nonviolence.[2] Gandhi did not invent *Satyagraha*, he discovered it, or rather re-discovered non-violence as a personal and public method for positive change. Gandhi said, " *Satyagraha* is as ancient as the hills".[3] He defined its principles and applied them on as large scale as possible to show its efficacy. *Satyagraha* has been described by Krishnalal Shridharani, [a disciple of Gandhi], as 'Gandhi's method of fighting the British'.[4]

*Satyagraha* or non-violent struggle — to the development of which Gandhi contributed so much — as a technique of great importance, is a practical method of resistance and for resolving conflict. He devised the technique of *Satyagraha* for the specific purpose of solving conflicts through the means of non-violence. It was his conviction that violence would aggravate the conflict out of all proportion. Therefore, non-violence was an alternative to violence in resolving conflict. It is a method which involves a breach of the law, but without causing physical harm to the agents of the law. It excludes the use of violence and hatred in any shape or form. *Satyagraha* is a relentless search for truth and determination to reach truth not by inflicting of suffering on the opponent, but on one's self.

In *Satyagraha* Gandhi demonstrated a method and a philosophy of engaging in conflict which can be developed as an effective substitute for political violence. *Satyagraha* shares with non-military defense the idea that harm shall not be inflicted on the antagonist. Gandhi was very explicit on this — he was against physical sabotage, against "scorched earth" policy.[5] The aggressor should be seen as misled rather than malicious beyond redemption. Cooperation with the aggressor is cooperation to evil. For the sake of aggressor and victim non-cooperation becomes a duty. In so doing the aggressed deprives the aggressor of possible gains which is also in accordance with a non-military defence programme.

Gandhi's approach, thus, relies on a pragmatic conception of nonviolence, namely that nonviolent methods are more effective than violent methods in that particular historico-poiltical situation of India. In other words, Gandhi's accurate understanding of the objective political situation of India and the Indian mentality combined with his own spiritual and ethical disposition made him adopt the method of non-violent resistance.

## Underlying Principles

Gandhian method involved three essential components which needed to work together: personal discipline; a programme for transforming society; and a method for engaging in conflict. It consists of three underlying principles.

(i) The first principle underlying Gandhi's *Satyagraha* is that it tries to resolve the sources of conflict by bringing out about a *conversion*, [i.e. we have much more to gain in harmony than in discord] — in an opponent. The optimal way of producing change in Gandhian approach is conversion through persuasive argumentation, through rational and gentle persuasion and not by coercion and compulsion. Gandhi's approach is based on a moral appeal to the opponent's conscience [amplified through personal suffering] and an approach based on undermining their sources of power. Gopinath Dhawan says, Gandhi's *Satyagraha* exerted "moral pressure" intended to evoke the best in the opponent.[6] The *Satyagrahi* undermines the moral defenses of the opponent and the pressure of the resistance, while compelling, is persuasive.

The strength of nonviolence lies in its ability to dramatically reduce the moral legitimacy of those who persist in using violent strategies against non-violent opposition. This loss of legitimacy can, in turn, contribute to coalition-building efforts leading to widespread condemnation of parties using violent strategies and often the imposition of sanctions by the international community.

Gandhi felt non-violent resistance, say such as a demonstration, will strengthen appeals to the opponent's conscience and may evoke their sense of justice; it may elicit the support of third parties. It is a means of strengthening self-control and discipline for the struggle against injustice generally "it frees one from the manipulative attempts of the other". Gandhi says, if the injustice remains unresolved, non-violent resistance [perhaps in another form] must continue until the opponent does change the attitude or opinion.

(ii) The second underlying principle in *Satyagraha* is that, Gandhi makes a clear distinction between the actor and the deed. According to Gandhi, British imperialism and the Indian caste system were both examples of structures that were perpetuated, in large part, as a result of people performing particular roles within them. The evil, however, was in the structure, not in the people who performed their duties. The essence of Gandhi's approach was to identify approaches to conflict that preserved the people while systematically demolishing the evil structure. This is the great spiritual teaching behind non-violent non-cooperation. As long as a people accept exploitation, both exploiter and exploited will be entangled in injustice. But once the exploited refuse to accept the relationship, refuse to cooperate with it, they are already free.

(iii) The third underlying principle in *Satyagraha* is the doctrine of self-suffering, willingness to suffer the violence of other without inflicting violence and suffering in return. Gandhi's non-violent resistance requires tremendous courage, self-control as well as a willingness to endure pain and sometimes even death. This will result in the least total loss of life and the greatest degree of moral enrichment for humanity as a whole. Key to the success of non-violent approaches is the willingness of the parties to base their resistance upon broadly supported moral principles and a communication strategy which publicizes for the world to see the immoral and violent behavior of their opponents.

## Types of Non-violent Action

Non-violent action is not passive resistance, but a technique capable of taking the initiative in active struggle. A link was forged between a means of mass struggle and a moral preference for non-violent means.

Gandhian non-violent action includes the types of behaviour known as non-violent resistance, non-violent direct action, and a variety of specific methods of action, such as strikes, boycotts, political non-cooperation, civil disobedience, non-violent obstruction, etc. in which the masses firmly reject the oppressive, insensitive and immoral alien authority through withdrawal of support [without resorting to use of force]. It remained for Gandhi to make the most significant political experiments to that time in the use of non-cooperation, disobedience and defiance to control rulers, alter policies and undermine political systems.

There are literally hundreds of different forms of non-violent resistance and struggle that may vary with circumstances, each with their own advantages and disadvantages. While analyzing Gandhi's approach to resistance and the various methods he used during his long span of freedom struggle, one might refer to the three categories of nonviolent action of Gene Sharp,[7] one of the leading scholars on nonviolent direct action. They are:

(1) *nonviolent protest and persuasion* (the mildest), includes symbolic actions such as marches or parades, picketing, teach-ins, or vigils—any action which voices peaceful opposition to a policy or a law. The intent is to persuade others to change their attitude toward that policy and to join the nonviolent struggle to overturn or correct the policy or law. The Champaran and Kheda *Satyagraha* movements are cases in point.

(2) *non-cooperation,* includes stronger actions which involve refusal to do things that are normally done to help a person, group, institution, or government with which one is in conflict. For example, people might refuse to pay taxes if they disagree with the government's actions spending those taxes; they might refuse to work, or stage a work slow-down to protest working conditions or business or government policies; or they might refuse to obey laws they consider to be unfair or immoral. Non-cooperation may be social, political, or economic, depending on what institution is challenged. The Triple boycott action is an example of this method.

(3) *Nonviolent intervention,* which is designed to interrupt an ongoing activity or process of the opponent, such as the Bardoli *Satyagraha*. Examples include "sit-ins" in which people will sit in a business or government office, stopping its functioning; or blockages of roads, railroad tracks, or the movement of ships at sea. Also included in this category are what Sharp called "psychological interventions," for example, self-inflicted fasting.

All of these forms of direct action are effective, Gandhi asserts, because they diminish the legitimacy, and hence the power of the opponent. "Nonviolent action tends to turn the opponent's violence and repression against his own power position, weakening it and at the same time strengthening the nonviolent group. Because violent action and nonviolent action possess quite different mechanisms, and induce differing forces of change in the society, the opponent's repression... can never really come to grips with the kind of power wielded by the nonviolent actionists."[8]

Yet, at another level of analysis of Gandhi's nonviolent approach may be described as principled and revolutionary,[9] as said by Robert Burrowes in his book, The Strategy of Nonviolent Defense. Many of his campaigns including the Salt Satyagraha were in this category. Gandhi may be described as a practitioner of principled nonviolence because he chose the path for ethical reasons and belief in the unity of means and ends. The Gandhian approach portrayed the struggle against the British as a moral battle in which the moral and spiritual strength of India which was supreme. For him, nonviolence was a way of life. He constructed a moral stance which cut across class, countries and rural-urban differences to create an anti-imperial front.

Gandhi's approach was also revolutionary in the sense of structural analysis of politics and relationships. His approach amounted to a non-violent revolution because it involved basic and rapid structural change. He believed there is a need for fundamental structural change and particular campaigns were conducted within the context of a long-term revolutionary strategy. Gandhi's Satyagraha campaigns were waged against political entities, not persons. His opponents included industries, local governments and'most notably, the British Empire. His approach was one between structure and counter-structure. It was aimed to bring about a structural change in the way in which the organization makes the policies i.e., it aims for a change in the structure that governs relationships – the organizational communities in which people live and work. Gandhi's concept of change was a change of structure, not redistribution or mobility of persons within the same structure.[10] It was a patient long-range strategy for changing the system by paralyzing the evil structure from the top. If that does not work it will have to be paralyzed from the bottom or from within. Gandhi's strategy aimed at making the unjust system unable to function by using non-violent measures and at the same time offering a constructive alternative.

## Constructive Programme

Considering that the struggle for independence was long-drawn battle in which open warfare had no role to play, Gandhi wanted to encompass the whole mass of people especially the women so as to establish close contacts with the masses.. For this, Gandhi's envisaged as 'Constructive Programme' that was intended to restructure the social and economic life of all Indians — a vital part of his strategy for the liberation of India. The constructive programme was designed to satisfy the needs of each individual member of society and was centrally concerned with the needs for self-esteem, security and justice. It was also a major aspect of his approach and national movement strategy of building counter hegemony.

This programme was an integral part and positive aspect of Gandhi's post-1920, *Satyagraha* movements. According to Gandhi, it was designed to build up the nation from the very bottom. It was adopted for the achievement of economic self-sufficiency and inculcation of *swadeshi* spirit amongst the masses. It was also employed for the promotion of communal harmony and removal of social evils like untouchability, unemployment and illiteracy.[11] For Gandhi, constructive work was the heart of the matter. He described it as the permanent part of the non-violent effort.[12]

The constructive work programme, as envisaged by Gandhi, had both inner and outer dimensions. At the inner level the workers were to be given moral and psychological training while at the outer level the constructive programme meant taking up of a proper kind of economic and social activity. J.V.Bondurant says, "The constructive programme was an essential component of the Gandhian revolutionary struggle for Indian independence. It was the constructive programme which gave content to the *Satyagraha* framework and applied Gandhian principles to the Indian circumstance."[13]

In the course of this movement that first started during the 1920s, national schools and institutions were started, arbitration courts and panchayats were established and spinning of charkha began with the sole object of replacing government schools and colleges, law courts and foreign goods which were to be completely boycotted.

Gandhi's constructive programme entailed many elements– one such was the campaign to liberate women and bringing them into the public sphere which was intended to secure self-esteem, security and justice for those most systematically oppressed by India's patriarchal society.

## Women's Participation in Freedom Movement

Gandhi's approach of non-violent resistance combined with the constuctive programme provided ample avenues for women's participation in politics in general and freedom struggle in particular. Gandhi's political belief and his idea of women's role or anticipation of the important contribution of women [from both their own and other families] to the nationalist movement carved a distinct negotiable space for women's political contribution. Gandhi had tremendous faith in women's inherent capacity for non-violence. And his experience of participation by women in politics from his days in South Africa till the end of his life bears testimony to the fact that they never failed his expectations. With Gandhi's inspiration, they took the struggle right into their homes and raised it to a moral level.

Gandhi-led mass movements emphasised the feminine culture as opposed to the basic character of the British rule wherein the symbols of power, prestige, status and individual successes represented a masculine character. The feminine traits such as simplicity, service, religion and dedication represented passive resistance while war or the use of brute force represented masculine traits. He thought the best way to counter 'male' symbolism [the British rule] was to project the alternatives — feminine vision in opposition to individualism competitive and aggressive self-development. In emphasising the virtues of female perseverance and non-violence, Gandhi gave the nationalist movement a moral quality and emphasised woman's moral strength.

Gandhi was of the firm conviction that women had a greater capacity to resist the temptation of foreign rule and to suffer non-violently for their beliefs.[14] He thought women were much better placed at the movement's cultural and ideological levels to attempt the method of non-violent passive resistance. His approach led to the juxtaposition and demands of domestic obligation and public participation of women in India.

He accorded political significance to the domestic sphere and women participated in public spaces through constructive practices like spinning khaddar, sacrificing for the family, acting as supportive wives and mothers to activists, serving as pillars of support and strength in families facing economic and emotional predicaments

For Gandhi, women's participation in national movement was necessary as well as for the practical reasons that with women involved the nationalist movement would be linked to every home in India.[15]

## Upsurge in Participation of Women

Gandhi's insistence on non-violence as a revolutionary weapon contributed to creating favourable conditions for mass participation of people, especially women. It is to the credit of Gandhi that women from all classes participated in large numbers in the national movement. . It was in response to the call given by Gandhi that women made significant contribution to the salt march, prison experiences, songs and cotton spinning.

Women were integral part of Gandhi's non-violence movement. The fact that there was no material weaponry involved, made women equal, and perhaps even better soldiers in Gandhi-led movements. Even the most common and uneducated women sacrificed time and materials, while volunteering, campaigning, protesting, fasting, and donating to the causes of freedom. Women organized public meetings, sold *Khadi* and prescribed literature, started picketing shops of liquor and foreign goods, prepared contraband salt, and came forward to face all sorts of atrocities meted out by police officers, bore the hardship encountered while picketing or demonstrating, courted arrest and even served prison sentences. When most of the men-folk were in prison, women came forward to take charge of the struggle. Uneducated and educated women sacrificed time and materials, volunteering, campaigning, protesting, fasting, and donating to the causes of freedom.

Women's traditional qualities, such as their lesser capacity for organised violence, were not downgraded but were held up as models of superior courage.[16] Gandhi tried to capitalise on women's feminine traits and traditional qualities by extending their traditional roles into the political sphere.[17] The symbolic representation of women constructed by the nationalist movement enabled women to play a political role through the avenues they opened, in both the public and domestic domain. He interpreted women's political participation as an extension of traditional and familial roles.[18]

Gandhi had sought the support of women for almost all of

his political movements. Consequently, women's involvement in the public sphere stretched from the Non-cooperation Movement of the 1920s to the Civil Disobedience Movement of the 1930s and to the Quit India Movement of the 1940s. Between 1920 and 1940 Gandhi came to advocate a greatly expanded role for women in political movements.

Initially in the 1920s, when he called the women to participate in the non-cooperation he wanted them to play a supportive role in *Swadeshi* and *Khadi/Charkha* movements. In the 1930s he called for broader participation in which they would take on the activity of picketing liquor shops and sellers of foreign cloth. By 1940s, Gandhi exhorted the women to play leadership role in the political movements

The non-cooperation movement saw the participation of women on a large scale in constructive programmes laid down by Gandhi like spinning and khadi work. Gandhi took up issues like *swadeshi* and prohibition and tried to motivate women to fight for them. During this period women's participation was limited to nationwide strikes, hartals, *Satyagraha* and breaking of government laws and only those women participated whose leaders made family members had joined the struggle serving jail sentences. By late 1920s women had started in increasing numbers in public bonfires of foreign cloth, even in the mill areas in the night, all-night dharnas consisting exclusively of women had begun to be organised.

In 1930s there was significant increase in the participation of women. Gandhi's special appeal to women provided impetus to their participation. By the time the first phase of the Civil Disobedience Movement ended in 1931-32, women were firmly entrenched in the mass movements, which encompassed diverse sections of women from the urban rich to the rural poor. The main body of woman participants were not from the intelligentsia or even big urban centres, thousands of rural women took recourse to defiance of the law in forests and villages where they stood with children around them. The myth of English-educated elite women had exploded by then. However, there were regional differences and variations in the intensity of women's involvement and the nature of activities.

During the Quit India Movement in the 1940s, twenty years after the Non-cooperation Movement and ten years past Civil Disobedience, more women came forward to participate because of the precedence in the past two decades. Gandhi wanted woman to be the true helpmate of man in the mission of service. Women extended the discipline and sacrifice of their homes to the nation as a whole.

Gandhi's involvement of women has been a carefully planned strategy that would fulfill a specific political purpose in the nationalist movement. First, he used household objects such as the *charkha* and *khadi* as an essential 'tool' to involve women in the national struggle. These were powerful symbolic domestic items which could be used by middle-class women with little or no formal education. Those women who could not cross the threshold of the domestic sphere engaged in activities which supported the movement from within the domestic sphere. Gandhi, thus, tried to use women's traditional qualities to extend their traditional roles into the political spheres.

Gandhi also realized that for mass mobilization, the nationalist symbols had to relate to the private lives of people and must touch their daily existence. The ability of Gandhi's leadership lies in the fact that he could successfully translate ordinary domestic items like salt, liquor and foreign cloth that were given [effective political] symbolic and nationalistic significance. Women's participation in the public domain was intricately tied with familial symbols, household dynamics and nationalist symbolism.[19]

Salt was an issue directly related to women's lives. It was a commodity which women from all classes bought, providing shared cultural context and constituting a shared national identity. There was a moral emphasis on including a special stress on the suffering of a helpless population and the suggestion that the resistance to the tax on salt must touch everyone and certainly the starving millions. It had a maximum appeal for the masses because salt was a commodity consumed daily by them. So also, foreign cloth that had long been important as a symbol of all foreign domination, hence foreign cloth boycott became a symbol of resistance

Here again, Gandhi understood the importance of family dynamics in encouraging or inhibiting women's involvement in public activities. Their dual stress on women fulfilling their duties as mothers within their homes as well as serving the nation was important because it enabled women to participate in the public sphere without dismantling the existing family situation and threatening the prevalent domestic ideology.

Gandhi outlined a clear and specific programme based on women's special virtues of patience and forbearance while picketing shops. Inherent in this was the idea that although men could participate in picketing, they would be less effective because violence was more likely to result. Gandhi suggested that successful picketing of the shops would dramatize the effective and important role of women. For Gandhi, picketing was more a matter of moral persuasion and conversion than coercion. His arguments provided women with a sense of moral and political power that inspired them to adopt a method of action.

The uniqueness of the Gandhian approach is underlined by the fact that thousands of women were able to take part in a myriad forms. Thousands and millions of women, educated and illiterate house wives and widows, students and elderly participated in the India's freedom movement under his influence.

To sum up, Gandhian approach of Non-violent resistance — the *Satyagraha* should be seen as a method of organising a movement for positive social change. Gandhi's perspective brought forth symbols which had mass appeal and comprehensive impactive potential. This explained a conscious endeavour to internalize the content and pruposes of nationalistic, self-respecting articulation and mass aggregration with a view to establishing mass identification with alternatives.It was also a matter of reaching out to resurrect national identitity.

A universal panacea or not, Gandhian approach to resistance served some political function in a particular historical context of India. Gandhi met the needs of the hour with his practical programme of *Satyagraha*. One can thus see how Gandhi's contribution to the Indian and the world culture was unique, varied and immense. Gandhi demonstrated a method and a philosophy of engaging in conflict which can be developed as an effective substitute for political violence.

## REFERENCES


1. Gene Sharp, Gandhi's political significance accessed fromwww.mkgandhi.org/g_relevance
2. Mark Shepard, *Mahatma Gandhi and His Myths Civil Disobedience*, Nonviolence, and Satyagraha in the Real World
3. Harijan: Sept 24, 1938
4. Krishnalal Shridharani, *War Without Violence,* Bombay: Bharatiya Vidya Bhavan, 1962, p. 15.
5. John Galtung, *The way is the goal: Gandhi Today*, Gujarat Vidyapith, Peace Research Centre, Ahmedabad, 1992, p.60
6. Dhawan. G. *The Political Philosophy of Mahatma Gandhi*, Ahmedabad: Navajivan, 1957, p. 190.
7. Gene Sharp, *The Politics of Nonviolent Action,* Vol. 2: The Methods of Nonviolent Action, Boston: Porter Sargent Publishers, 1973, p. 111
8. *Ibid.,* p. 113.
9. Robert, J. Burrowes, *The Strategy of Nonviolence Defense: A Gandhian Approach* Albany, NY: State University of New York Press, 1996.
10. John Galtung. *The Way is the goal: Gandhi Today,* p. 73
11. Surjit Kaur Jolly (2006) (ed.), *Reading Gandhi,* New Delhi, Concept.
12. M.K.Gandhi, *Constructive Programme,* 1941, p. 29.
13. Bondurant, J.V., *Conquest of Violence: The Gandhian Philosophy of Conflict,* University of California Press, 1965. p. 180.
14. Anup Taneja, *Gandhi, Women, and the National Movement,* 1920-47, Har-Anand publications, 2005, p..51.
15. Gail Minault, *The Extended Family: Women and Political participation in India and Pakistan,* Chanakya Publications, New Delhi, 1981, pp. 10-11.
16. Kishwar, Madhu, 'Gandhi on Women', *Race and Class 28/1,* 1986 p. 52.
17. Gail Minault, *The Extended Family: Women and Political Participation in India and Pakistan*
18. Anup Taneja, *Gandhi, Women, and the National Movement,* 1920-47, p. 52.
19. Suruchi Thapar-Björkert, *Women in the Indian Nationalist Movement: Unseen faces and unheard voices, 1930-04,* SAGE, 2006, p. 55.

# 8

# Mahatma Gandhi Won and His Challenge to British Imperialism

*Sona Kanti Barua*

## Introduction

Massive humanitarian crisis was occurring in British dominated South Asia (India, Bangladesh, Pakistan, Sri Lanka and other countries) from 1765 to 1947. Resistance to foreign rule began mid-19$^{th}$ century, even though the first War of Independence failed in 1857, the dreams and sacrifices of its leaders inspired the generations to come. In the late 19$^{th}$ century and early 20$^{th}$ century, political aspirations were shaped by solid work for the country's social reform of the Congress Party founder Surendranath Banerjee and his team leaders. First Indian National Congress meets in Bombay. Great writer Bankim Chandra Chattopadhay wrote "Vande Mataram," the wonderful national Song – that soon became the famous among several generations that bravely fought the British Crown. It defied India, its fertile soil, beautiful landscape and relegated its governance and defence to no emperor or general but its masses." Logic is: if there is foreign rule, we have to fight for Home Rule (Swaraj). Arabian and Turks Muslim soldiers and rulers conquered India and Islamic Mogul Empire was established in South Asia before the British took over it. Is Muslims' rule foreign in India? Was there Home Rule in Moghul Empire? In Sonar Ga Bengali Nawab Isha Khan was revolt against the Emperor Akbar's Commander-in-Chief Man Singh and fought against Mogul crown. There are two main faces (Hindu and Muslim) of India. Alongside "Allah ho Akbar" with Vande Mataram was the slogan of the Khilafat movement in 1920. Might is Right. Today's Taliban, Al-Qaeda and Pakistan's Red mosque problems are the results of blind Islamic radicalism. Even Mohammad Ali Jinnah banned the Bengali language in 1948 to save Pakistan brand Islam. Such a great man (Mr.Jinnah, National Father of Pakistan), forgot the universality of Islam. Mr. Jinnah did not get any lesson from the non-violence movement. He had sinister conspiracy to rob Bangladesh (East Pakistan). Gandhi came to Noakhali to stop Hindu – Muslim riot. Mr. Jinnah came to Dhaka to confiscate Bangladesh people's mother tongue in the name of Islam. Bangladesh people express shame on him. The people of Bangladesh have been suffering by the Jamat and Islamic Fundamentalists ages after ages.

Mohandas Karamchand Gandhi (1869 – 1948) fought to defend the East Indians at home and South Africa. He was combined brilliance, humanism and courage with indomitable will brought a revolutionary change in the East Indian Community in South Africa and India. He became an icon of world peace and India. He brought dignity of Man to the East Indian Community. Gandhi encouraged us that the triumph over prejudice and ignorance is a triumph for us all. Humanity is like the ocean. Nobody could divide it in a name of politics and religion. Greed and hatred are roots of many problems, it is necessary to bring greed and hatred under control. This is message of Gandhi for his Swaraj or Home Rule. It is remarkable that the author Michael Adas writes, "In the long term interests of the peoples brought under European rule." It quotes in his famour book (p. 200) entitled "Machines as the Measure of Men: Science, Technology and Ideologies of Western Dominance." Gandhi protested against Britian's injustice.

Gandhi said, "Great as the Buddha's contribution to humanity was in resorting God to His eternal place, in my opinion, greater still was his contribution to humanity in his exacting regard for all life, be it ever so low. The Buddha said, if you want to do any sacrifice, sacrifice yourself, your lust, all your material ambition, all worldly ambition. That will be an ennobling sacrifice."

### Setting the Scene

Indian community at home and abroad truly amazed to see

Gandhi's commitments by dedicating his time, money and life. He was the supreme leader of the Congress Party of India years 1918 – 22, who could lead India as he (Gandhi) wished. In simple words everyone is free in his home and country. We want our rule in our country. Gandhi discovered his country's self rule (swaraj or home rule) and his leadership helped introduce to India and the world a completely new set of opinions to fight foreign rule, namely civil disobedience based on truth and non-violence and mass participation in peaceful, political action against colonialism. In "Gandhi" (through Richard Attenbourough's 1982) film as we watched, "They (police) beat us, but should not beat them." It is impossible for human nature. But Gandhi found the kingdom of God in human minds. So we respect Gandhi for his self rule (swaraj) relating to India's freedom.

Under Mahatma Gandhi, a unique mass mobilization was started to take shape. The foundation of Gandhi's advocacy for freedom and self-rule was based on the truth and Ahimsa or non-violent protest revolution against the British Government. India's independence movement is also characterized by largely nonviolent methods of resistance to the British rule. The Indians adopted the West minister parliamentary model as their ideal. It reminds me the 1916 Rising and the Irish War of Independence. When I study Gandhi's self rule in India, then I discover similarity relating to Northern Ireland and IRA terrorism, political prisoners and hunger strikes.

## Gandhi is a Challenge to Violent World

Many freedom fighters became terrorists in India, Ireland and other countries who dedicated their lives for the sake of their mother lands or home land's home Rule (Swaraj). The purpose of this essay is to give a short outline of "Mahatma Gandhi's) (1869-1948) freedom struggle was started with Home Rule (Swaraj) movement in South Africa and Non-cooperation movement (Satyagraha) including Crime and Society in British India. Mohandas Karamchand Gandhi (Sanskrit word Mahatma means in English language great mind)ever to have walked on the planet who is one of the most famous Indians who followed Buddha, Jesus and Tolstoy." East India Company and British corrupt bureaucrats made irregularities and corruption in the administration.

Mohandas Karamchand Gandhi (Mahatma Gandhi) designed a campaign which came to be known as the "Rowlatt Satyagraha" the first experiment with non-violent resistance on a national scale. I have to define Gandhi's Swaraj or Indian Home Rule in the British India. As we study on Michael Collins (1890-1922) leader of Irish Revolution and watched his (M.Collins) movie in our class, feelings of freedom in Ireland and India alike. British Government tortured us (Indians and Irish people). Our events and modes of expression of freedom are parts and parcels.

## Crime and Society in British India

Native East Indians are over represented as victims, offenders, and prison immates, due to (1) unemployment and homeless create higher rates of criminal activity and (2) discrimination in the system of colonial criminal justice. There WAS hypocrisy of British Justice, Law and order. There was the Mutiny of the Indian soldiers of the army of the East India Company and revolt of Oudh and of some Indian princes.

## Gandhi in South Africa (1893-1914) and 'Self Rule'

In May 1893 Gandhi arrived in Cape Town, South Africa. Law in Durban, South Africa, Gandhi wore a turban and entered into the Court and the British judge ordered him (Gandhi) to remove the turban. Gandhi refused to do so and left the chamber in protest. Due to racism a British ticket master insulted Gandhi and he was ejected from the train at Pietermaritzburg Railway Station despite holding a first class ticket. Gandhi was insulted by the South African Government and he became the victim of racism as he discovered the 'deep disease of color prejudice' in British dominated South Africa.

Deeply influenced by the South Africa's racism toward East Indians, Gandhi founded Natal Indian Congress to agitate for Indian Rights in 1894. In retaliation British Government imprisoned Gandhi and he was harshly beaten several times and he was twice imprisoned. During the Boer War in 1899 Gandhi raised an ambulance corps and sincerely he served the South African British Government. There were thousands of Indians Who joined him in civil disobedience campaign.

*In India Swaraj (home Rule or Independence, May 1921) in one year*:

There were Gandhi's "the Rowlatt Satyagraha (Resistance of tyranny through civil disobedience)" and Swaraj (Home Rule) are adding fuel to the fire in the Crown of British India. The leadership of Mohandas Karamchand Gandhi (Mahatma Gandhi) helped introduce to India and the world a completely new set of weapons to fight foreign rule, namely civil disobedience based on Truth and Non-violence and mass participation in peaceful political action against colonialism.

There was historic movement in 1920 which Gandhi launched as non-cooperation movement against British Government and urging Indians to spin their own cotton and boycott British goods, courts and government. He was arrested and confined in jail from 1920-1924. In the history of man so many conflicts and persecutions have been provoked and so many wars precipitated in the name of politics or religions. Gandhi researched and found all human beings equally worthy of dignity and respect. Another important in protest salt tax movement launched by Gandhi and thousands of Indians on the 200 miles (320 km) march to the Indian Ocean to make their own salt. British Government arrested him again. Lord Irwin's declaration on 'Dominion status' does not satisfy Indian Congress.

Gandhi conquered hearts of East Indian people by his highly compassion, sincerity and honesty. Relating to the Swaraj (Indian Home Rule) Gandhi explained, "My countrymen impute the evils of modern civilization to the English people and, therefore, believe that the English people are bad, and not the civilization they represent. My countrymen, therefore, believe that they should adopt modern civilization and modern methods of violence to drive out the English, '*Hind Swaraj*' has been written in order to show that they are following a suicidal policy, and that, if they would but revert to their own glorious civilization, either the English would adopt the later and become Indianized or find their occupation in India gone."

"I (Gandhi) have written some chapters on the subject of Indian Home Rule which I venture to place before the readers of Indian Opinion.....He added, "I should prefer to be killed by the arrow of a tribal person (Bhil) than to seek unmanly protection. Macaulay betrayed gross ignorance when he labeled Indians as being practically cowards." (Hind Swaraj). Gandhi writes to J.Nehru, (first prime minister of India), "The real question, according to you, is how to bring about man's highest intellectual, economic, political and moral development. I agree entirely, (2) In this there should be equal right and opportunity for all, (3) In other words, there should be equality between the town dwellers and the villagers in the standard of food and drink, clothing and other living conditions. In order to achieve this equality today people should be able to produce for themselves the necessaries of life, i.e. clothing, foodstuffs, dwellings, lighting and water. (4) Man is not born to live in isolation but is essentially a social animal independent. No one can or should ride on another's back. If we try to work out the necessary conditions for such a life, we are forced to the conclusion that the unit of society should be a village, or call it a small and manageable group of people who would, in the ideal, self sufficient (in the matter of their vital requirements) as a unit and bound together by its bonds of mutual cooperation and inter-dependence.")

## *Abuse was wrong in British India (1757-1947)*

East Indian people had been abused by the rulers of East India Company, British Army & its Government for 200 years. The abuse could be physical, sexual, emotional, psychological or financial. Indian people experienced more than one type of abuse. Examples of physical abuse were (1) hitting (2) pinching (3) slapping (4) pushing (5) punching (6) kicking (7) burning (8) shooting (9) stabbing and (10) cutting.

According to the British law Gandhi could not enter into Punjab state due to the general strike (haratal). There were about 10,000 people gathered on the 13 April 1919 in the Jalianwala Bagh square, Amritsar, Punjab. Without any warning suddenly Brigadier General Reginald Dyer ordered his troops to open fire on the unarmed crowd. There was no moral value in British Army. There were 379 civilians were killed and 1000 wounded. British Government wanted India for money and its wealth, not its people. Gandhi's social movements are enduring by collective attempts to change all of the social order by means of non-violence.

It is also remarkable that military's demands get articulated and implemented, while public demands get ignored and suppressed. It is abundantly clear that British Government made a mockery of civilization and its principles by hypocritical actions throughout India and the World. It was no exaggeration to say that the concept of British democracy has been one of the most tossed about misused, confused, misunderstood and abused terms ever since it came into use and applied specially to governance.1906-1907 Recording companies recorded the first national song (Vande Mataram) in the voice of Rabindranath Tagore and other artists released a version commercially in 1907. Police destroy the factory, as well as the disc, however, survived in Belgium and Paris, where the record was released. (Desi Talk, Indian Community New Weekly, Toronto, May 11, 2007).

## Gandhi in South Africa and India: Comparative study

To my mind, in South Africa Gandhi "Learned to see all Indians as one, regardless of class and caste, religion and regional origins." (p. 49, Gandhi, David Arnold). But in India when Gandhi demanded immediate Independence as India price for helping Britain during World War II. British Government imprisoned Gandhi from 1942-1947. Gandhi could not save one India as Muslims created Pakistan by Muhammad Ali Jinnah. Again Gandhi started fasting for non-violence until Delhi rioters pleaded peace to him. On the January 30, 1948 while Gandhi was on way to prayer. Naturam Godse assassinated Mahatma Gandhi by three bullets. Life of Gandhi mirrors the fate of violence, "As war begins in the minds of men, it is in the minds of men that the defenses of peace must be constructed." Gandhi said, "Hinduism absorbs the best in other religions and there is a scope for expansion in it."

## Conclusion

However, every day we discover Gandhi's dream of happiness for mankind in his thoughts. Gandhi said, "A time is coming when those who are in the mad rush today of multiplying their wants, vanity thinking that they add to the real substance, real knowledge of the world, will retrace their steps and say what have we done? Civilizations have come and gone and in spite of all our vaunted progress, I am tempted to ask again and again: To what purpose?"

Recently U.N. declares Gandhi's birthday "International Day of Non Violence." M.K. Gandhi said, "An eye for an eye makes the whole world blind." Mahatma Gandhi's philosophy of brotherhood and peace was immortalized when the UN General Assembly declared October 2, Mahatma Gandhi's birth anniversary as the International Day of Non-violence." My interpretations of Gandhi's Home Rule (or self rule Swaraj) and his freedom struggle followed several books, experiences and exhibitions etc. I respect the glorious remarks of Albert Einstein in 1944, "Generations to come, it may be, will scarce believe that such a one as this ever in flesh and blood walked upon this earth."

Historians have judged India's National Movement as a unique struggle by a people, inspired by a shared vision. Mahatma Gandhi's teaching inspired us according to the International law, Universal Declaration of Human Rights, Convention against torture and crimes against humanity to which Britain is a signatory. Home Rule (Swaraj), Indian and Ireland people's rights had been severely violated by the British Government. We have to recognize all human beings are endowed with dignities of equality and uniqueness which makes each of us precious beyond measure. We are governed by our compassion of each other, our humanity and common family in our "Home Rule (Swaraj)."

## REFERENCES

1. Desi Talk, *Indian Community News Weekly*, Toronto, p.15, dated May 11, 2007.
2. David Arnold, *Gandhi*, p. 105.
3. *Ibid.*, p. 61.
4. Autobiography by M.K. Gandhi, p. 114.
5. Hermann Kulke and Dietmar Rothermund, *A History of India*, p. 358.
6. H. Kulke and D. Tothermunkd, *A History of India*, p. 357.
7. Instructor V. Ravindiran, *History of India*, Part II, Summer Term 2000, U of T. pp. 66-71.
8. V. Ravindiran, *History of India*, Tutorial 7, : Gandhi's Vision of India, 12-57.
9. V. Ravindran, *History of India*, supplementary writings, University of Toronto, p. 155.

10. Hermann Kulke and Dietmar Rothermund, *A History of India*, p. 246 & 267.
11. Desi Talk, Indian Community Weekly, Toronto, Toronto, p.15, dated May 11, 2007.
12. David Arnold, Gandhi p.41.
13. Anthony Copley, Against the Tide, p.65, Oxford, 1987.
14. Publication Division, Ministry of Information and Broadcasting, Govt. of India, *The Way of the Buddha*, p. 5.
15. David Arnold, *Gandhi*, p. 5.

SECTION - 2

GANDHIAN APPROACH TO CONFLICT RESOLUTION

# 9

# Conflict Resolution: The Gandhian Way

*A.N. Panda*

The contention between harmony and confrontational models has gripped the attention of mankind since time immemorial. Wise and sensible men have always tried to evolve an arrangement in which people can live in agreement and they have devoted their life to outline a theory of harmony. As competition and conflict are the integral features of human society and more so, in case of the modern societies because those are more scarcity ridden, there is always a need to develop a mechanism to contain conflict among individuals. So, all the time there is a need to think about the methods to resolve conflicts which take place in different situations and arising out of different reasons.

Conflict resolution is the process of attempting to resolve a dispute or a conflict. Successful conflict resolution occurs by listening to and providing opportunities to meet each side's needs, and adequately address their interests so that they are each satisfied with the outcome. Conflict Practitioners talk about finding the win-win outcome for parties involved, vs. the win-lose dynamic found in most conflicts. Conflict itself has both positive and negative outcomes. Practitioners in the field of Conflict Resolution aim to find ways to promote the positive outcomes and minimize the negative outcomes. Conflict resolution engages conflict once it has already started and aims at ending conflicts or lessens their negative impact.

There is a debate in the field of conflict work as to whether or not all conflicts can be resolved, thus making the term conflict resolution one of contention. Other common terms include Conflict Management, Conflict Transformation and Conflict Intervention. Conflict management can be the general process in which conflict is managed by the parties toward a conclusion.

Conflict Practitioners work on conflict in many arenas, internationally, domestically, interpersonally and intrapersonally. Conflict resolution processes can vary. Conflict usually involves two or more parties with opposing views regarding specific issues. Resolution methods can include conciliation, mediation, arbitration or litigation.

These methods all require third party intervention. A resolution method which is direct between the parties with opposing views is negotiation. Negotiation can be the 'traditional' model of hard bargaining where the interests of a group far outweigh the working relationships concerned. The negotiation model is where both the interests and the working relationships concerned are viewed as important. Often, face saving and other intangible goals play a role in the success of negotiation.

It may be possible to avoid conflict without actually resolving the underlying dispute, by getting the parties to recognize that they disagree but that no further action needs to be taken at that time. In many cases such as in a democracy, a dialogue may be the preferred process in which it may even be desirable that they disagree, thus exposing the issues to others who need to consider it for themselves: in this case the parties might agree to disagree and agree to continue the dialogue on the issue. It is also possible to manage a conflict without resolution, in forms other than avoidance.

## The Gandhian Idea

Mahatma Gandhi has a special place among the leaders of the world who had concerned themselves with the intricacies of conflict resolution. Gandhiji not only led India's freedom movement and contributed for building a modern India but also outlined his own theory of conflict resolution. He put forward his method of dealing with an adversary. Because of his own experience and pragmatic mind he was able to provide an alternative way to tackle a crisis situation. Therefore, Mahatma Gandhi has a unique position among the different leaders of the world.

He shouldered the leadership of Indian freedom movement when it was in search of a leader. Gandhi guided the Indians in their fight against the foreign rulers and helped them to attain their independence. The magnitude of the Mahatma's leadership can be appreciated if an attempt is made to understand the strategy he adopted during the independence movement to confront the mighty British rulers in India.

By the time Gandhiji took up the leadership for Indian freedom struggle both the moderates and the extremists were losing their hold over the situation. The moderates had failed to attain their goals through the technique of appealing to the government and the extremists had failed to sustain the initial gain achieved by them through violence. The freedom movement was in search of a leader who would provide it unity and success.

Further, the Jallianwalabagh massacre in 1919 had created a widespread resentment against the British and there was a crave for revenge against the perpetrators of the cruelty. The people were demanding quick retribution for the tragedy and expected the freedom lighters to punish the wrong doers. They were clamouring for the blood of the persons responsible for the bloodbath and the situation was favourable for the occurrence of violence. Against all these backdrops Mahatma Gandhi assumed the responsibility of the freedom struggle by taking over the leadership of the Indian National Congress and undertook the burden of guiding the national movement.

## Gandhian Idea of Ends and Means

To meet all these challenges Gandhi had to choose the right method. He had to gain the confidence of the people and lead them in their opposition against the foreign rulers. However, as a champion of peace and non-violence, he could not approve the violent method of the extremists and as a man of action, he could not follow the method of appeal as preferred by the moderates and wait for things to happen; he neither wanted to make India free through bloodshed nor wished to be a mute onlooker to the misrule of the British. In his wish to bring independence to India, Gandhi also could not favour a means which was unacceptable to his conscience. He was not unscrupulous while he attempted to achieve his objective.

In the opinion of Gandhi, both means and end were of equal importance; they were two sides of the same coin. In his view, "The means maybe likened to a seed and the end to a tree; and there is just the same inviolable connection between the means and the end as there is between the seed and the tree." Unlike some other thinkers such as Machiavelli, he did not follow the precept of 'end justified the means'; rather for him, if the means were good automatically the end would be good. Therefore, the selection of a just method was as important as the attainment of the end.

Though Mahatma Gandhi earnestly desired to free India from the British rulers he did not want to do it with the help of a method which was not honourable or moral. He believed that an unethical means never brought a good result and to him violence was unethical. Hence, he did not prefer the means of violence for challenging the bad governance of the rulers. He felt that in stead of adopting the principle of 'blood for blood' it was easier to win over the enemy with the help of non-violent means. According to him, violence resulted in more violence and there was the possibility of inviting the severe oppressive power of the government if a violent means was opted for opposing the government. He was certain that it would be impossible for him to face the British rulers with any unethical and immoral method. Therefore, he chose to confront them by attracting the attention of their conscience and reason to their own misdeeds. He wanted to challenge the rulers on moral ground. He preferred to awaken their conscience by his rational approach. Gandhi decided on this method to attain his objective as he was convinced that violence would be a failure in the long run and only a peaceful means would bring an everlasting result and independence to India. And ultimately, he proved him to be right.

## The Gandhian Method of Protest

But at the same time he also provided a new answer to the naughty question of resolving conflicts. Gandhi had already experimented his formulas of truth and non violence in South Africa where he had ably opposed the practice of discrimination against the blacks and propagated for the principle of racial equality. After coming to India, he applied those methods to win freedom for his countrymen. Gandhi supported the cause of peaceful resolution of conflicts and preferred a method sans violence in an age when the principle of humanism had been savagely attacked by the might of the weapons of mass destruction. Therefore, he got the recognition of being the apostle of peace who vindicated the cause spiritual and moral approach to political problems.

Though like Gokhale, Mahatma Gandhi wanted to spiritualise politics and inject moral values into politics, he went a step further in his effort to cleanse politics by bringing religion into it To him, politics without moral principles did not serve the cause of soul. For him, the road to salvation lied in the service of his country and of humanity. He wanted to love both his friends and foes. He also believed that a bad means could not be justified because it would not good end. All these might have made it difficult for some other leader but not for the Mahatma. Against all odds Gandhi selected the peaceful means to fight the powerful British and achieve freedom for the country. This accorded him the position of the most important leader of the Indian independence movement and distinguished him from other leaders of the country who had fought for the countrys freedom.

Mahatma Gandhi was a very pragmatic leader. He had a clear understanding of his position. He was quite aware of his own strength and the power and limitations of his adversary and accordingly selected his means to achieve his target. He had evolved his own method o resistance and perfected it in South Africa. He had applied this method to wage a war against the British without compromising his conscience. His experience in South Africa had convinced him that if an appeal was made to the soul of the adversary and the reason of the opponent was awakened it would not be difficult to achieve the goal. He had realised that even a very powerful opponent would succumb to the pressure of his o reason.

To him, the eastern culture strongly supported the notions of peace and non-violence. As Gandhi had remarked, "Two paths are open before India today, either to introduce the western principle of 'might is right' or to uphold the eastern principle that truth alone triumphs, that truth knows no mishap, that strong and weak have alike a right to secure justice." He believed, "To use violence for securing rights may seem an easy path, but it proves to be thorny in the long run, those who live by sword also die by sword." He felt that violence bred violence and it would not bring a good result.

Mahatma Gandhi was against any form of exploitation and injustice. He did not support tyranny of anybody. He propagated that evil must be opposed. But he insisted that the weapons must be non-violent and moral ones. The opponent must be dealt with mutual respect and love. He believed that only through love an enemy could be permanently won.

Gandhi had a deep feeling with regard to the futility of violence as a method to solve a problem and because of this attitude he did not want to be a follower of violence. He had a strong conviction that the means of violence was an uncivilized method and ultimately it would fail to achieve anything. Thus he said, "The barbarous method is warfare, open or secret. This must be ruled out if only because it is impracticable. If I could but persuade everyone that it is always bad, we shall gain all lawful ends much quicker. The power that an individual or a nation forswearing violence generates is the power that is irresistible. But my argument against violence is based upon pure expedience, i.e. its utter utility." He was so much against violence that 'he desired no emancipation, no Swaraj through the sword' To him, non-violence was the weapon of the strongest and unless a person had sufficient moral strength he would not use non-violence as a means to achieve something.

His idea of protest was based on peace and non-violence and had the support of moral principles. He believed that with the help of ethical methods he would be able to reach his targets. His conviction in truth .gave him the moral strength to opt for an unconventional means during a time when extremism and violence were the most preferred weapons of resistance. He wanted to achieve his goals with the support of non cooperation and satyagraha.

Gandhi thought non-violence would serve double purpose; it would counter the vindictiveness of the Government and also unite the common mass in their struggle for independence. His experiment with truth and non-violence as methods of resistance as applied in South Africa helped him to consider peaceful Non-cooperation as the most suitable technique to be employed in the freedom movement in India. He understood that it would be impossible for the innocent peace loving people to oppose the powerful rulers through violent means; rather if the conscience of the British was awakened and if the British were to see reason it would be easier for the Indians to gain freedom. He concluded. "Non-cooperation is therefore the only remedy left open to us. It is the cleanest remedy as it is the most effective, when it is absolutely free from all violence." He further stated, "Non-cooperation is the only method which will either bring freedom or purge the regime of its evils."

Mahatma Gandhi believed that people's mind could be changed by the impact of love and reason. If the heart of the opponent could be touched by the power of love and reason, it would not be difficult for somebody to win over his opponent and reach his own objective. Gandhi thought that Swaraj could also be achieved through the power of love and reason. He asserted, "We want to win Swaraj by changing people's ideas through the force of love and reason and this has obliged the government also to rely on reason."

Gandhi was an avowed supporter of peace. He had always put emphasis on the peaceful method of resistance. Even in Non-cooperation movement he did not want anybody to be a party to any violent activity. He was so much attached to non-violence that he considered non-violence was the essential part of the Non-cooperation movement. He declared, 'Non-violence is the most vital and integral part of noncooperation."

While fighting for Khilafaf, expounded the uselessness of the power of the sword. He believed that the power of the sword was less effective than that of love. According to him, "The sword makes men equal. After fighting with one another like so many bulls, till they all get exhausted, the opponents salute each other and become friends. Anyone who shows weakness will humiliate himself. The other method is, instead of using physical force against the opponent to employ soul force and win ascendancy over him. This ascendancy is accepted not out of fear but out of love, and so both become equals. One does not consider it humiliating to admit another's moral superiority. The other takes no pride in being morally superior. Hence both behave respectfully towards each other. We must give up the very thought of overcoming the British sword."

Gandhi said that the practitioners of non-cooperation needed to purify themselves. Unless one was purified one was not capable of becoming a true soldier of the non-cooperation movement. Taking his argument a bit further he stated that the practice of untouchability prevalent in the Hindu society was against the principle of purification a it would hamper the non-cooperation movement. Non-cooperation required the active involvement of all sections of the Indian society and the involvement would be possible only if there was unity among all sections in India. Therefore, he pronounced, "Non-cooperation is a science of purification. Unless we have purified ourselves, we cannot employ it. So long as we regard one of limbs as untouchable, we ourselves, the Hindus, and our neighbours, the Muslims and others, will remain the untouchable that we have become."

Mahatma Gandhi advocated that an opponent could be reached through non-cooperation. The heart of an adversary could be changed by putting moral pressure on him through non-cooperation. At the same time he also warned against the misuse of the power of non-cooperation. He directed that a person practising non-cooperation must observe strict discipline in his conduct and maintain restraint in his behaviour towards others. In the opinion of Gandhi, "Non-cooperation is a process of purification and we must continually try to touch the heart of those who differ from us, touch their minds and their emotions but never their bodies. Discipline and restraint are the cardinal principles of our conduct and I warn you against any sort of tyrannical social ostracism." Thus, Gandhi was aware of the effectiveness of Non-cooperation to confront an enemy, but also he was conscious of its susceptibility to be misused.

Gandhi contended that while a person remained engaged in non-co operation it was imperative for him to avoid violence as violence had no place in non-cooperation. Adoption of violence even in an indirect form w prohibited by Mahatma Gandhi. Therefore he said. "So long as we are associated with the movement of non-co operation, we shall not directly or indirectly advocate violence at present or in the future nor create an atmosphere of preparedness for violence. Indeed we hold it contrary to the spirit of non-violent Non-cooperation to which we have pledged our word."

Mahatma Gandhi was more concerned with the cause of the evil than its symptoms. He had given more importance to wipe out the cause of the evil than to do away with the evil doer. According to the Mahatma, Non-cooperation was a process which would cure the system from all evils. He advised that the aim should be to go to the root of the problem and think of the remedy to purge the system of its defects. He regarded Non-cooperation as an effective way to tackle the cause of a problem. "Non-cooperation is essentially a cleansing process. It deals with causes rather than symptoms."

Mahatma Gandhi was a sincere fighter in the war of Indian independence. He was prepared to suffer for the sake of the nation. He honestly believed that through sacrifice India could be made independent. He felt, to make India free from the foreigners all should be prepared to make sacrifices. There was nothing to boast or bluff about non co-operation. By becoming a participant in Non-cooperation one works for the Nation. To Gandhi. "Non-cooperation is not movement of brag, bluster, or bluff. It is a test of our sincerity. It requires asocial and silent self sacrifice. It challenges our honesty and our capacity for national work. It is a movement that aim's at translating ideas into action. And the more we do, the more we find that much more must be done that we had expected. And this thought of our imperfection must make us humble."

Gandhi had differentiated Non-cooperation from passive resistance and civil disobedience. He thought that a weak person adopted the method of passive resistance to challenge his opponent. It also did not disallow violence. The weak did not employ violence in passive resistance because he could not use it due to his weakness, but use of violence was not excluded from passive resistance. Passive resistance, according to Gandhi "covers the suffragette movement as well as the resistance of the nonconformists. Passive resistance has been conceived and is regarded as the weapon of the weak. Whilst it avoids violence, being not open to the weak, it does not exclude its use if in the opinion of the resister, the occasion demands it."

By civil disobedience Gandhi meant refusal to render obedience to law made by the state. According to Gandhi if it was felt that if the law of the state was discriminatory and immoral the citizens had the right to disobey the law. Thus he said, "Civil disobedience is civil breach of immoral statutory enactments." By civil disobedience the evil intentions of the state could be exposed.

## Methods of Non-cooperation

While describing the process in which the Non-cooperation movement could be waged Gandhi explained that "Non cooperation predominantly implies withdrawing of cooperation from the state that in the non-co-operator's view has become corrupt and excludes civil disobedience of fierce type described above By its very nature it is even open to children of understanding and can be safely practised by the masses. Civil disobedience presupposes the habit of willing obedience to law, without fear of their sanctions. It can therefore be practised only as a last resort and by a select few in the first instance at any rate." Thus according to Gandhi, it was possible for all the people who were of sound mind to be the participants in the Non-cooperation movement whereas civil disobedience was for the few selected people who had the deep conviction of the faulty nature of the law made by the state. A meek and mild person could also start non co-operation against his powerful opponents and show his resentment against them.

Mahatma Gandhi had described in detail the various weapons to be used by the practitioners of Non-cooperation. He explained that in Non-cooperation movement the people could adopt different means for not cooperating with their adversaries. Besides boycotting the wrong doers, those who practised Non-cooperation might observe strike or they could cease work or could begin hartal. Gandhi believed that opposition to the immoral conduct of an authority or a person could be expressed through these means peacefully. At the same time he also warned against the misuse of these means. He stated, "Strike, cessation of work and hartal are wonderful things no doubt, but it is not difficult to abuse them."

## Satyagraha

Gandhi contended that the most effective means for a fighter in non-co operation was the weapon of Satyagraha. According to him, Satyagraha had a far more superiority than any other means because it had a moral foundation. Satyagraha gave importance to Truth and Truth alone was more desirable than anything else. In Gandhi's view, there was no substitute for Truth and ultimately only Truth prevailed. Satyagraha "is literally holding on to Truth and it means therefore, Truth force. Truth is soul or Spirit. It is, therefore, known as Soul-force. It excludes the use of violence because man is not capable of knowing the absolute truth and therefore not competent to punish."

Narrating the meaning f Satyagraha Mahatma Gandhi said, "Its root meaning is holding on to truth'; hence, truth force. I have also called it love force or soul force. In the application of Satyagraha I discovered in the earliest stages that pursuit of truth did not admit of violence being inflicted on one's opponent, but that he must be weaned from error by patience and sympathy. For what appears to be truth to one may appear to be error to the other. And patience means self-suffering. So the doctrine came to mean vindication of truth, not by infliction of suffering on the opponent, but one's own self."

The Gandhian concept of Satyagraha is a natural outcome of his faith in the supremacy of Truth. It was the result of his sincere realization of Truth. Gandhi regarded Truth as the ultimate reality. He believed that it was the moral duty of everybody to protect the foundation of Truth. According to him a supporter of Truth should put all his might to safeguard the basis of Truth. A votary of Truth must work with determination to establish the supremacy of moral and spiritual principles. Propagation of Truth was the final goal of a lover of Truth and Satyagraha was the practical application of Truth.

The term Satyagraha was coined in South Africa to distinguish the resistance of the Indians from the contemporary passive resistance of the suffragettes and others. To Gandhi a satyagrahi acknowledged the omnipotence of Truth in his heart. Within his heart a satyagrahi knew that Truth must be established, if necessary even at the cost of one's life. "It (Satyagraha) is also called Soul force because a definite recognition of the Soul within is a necessity if a satyagrahi is to believe that death does not mean cessation of the struggle but a culmination."

satyagrahi should be prepared to make any sacrifice for the protection of the basis of Truth.

According to Gandhi Truth did not need the support of others. It was self reliant. He contended, "Satyagraha is self dependent. It does not require the assent of the opponent before it can be b into play." Gandhi thought that a satyagrahi would try to change the heart of his opponent by making an appeal to the reason of his adversary. By gentle arguments a satyagrahi would attempt to make his opponent see reason and be aware of his misconduct. Through his self sacrifice a satyagrahi would make effort to bring changes in the thinking of his enemy. "And a Satyagrahi never injures his opponent and always appeals, either to his reason by gentle argument, or his heart by the sacrifice of self, satyagraha is twice blessed; it blesses him who practises it, and him against whom it is practised." Gandhi thought that everybody had a soul and in his heart everybody knew what was right and what was wrong; if an attempt was made, everybody would see reason. In his view, even the hardest opponent's heart could be changed by self-suffering. Differentiating Satyagraha from passive resistance Gandhi said that passive resistance was a weapon of the weak. If a person was unable to openly resist his opponent he adopted the method of passive resistance. In contrast, Satyagraha was the weapon of the strongest. It could be practised by only such persons who had total conviction about the importance of Truth and because a satyagrahi was convinced of the supremacy of Truth he was not in need of any violent means. In Gandhi's opinion, "Satyagraha differs from passive resistance as the North Pole from the South. The latter has been conceived as a weapon of the weak and does not exclude the use of physical force or violence for the purpose of gaining one's end; whereas the former has been conceived as a weapon of the strongest, and excludes the use of violence in shape or form." It was the sacred duty of a satyagrahi to make endless endeavours for the vindication of Truth.

While Gandhi narrated the concept of Satyagraha he drew an analogy between the relationship within a family and the outside world. He believed that law of love regulated the domestic life within a family and because there was no use of violence in the family; the family life had been continuing since time immemorial. Within a family there was mutual respect among the members in spite of the many differences among them. One of the basic foundations of the family structure was the sacrifice of its members. Thus he asserted, "This doctrine of satyagraha is not new; it is merely extension of the domestic of life to the political Family disputes and differences are generally settled according to the law of love. The injured member has so much regard for the others that he suffers injury for the sake of his principles without retaliating without being angry with those who differ from him....his actions, whether he resists or resigns, is always calculated to promote, the common welfare of the family. It is this law of love, which silently but surely, governs the family for the most part throughout the civilized world."

The Gandhian concept of Satyagraha did not presuppose disobedience to the law of the state. By nature Gandhi was a law abiding person and he respected the laws of the society; however, he objected to the laws which were immoral and against the principle of justice. He advocated that any laws which were against the interest of the citizens must be resisted. At the same time he clarified that he was not deliberately trying to creating problems for the government. In his words, "It is contrary to my creed to embarrass governments or anybody else...But I should not hold myself responsible for having caused embarrassment when I resist the wrong of a wrong doer by refusing assistance in his wrong doing."

## Duties of a Non-cooperator

The idea of Non-cooperation as conceived by Gandhi did not presume social and political disintegration. It did not believe in the subjugation of one by the other. It taught to respect even the rights of an opponent. Non-cooperation, he opined, "will not succeed unless we create an atmosphere of perfect freedom, unless we prize our opponent's liberty as much as our own. The liberty of faith, conscience, thought and action which we claim for ourselves must be conceded equally to others."

Mahatma Gandhi was so deeply attached to the principle of non-violence that he always emphasised on the use of this method to gain one's objectives. Non violence and love should be the only weapons in the fight for a just cause. According to him, violence should never be used as a means by a practitioner of Non-cooperation movement. This means should never be used even as a last resort. He felt that when people became restless, impatient and vindictive they used to adopt violent methods to achieve their goals. Hence he had warned against the use of violence in the movement, "The real danger of violence lies in the people resorting to Non-cooperation becoming impatient and revengeful."

Gandhi believed in self-discipline. According to Gandhi, those who were participants of Non-cooperation should observe certain restraints. A non-cooperator should always consciously avoid violence; even the very thought of violence should be abominable to him. Prescribing what to do while practising Non-cooperation Gandhi advised, "It is infinitely more necessary that we non-co-operators control our speech, control our movements and free them even from any danger or any smell of violence. Let our speech and our pen be free from any violent thing." him, non-violence was not merely abstention from physical violence; it included violence in any form.

Mahatma Gandhi emphasised that a participant of Non-cooperation movement had certain duties towards others. Non-cooperation movement did not mean disregarding the sentiment and feeling of others. Rather a non-cooperator should be respectful towards others. He must be humble towards all. Gandhi said, "Anon-co operator must remain respectful, peaceful and humble towards all." Thus Gandhi's idea of Non-cooperation made one to be more aware of his duties. Involvement in the movement was not a license to do whatever one wished. On the other hand, it put many limitations on the conduct of a participant of the movement. In the opinion of Gandhi, Non-cooperation movement was a voluntary movement and the participants were such persons 'ho were convinced of its utility and were prepared for making sacrifices for the success of the movement. In Gandhi's view, only a person who had a genuine commitment would be willing to suffer for the cause for which the movement had been launched. He said, "Non-cooperation as a voluntary movement can only succeed if the feeling is genuine and strong enough to make people suffer to the utmost."

Gandhi said that Non-cooperation movement aimed at establishing the superiority of Truth. As Truth did not need the support of others for its vindication and it was the ultimate reality there was no need for any violence for establishing its supremacy. In Gandhi's view, the movement was for the vindication of Truth. He clarified, "Non cooperation too like civil disobedience is a branch of Satyagraha which includes all non violent resistance for the vindication of Truth."

## Process of Non-cooperation

Besides describing the meaning of Non-cooperation and the duties of a non-co-operator Mahatma Gandhi also narrated how the movement could be started and how an opponent could be faced during the movement. According to him, when the government became tyrannical and began tormenting the people it was the right and duty of the people to oppose the government. The people should not be associated with such a government which did not serve the interests of the people; they should not become party to the tyranny of the government. Thus he said, "Non cooperation means refusing to associate ourselves with or be a party to the tyranny of the Government and to render any support, direct or indirect, to such tyranny."

Gandhi contended that it was the prime duty of the government to protect the interest of the people and if the government failed in its duties it had no right to demand the obligation of the people. He asserted that without the willing acceptance of the people that the government had the legal right to control over them, no government had the capacity to regulate the people, however powerful it might be. It was also the duty of the people to protest such a government which did not safeguard their interest. They should not be the willing abettors of the tyranny of the rulers. Therefore Gandhi said, "As there can be no cooperation between virtue and sin, between darkness and light, so there can be none between the people and a government opposed to their interests; by means of non cooperation, we are proving that even the most wicked policy cannot survive if the people do not tolerate it, refuse to be a party to it."

In accordance with Gandhi, all the people were to be involved in the movement of non-cooperation for the movement to be successful. However, while launching the non-cooperation movement Gandhi first targeted the classes which were trapped by the government to execute its policy of oppression. Gandhi felt that the school going youths were lured by the faulty policies of the government and they were the first group of persons who were to be warned of the evil designs of the government; if the students could be convinced of the utility of the Non-cooperation movement then it would be easier for the movement to succeed. Thus he said at the beginning of the movement. "Non cooperation deals first with those sensitive classes upon whom the Government has acted so successfully and who have been lured into the trap consciously or unconsciously as the school going youths have been."

Delivering a speech at the students' meeting at Banaras on November 27, 1920 Mahatma Gandhi said. Now I want to tell you why in the scheme of non-co operation I h included the sacrifice from students. It is my firm conviction that the main reason why the present regime goes on and continues to perpetrate the atrocities that it does, is that we have come under the spell of its education. Before its intrusion we were self reliant and not dependent as we are today. The present system of education has rendered us more dependent."

Mahatma Gandhi was convinced that the system of education that the British introduced in India aimed at creating dependency in the country. The people who were educated by the British were blindly following the British dictates because of their educational background. They were the people who were acting as supporters of the tyranny of the government. So unless those people changed their attitude, it would not be possible to counter the evil design of the British government.

Mahatma Gandhi had evolved his own method of peaceful resistance and applied it in the freedom movement in India. He launched the Non-cooperation movement in 1920-21 and continued to use this method till the attainment of freedom by India. Though initially the movement was regarded as a failure by some, it provided an example to others about the relevance of peaceful means in a violent situation. Gandhi could prove to the world that even a powerful opponent could be successfully challenged by non-violent means and he could be changed through the power of love. He taught the world how to manage a crisis without invoking the power of sword.

If the whole concept of Non-cooperation and its application

as expounded by Gandhi is analysed it can be deduced that Gandhi had given a new answer to conflict resolution and resistance. He expounded a new theory with reward to solving a problem. He prescribed how to meet one enemy in a world torn by violence. He experimented the formulas of truth and non-violence during the Indian freedom struggle and came to the conclusion that if a person had moral force he could face any challenge and fight against any enemy, however powerful he might be.

Gandhi was a firm believer in the inherent goodness of man. To him, everybody had a conscience and if he was made aware of his own misconduct he would see reason and behave differently. So it was not necessary to threaten him with physical violence and further incur his wrath; it would be better to convince him with rational and gentle persuasion and settle the disputes peacefully.

Mahatma Gandhi was a man of moral conviction. He believed in the supremacy of moral and ethical values. He had a strong belief that freedom could be brought to India only by such methods which were supported by the principles of morality. Moral superiority would enable the Indians either to bring freedom in the country or eliminate the evils from the regime. In both ways, they would be 'gainers. Ultimately, he proved to be right.

The credit of Gandhi lies in the fact that in stead of an aggressive and militant struggle he built up a popular movement of peaceful resistance in the form of Non-cooperation in which the Indian masses were transformed into active participants in the fight against oppression, injustice and violence. Only a person of the Mahatma's stature could transform the docile people into vigorous soldiers in the war of Indian Independence who could face the powerful British Empire with conviction and courage. Because of his moral strength he could lead the people of India to their freedom and he could do so with the support of only Truth and non-violence.

The Gandhian techniques of conflict resolution were based on peace and non-violence. Mahatma Gandhi always emphasised on attaining a goal with the help of an ideal method and any means associated with immoral and unethical elements was not acceptable to him to reach any end however desirable and noble it may be. Thus, his manner of resolving a conflict was not only ideal but also pragmatic. He accomplished his goal by following a simple method directly confronting his adversary and without any third party intervention. Moreover, he prepared the mankind for facing the crisis of a world full of strife and hatred. He showed a way in which people can peacefully live in a violent world and work together on the basis of cooperation and harmony. His means of Satyagraha is a substitute for war and the concept of Non-cooperation is a different method of conflict resolution. For all his contributions he is deservingly acclaimed as the champion of peace and non-violence and hailed as one of the greatest personalities mankind has ever produced.

## REFERENCES

1. Gandhi, M.K. *Hind Swaraj*, p. 60.
2. *The Collected Works of Mahatma Gandhi*, Vol. XVII, The Publication Division, Ministry of Information and Broadcasting, Government of India, New Delhi, 1965, p.17.
3. *Ibid.*, pp. 17-18.
4. *Ibid.*, p. 75.
5. *Ibid.*, Vol. XIX, The Publication Division, Ministry of Information and Broadcasting, Government of India, Delhi, 1966, p
6. *Ibid.*,, Vol. XVII, p. 75.
7. *Ibid.*, Vol. XIX, p. 36.
8. *Ibid.*, p10.
9. *The Collected Works of Mahatma Gandhi*, Vol. XX, The Publication Division, Ministry of Information and Broadcasting, Government of India, Delhi, 1966, p439.
10. *Ibid.*, Vol. XVII, pp 105-106.
11. *Ibid.*, Vol. XIX, p 8.
12. *Ibid.*, pp. 104-105.
13. *Ibid.*, Vol. XX, pp93-94.
14. *Ibid.*, Vol. XIX, p.145.
15. *Ibid.*, p. 220.
16. Ibid., p. 466.
17. *Ibid.*, p. 466.
18. *Ibid.*, 466.
19. *Ibid.*, Vol. XVII, p. 17.

20. *Ibid.*, Vol. XIX, p. 466
21. *Ibid.*, Vol. XVII, p. 152.
22. *Ibid.*, pp. 153-154
23. *Ibid.*, p. 153.
24. *Ibid.*, p. 154.
25. *Ibid.*, p. 152.
26. *Ibid.*, p. 153.
27. *Ibid.*, p. 350.
28. *Ibid.*, Vol. XIX, p. 104.
29. *Ibid*, Vol. XVII, p. 352.
30. *Ibid.*, Vol. XIX, p. 545.
31. *Ibid.*, Vol. XX, p. 513.
32. *Ibid.*; Vol. XVII, p. 390.
33. *Young India*, 23.3.1921.
34. *The Collected Works of Mahatma Gandhi*, Vol. XIX, p. 250.
35. *Ibid*, p. 284.
36. *Ibid*, p. 234.
37. *Ibid*, p. 37.

# 10

# Gandhian Approach to Conflict Management: HRM Perspective

*Naga Raju Battu*

Conflict is a part of normal life. The conflicts we experience range from the micro-level (an individual's conflict, intrapersonal or intrapsychic conflicts) to the macro-level conflicts (International conflicts). Individuals with a high need for results and excellence fight the battle alone. They tend to avoid situations of conflict, or if conflicts do arise they arbitrate to impose the best solutions according to their own wisdom. This makes collaboration more difficult. Thus they are caught in a vicious circle. This paper makes an attempt to deal with this critical dimension. Main focus of this is to briefly discuss the role of conflict and cooperation, their nature and dynamics with a view to increasing effectiveness of managing these more effectively in organizations. Management of these phenomena would involve both the utilization of their positive contributions and minimizing their negative aspects. Gandhian principles of managing conflicts, it would involve their effective use for strengthening individuals, groups and organizations. The functional aspects need to be developed and utilized. The dysfunctional aspects need to be prevented, reduced and soled. In order to resolve conflicts and develop collaboration effectively in organizations, it is indispensable to understand the Gandhian perspectives and its relevance in Globalised and liberalized society.

## Conceptualization

### Gandhian philosophy

Gandhiji never liked phrases like 'Gandhism', 'Gadhian

ideology' or 'Gandhian Philosophy'. He claimed only that he attempted to apply the ancient principles of truth and non-violence to the problems of mankind. When charged with being 'an idealist', Gandhi was a social scientist who tried to analyse the ills of society and find a cure for them in the content of all facts involved. It is a good augury that the youth of the country are reposing their faith in Gandian ideology – Gandhigiri, let us rededicate ourselves to revive the truth.

## Conflict management

Conflict is inevitable in an organization. It is now a generally accepted fact that, whether we like it or not, conflicts continually occur in our social life. Conflicts occur at various levels within the person, between persons in a group and between groups – and may have important implications for work and the effectiveness of the persons and groups involved. The nature and intensity of conflict may vary from persons to person, group to group and society to society, but except perhaps in utopia, it takes place in all individuals, groups and societies.

## Approach to conflict resolution

Conflicts are so pervasive in human society. In so far as conflicts are disruptive of our social goals (Productivity, Public welfare etc) what and how the Gandhian approach to the resolution of conflict. Gandhian followers developed a model of industrial relations/people management based on the lectures, writings and statements of Gandhi on various issues relating to industrial relations. This is an effort to analyse Gandhi's view point on various matters of labour management problems and resolve their conflicts.

## Gandhian Approach to Conflicts/Management

It seems impossible that any set of reforms of the existing system, with its structural characteristics kept intact, can improve the situation for the poverty ridden people of India as well as the third world. Some countries may benefit from reforms, but by and large what goes under the general demand of a New International economic order is either impossible to or irrelevant for the poor of the third world. Therefore, in our view, the only alternative approach can be Gandhian. First of all everyone has to accept Gandhi is Management Guru.

## Mohandas Karamchand Gandhi as Management Guru

Management is as old as human civilization. Professor Peter Drucker has been acclaimed as the founder of the management discipline and was being looked upon as a pivotal figure for making management one of the most sought after subjects in most of the countries. After more than six decades of the introduction of management as a vibrant discipline one is pleasantly surprised to find that Mahatma Gandhi has been acknowledged as a Management Guru. The Harvard School of Business Management has hailed Mahatma Gandhi as Management Guru of the 20th Century. Boston Consulting Group's CEO Anen Maira, prominent professors of Management professor C.K. Prahlad and Prof. Arindam Chaudhury are now advocating to rediscover Mahatma Gandhi's ideas and leadership qualities for making managers more successful, humane and compassionate.

Mahatma Gandhi was a Manager par excellence. His management was not based on any strategy or calculation but on deep conviction on certain fundamental principles and values which govern the whole universe. His approach was much based on spontaneity of action as on careful consideration of diverse issues confronting the nation, humanity and nature as a whole. His approach was far above the common place approach which stressed on outlays and outcomes and believed in a specific calculus to reach the goal. His management was born out of non-violence, care, compassion and modern values of liberty, equality and fraternity.

Mahatma Gandhi stood for decentralization to devolve power and involve people in the process of governance. He did so when centralization was the governing norm. Through decentralization alone people can be given opportunities to play a meaningful role in running the affairs of the nation. Adoption of the principles and practices of decentralization in the management domain is yet another example to Gandhi's relevance as Management Guru.

## Fundamental Principles of Gandhi

Gandhi's views are based on some of his fundamental principles such as morality, truth, non-violence, humanity, fearlessness, non-possession, Swadesi and tolerance, these principles are the basis for his concepts of Trade Unions, Trusteeship, non-cooperation, minimum living wage, business ethics and values.

## Philosophy of Trusteeship

According to Gandhi men should renounce the desire to possess wealth in excess of what was necessary to satisfy the essential wants. As applied to industry, this meant that the capitalist should use only that much of wealth as was absolutely necessary to satisfy his wants. The wealth that was found in excess of this should be held by him in trust for the benefit of all. From the principle of non-possession thus emerged the theory of trusteeship.

The trusteeship theory is the cornerstone of the economic system which Gandhi envisaged. He believed that this theory provided a means of transforming the present capitalist order of society into an egalitarian one. Elaborating this point further he observed that trusteeship did not recognize the right to property except to the extent permitted by the society for its own welfare. While the capitalists expected to hold industry in trust for the community it was envisaged that as workers in collaboration with the employer they too were expected be 'co-trustee' with the latter. Gandhi expected that the employees take workers into confidence regarding financial and other related matters of the industry. Hence in the context of trusteeship theory of Gandhi the employee-employer relations are characterized as 'co-equals' or 'co-owners'. He strongly believed though legally wealth belonged to owners, morally it belonged to the society and workers were co-equals or co-trustees. Hence Gandhiji believed that under the philosophy of trusteeship there *is no room for conflict of interests between workers and management.*

## Awakening and unity among workers

Gandhiji advocated awakening and unity among workers. By awakening among workers, what Gandhiji meant was growth and development of faith in their moral strength and consciousness about its existence with this awakening and unity. Gandhiji believed that, working class could always face up the tricks of the capitalists. He stated that capital was perfectly useless without labour and he believes that without workers cooperation capitalist could not expect labour. He observed "rich cannot accumulate wealth without the conscious cooperation of the poor in society. If workers resorted to non-cooperation the exploitation of labour by capital would stop."

## Unionization of workers

Gandhiji advocated for the unionization of workers. He observed that "Everyone has to help himself, no one from outside can help any one" they could be better able to help themselves if they were stronger organized into trade unions. He proposed the following objectives of the trade unions:

i) Cooperation and collaboration with the capitalists in running the industry.
ii) Safeguarding themselves from the exploitation of capitalists.
iii) Internal reformation i.e. stopping quarreling within the works, giving up bad habits of drinking, gambling etc., and
iv) Moral education and training.

The Ahmadabad Textile Labour Association (henceforth ATLA) was the model trade union in Gandhiji's view. About it he said "I am responsible for the organization of Ahmadabad Labour. I am of the opinion that it is a model for all India to follow. Its basis is non-violence, pure and simple. It has never had a setback in its career.

## Fixation and regulation of minimum living wage

Under the trusteeship situation in industry the capitalists were expected to pay a minimum living wage to the workers which should be adequate to cover basic needs of workers. He advised the workers to give up bad habits and make good use of their earnings and has also advised the capitalist that if they could not pay the minimum living wage to the workers, better close down the shop. Thus Gandhiji felt rather strongly against those who could not pay such a wage.

To a large extent Gandhiji pleaded for no reduction in the existing levels of wages. If the capitalists failed to pay such living wage or reduced the existing wages, workers should first appeal to the conscience of the capitalist. If this did not work they should resort to non-violent non-cooperation.

## Mahatma Gandhiji's views on the role of Trade Unions

Rolė of Trade Unions were contrary to those of Marx. Marx believed in class struggle. Gandhiji admitted the existence of the two classes; but, with his faith in the goodness of man, he ruled out the need for class struggle. Many of Gandhiji's views have arisen out to the Fundamental Principles of his idealism, such as faith in the goodness of the individual, purity of means, economic equality, trusteeship, removing the evils of industrialization. He believed that the trade unions should be internally used for the reformation of workers as good citizens, as for their defence against assaults from outside. Unions are not anti-capitalistic organizations. They are the least degree political. Their main aim is to increase their internal strength to work conscientiously and to take from the employer no more that what is rightfully due to the labourers. Trade Unions can be moral institutions for the improvement of behavior, and belief in the dignity of labour. Gandhiji advised workers to organize because then they would have more wealth and resources through their labour than the capitalists through their money. He established the Textile Labour Association (TLA) at Ahmadabad on the lines of these principles.

## Industrial Conflict and its Resolution

The basic aim of Gandhian philosophy is the realization of Sarvodaya i.e. the good of all. It is intended to elimination of conflict of interest and restoration of peaceful and harmonious relations. As applied to industry, this actually means a peaceful coexistence of capital and labour. However where conflicts exist, they should be resolved by 'Satyagraha' i.e. non-violent, non-cooperation. It postulates the conquest of the capitalist by self suffering and self purification.

Self-sufficiency is intended to awaken and educate the public opinion which is considered as mighty force than gun powder. However, Gandhiji contained that such suffering should be accompanied by perfect patience and equity. Gandhiji advocated the other methods of conflict resolution such as collective bargaining, arbitration and as a last resort peaceful strikes under certain conditions. He laid down certain conditions for a successful strike. They are:

i) The cause of the strike must be just.

ii) There should be non-violence and non-strikers or "black legs" should never be molested.

iii) There should be unanimity among workers.

iv) Strikers should be able to maintain themselves during the strike period without falling back upon union funds and should therefore occupy themselves in some useful and productive temporary occupations.

v) A strike is no remedy when there is enough of other labour to replace strikes. Gandhiji regarded strike as the inherent right of workers, but in his opinion it was criminal, if it was continued as soon as the arbitration for the settlement of demands for which it was called out was accepted.

vi) He pleaded strike is the last weapon in the armoury of industrial workers and hence should not be resorted to unless all peaceful and constitutional methods of negotiations, conciliation and arbitration are exhausted.

## Application of Gandhian Model

Gandhian philosophy on industrial relations influenced the industrial relation policy of India. The methods and machinery available in India should act as trustees. Workers should get unionized. The Conflict for prevention and settlement of industrial disputes reflects some of the ideas of Gandhi and Public Policy expects to settle the industrial disputes peacefully. The provisions of the Act relating to strikes and lockout legally discourages direct actions. Indian Labour conference laid down code of discipline and code of conduct in tune with Gandhian philosophy. One of the central federations of trade unions in INTUC was built on the lines of ATLA – an organization profounded by Gandhiji. The leaders of the INTUC claims that they are following the Gandhian principles in their dealing with the employers.

## Gandhian Theory of Collective Bargaining

Gandhiji can be called one of the greatest negotiator and labour leader of modern India. His theories to labour issues, negotiations were completely new and refreshingly human. He held different strategic views regarding collective bargaining which is heart of industrial relations management. He strongly supported and explained "collective bargaining is a bi-partite democratic decision-making process. Even though both parties are having antagonistic interests, both strategically negotiate and win what the other party has". He is conscious in the process of negotiations on conditions of work and life, duties of workers, work rules and interpretation, responsibilities of bargaining agents before and after collective bargaining agreement. He believed this voluntary method enables the workers' organizations and reserves the bargaining power.

## Gandhiji and Voluntary Arbitration

The principle of arbitration was the main principle of Gandhian philosophy in industrial relations. In disputes and differences between employers and workers, each side considers itself to be right and just and the problem arises as to who should judge the merits of the case. Gandhiji's answer to this problem was arbitration. The public has no means of judging the merits of a strike, unless it is backed by impartial persons enjoying public confidence. Interested men cannot judge the merits of their case. Hence, there must be an arbitration if they are ever to live in peace. He said, "Strikes must be considered crime if the capitalists accept the principle of arbitration". An impartial tribunal for setting disputes should always be accepted. Refusal is a sign of weakness. As a true satyagrahi, he was not against strikes, but did not consider them as the only means for resolving disputes. He strongly favoured the system of arbitration between the parties. It is our experience that settlement of disputes through courts takes a lot of time and it engenders bitterness and develops estrangement between employers and employees, which ultimately leads to deteriorated industrial relations. It is, therefore, becoming inevitable to once again go back to the method of voluntary arbitration suggested by Gandhiji.

## Observations of Gandhi on Customers and Stake-holders

His remarkable observations on customers as stated that "*A customer is the most important visitor on our premises. He is not dependent on us. We are dependent on him. He is not an interruption in our work. He is the purpose of it ... we are not doing him a favour by serving him. He is doing us a favour by giving us an opportunity to do so.*" The above observations on customer makes Mahatma Gandhi one of the foremost modern day managers whose thinking goes beyond the conventional understanding of management and covers the interests of customers and stakeholders who are the main purpose of business and commerce.

Again if we look at the idea of the stakeholder which is the governing principle of modern day business and management we find that Mahatma Gandhi had articulated such ideas much before the management authorities and experts had highlighted them. In one of the interesting books on Management written by Wayne Visser and Clem Sunter on the them "*Beyond Reasonable Greed: Why sustainable business is a much better idea*?", it is stated that most of the modern day managers are driven by unreasonable greed and neglect the interests of the customers and shareholders. If we examine writings of Mahatma Gandhi from his collected works, we find that he gave importance to the workers and labourers in a factory as major stakeholders.

As early as August 1927, Gandhiji wrote in *Young India*, "In my opinion, the millhands are as much the proprietors of the mills as the shareholders and when the millowners realize that the millhands are as much millowners as they are, there will be no quarrel between them". He further emphasized that "workmen should be regarded as equals with the shareholders, and they should have, therefore, every right to possess an accurate knowledge of the transactions of the mills" (Harijan, 13-2-1937). He recognized the need for higher productivity and pleaded that "the management should share with the workers the gains from higher productivity." He also laid stress on the importance of job enrichment and observed: "A spinner may not dream of earning as much as the manager know, but he refuses to be ignored. If his work and talents are ignored and if his contributions to the industry are never to be measured by any other yardstick except of selling price at the lowest or static level, he will never give his best" (*Harijan*, 10-8-1947)."

On 31st March, 1936, he visited the Kolar Gold Mines and found that the small dwelling units of labourers lacked adequate space. He expressed deep regret that the mill owners were not giving adequate attention to the needs of the labourers. He then wrote "If the workers only knew what they could do for themselves by combining the training and intelligence they would realize that they were no less proprietors of the mines than the managers and the shareholders." By juxtaposing labourers with managers and shareholders, Gandhiji was emphasizing on a management method which if followed would ensure efficiency and effectiveness of an organization. This is what exactly the global managers are doing while talking about maximizing the productivity of an organization.

## Gandhi in the 21st Century

The former President of South Africa and the ardent follower of Mahatma Gandhi, Nelson Mandela in 1999 aptly pointed out that the twenty-first century would be the Gandhian century. In this line of thinking, the world leaders at United Nations had declared this first decade of the twenty-first century (2000-10) as the 'International Decade of Culture of Peace and Non-Violence' to explore the possibilities for implementing Gandhian techniques for managing the problems of the world ranging from politics to economics. Twenty Nobel Laureates have pledged their commitment to this cause and have emphasized the need to spread the message of non-violence at every level of society during this decade. 189 countries have adopted this historic 'Millennium Declaration' in their national agenda and have been working for achieving peace, prosperity and human development in the twenty-first century through the set agenda of the UN: Eradicate extreme poverty and hunger; Achieve universal primary education; Promote gender equality and empower women; Reduce child mortality; Improve maternal health; Combat HIV/AIDS, tuberculosis, malaria and other disease; Ensure environmental sustainability; Promote peace and human right. It should be noted here *that most of the schemes of the UN are from Constructive Programme of Mahatma Gandhi* devised during 1920-47. Thus, Gandhian ideals have become much more important than ever before for managing the problems of world community. The *United Nations General Assembly will declare October 2 the birth anniversary of Mahatma Gandhi as International Day of Non-Violence* in recognition of his role in promoting the message of peace around the world.

## Conclusion

This approach holds that conflict between workers and capitalists should be resolved peacefully either by moral appeal, or by arbitration or by non-violent non-cooperation methods. An evolution of Indian industrial relations reveals that public policy incorporated the Gandhian ideas on industrial relations. Many of his ideas were implemented by the ATLA, a unique and a successful experiment in Gandhian Trade Unionism. Gandhiji had immense faith in the goodness of man and he believed that many of the evils of the modern world have been brought about by wrong systems and not by wrong individuals. He insisted on recognizing each individual worker as a human being. He believed in non-violent communism, going so far as to say that "if communism comes without any violence, it would be welcome".

## REFERENCES


1. Udai Pareek (1992) *Conflict and Collaboration in Organizations* (Second edition), Oxford and IBH Publishing Co. Pvt. Ltd., Calcutta, pp. 18-19.
2. Hymen R. (1975) Industrial Relations, *A Marxist Introduction*, MacMillan.
3. Rama Swamy E A and Uma Rama Swamy, (1981) *Industry and Labour, An Introduction*, Oxford University Press, New Delhi.
4. Abdul Aziz, (1984), *Labour Problems of Developing Economic*, Asish Publishing House.
5. Pramod Verma (1990) Management of Industrial Relations: Readings and Cases (Fourth Edition), Oxford & IBH Publishing Co., Calcutta. pp. 238-240.
6. Sarma A.M. (2007 *Industrial relations (conceptual and legal frame work)*. Himalaya Publishing House, Nagpur, pp. 17-19.
7. Waly, Thomas (1986) "Organisational Behaviour and Non-violent

Management: A Gandhian analysis" *Gandhi Marg*, A Journal of Gandhi Peace Foundation, New Delhi, February.

8. Sharma, Jai Narain (2003), *Alternative Economics* (New Delhi: Deep and Deep) p. 33.
9. Hussain G. (2007) 'Gandhigiri – Reviving the Truth' in Jagriti, Khadi and Village Industries Commission, Mumbai, June.
10. Narendra v Shukla (2004) *Gandhian Philosophy and its contribution to Trade Union Movement*, Workers Education, Central Board for Workers Education Nagpur, pp. 16-21.

SECTION - 3

GANDHI'S CONSTRUCTIVE PROGRAMME

# 11

# Gandhian Economic Ideas and Its Relevance Today

*B. Lilly Grace Eunice & Mande Ramesh*

Sixty one years ago when we broke the shackles of the alien rule, "We, the people of India .... Resolved to secure to all its citizens justice—social, economic and political, equality of status and opportunity." We embarked upon a programme of planned development to eradicate poverty in rural India. Since then eleven five year plans have been implemented and now we are in the 21st Century. Despite all this, we still find ourselves overwhelmed by poverty, unemployment, illiteracy, untouchability, low-wages, lack of infrastructure, sky rising prices of all essential goods and services, transportation facilities etc.

It is an undisputable fact, that India secured a notable place in the fields of atomic energy, Information Technology and science and technology. Yet, the government is faced with enormous resources crunch. When we look back, we find that the lot of poor has not improved despite of anti-poverty schemes. Is it because, we are drifted away from the Gandhian path of rural development? Or why the path which we choose dearly to tread on has not produced the desired results? Against this backdrop, in this paper an attempt is made to analyse the economic ideas of Gandhi.

## Fundamentals of Gandhian Philosophy

The main problem in understanding Gandhian philosophy is the problem of mis-interpretation and mis-conceptions. Gandhi went through an evolutionary process of formulating ideas, approaches and development models. There was a great flexibility in him based on his experiences. Gandhiji was not a philosopher, academician or system builder. He was a path-finder with definite source of economic goals. Any path is futile if it is goalless. Gandhian philosophy is comprised of seven basic concepts. These are: *truth, non-violence, swadeshi, satyagraha, equality, bread labour* and *aparigraha.*

To Gandhi, the truth, the reality is more important than any doctrine. For him, truth is not only self-evident in a given situation but it is self-sufficient as well. He stressed the necessity of following the truth as much as he explained all other things in the light of truth. According to Gandhi non-violence is not restricted in actions only but it was to be manasa, vacha and karmana. On the contrary, it is the most abused concept, Gandhian doctrine of non-violence desired total abolition of violence. The fact is that he wanted violence to be reduced to its minimum and not to use it unnecessarily. The selection of violence and non-violence is totally dependent on the nature of the situation concerned.

The third doctrine of Gandhian philosophy is Swadeshi. Gandhi advocated self-reliance of individuals and that of nations. He opposed individual to depend upon another individual or a nation on another nation. For the sake of Swadeshi, he opposed the science and technology. He realised that modern science and technology is useful when it serves our socio, economical and political requirements of rural poor. The fourth major concept of Gandhian philosophy is Satyagraha. It means non-violent resistance for the cause of truth. In fighting the cause of truth one must not fear for anything. The essence of Satyagraha is fearlessness, truth and actions.

The fifth fundamental of Gandhian philosophy is equality. The concept of equality is basic of all economic concepts. He put forward the nation of not differentiating the human beings on the grounds of caste, creed and colour. Originally he applied the concept of equality in India and latter extended it to the whole world. The sixth basic concept of Gandhian Philosophy is bread-labour. He was of the view that every individual should work to fulfil his basic needs food, shelter and cloth. He asked every body to weave the yarn as much as necessary for his clothes. He established the dignity of labour in the society. He said that one who eats without doing necessary labour is a thief and he is therefore sinning. The last important basic concept of Gandhian philosophy is *aparigraha*. Aparigraha stands against the acquisitive spirit of man. Gandhi believed that possession of more things than necessary is a crime against manhood and society.

The above philosophy was evolved from these seven basic concepts. Truth can be achieved only through "Ahimsa" humility which means infinite love and infinite capacity for suffering. Gandhi did not study economics nor propounded any economic theory. His economics was based on his personal experiences. He developed doctrine of trusteeship which alone can be the solution for the present day mal-distribution of wealth. There should be minimum and maximum ceiling for the accumulation of wealth. A large number of economists believed that Gandhian theory of "Trusteeship" should be given a legal status because that is the only answer to the challenges of 21st century.

## Economic Ideas of Gandhi

Many writers, such as Tolstoy, Ruskin, James, Yen, Paulo, Ferrier etc., did not have formal economic base but they exercised considerable influence on economic thinking. Similarly Gandhi is also not an economist but contributed much to the economic ideas and social well being. An analysis on Gandhian ideas will reveal their greater relevance to uplift the poor from poverty. Gandhi's economic ideas basically emanated from a strong argument to remove poverty, distress and reduce the gap between poverty and prosperity.

- The villages should be made self-sufficient and self-reliant.
- Grass-root level decentralised planning and implementation should be initiated.
- Cottage and small scale industries should be encouraged by avoiding capital intensive technology.
- Co-operative and community farming be promoted.
- Income inequality should be reduced by changing the attitudes of the rich.
- Capitalists, businessmen and landlords have to serve as "Trustees" for the whole community.

John Ruskin book "*Unto the Last*" influenced Gandhiji's basic economic philosophy. Leo Tolstoys *Bread Theory of Labour* inspired Gandhi strongly to believe that no man was frees from the obligation of production of the elementary necessities of life. Gandhi was influenced by James Yen who was founder of International Rural Reconstruction Movement Institution of Philippines. He studied Paulo Ferrier, "Pedagogy of Oppressed." Such philosophical base is related to the structure of Gandhian economic desire.

He rejected the class conflict theory of Karl Marx and passionately wanted the existence of a harmonious living of different sections of society. Gandhian crusade was for the equality of man both in economic and social spheres. He repeatedly emphasised that the people were exploited by the rich and rich accumulated wealth from the blood of the poor. His concept of economic equality did not mean that everybody would literally have the same amount. So, the real meaning of economic equality was "to acquire each according to his needs". The poor villagers produce the food and go hungry. They produce milk and their children go without milk. This constitutes the picture of economic inequality. Accumulation of wealth is not opposed by Gandhian economic reforms. The means to achieve this equitable distribution of income and wealth in Gandhian economics is not violent practice of trusteeship. A moderate attempt in the recent past was to achieve land distribution through Bhoodan movement in reply to a question on the 1947 Tebhaga Movement in Bengal; Gandhi said that he did not feel that the landlords would be ruined if they got 1/3 of the output instead of 1/2 output.

Gandhi worried about unemployment, underemployment and disguised employment in agricultural sector. So as to tackle this problem he laid emphasis on the development of village industries, cottage industries as an effective remedy to of solve the problem of unemployment. Further he emphasised on labour intensive rural industries and crafts. Development of khadi and handicrafts could provide employment to women and child at home during spare time occupied a central place in Gandhian economic model. It is important to note here that Gandhi was adverse to modern industrialisation. He preached that mass unemployment could be eradicated through development of rural industries.

## Gandhian Attitude to Machinery

According to Gandhi the usage of machines should be minimum when are inevitable only but must not be allowed to displace the human labour. Gandhiji wanted that the labour, cottage and small scale industries and labour intensive industries should be the means of production in rural areas. The argument is even tenable today. The hue and cry against incoming of multinational corporations in the wake of new economic policy is essential due to the fear of usurpation of labour intensive, small-scale industries and concentration of economic power. Gandhiji was convinced that large-scale industries were not suitable. An analysis of Gandhiji ideas on modern industrialisation will reveal that large scale centralisation and supply of simple tools and machinery to the millions of small production units would be necessary under the management of public sector. The core contents of Gandhian economics related to village self-sufficiency, removal of income inequality, poverty and employment generation. Gandhi did not rule-out the necessity of central control over decentralization of administration. Large part of planning could emerge from the grass-roots and implemented by the local self-government under general direction of central government. Gandhi clearly visualised the development of country was not possible without growing rural economy. This was proved in the post and pre-independent era with high prices and shortage of mass consumption goods due to rapid industrialization. The advocacy of Gandhiji for decentralization of political and economic power has been revived and revitalised with greater powers and functions in the wake of 73rd and 74th Constitutional amendments.

## Eradication of Poverty

In 1994 U.N. General Assembly proclaimed 1996 as the International year of the eradication of poverty. Its objective was to create "a greater awareness of the fact that the eradication of poverty is - fundamental to reinforcing peace and achieving sustainable development". Poverty has individual, social and economical dimensions. Individually every man should have basic requirements like food, shelter and clothing etc., Gandhiji was concerned with the restoration of cardinal virtues and values. Aparigraha is one of the cardinal virtues which Gandhiji enunciated. According to him, practice of cardinal virtues will eradicate poverty and leads to economic and social justice. Poverty alleviation and population issues are very closely related to each other. Gandhi views on poverty are a spectrum of thought which reveals to us several aspects. According to Gandhi's representative democracy, participative democracy is needed at grass-root levels to manage their own affairs. Drive against poverty has taken added significant. Since the then Prime Minister Smt. Indira Gandhi has started "Garibi Hatao" movement. In the field of poverty eradication, India has made significant efforts. Poverty is defined as that state in which a family is unable to fulfil their basic needs. Globally speaking, drastic policy changes are necessary in order to have successful assault on poverty. The 73rd Amendment has given paramount importance to eradication of poverty. To eradicate poverty the government of India has introduced so many programmes since inception of the independence.

There are three broad categories of Anti-poverty programmes implemented in India. They are Income-Employment generation Programmes, Wage and Infrastructure Development Programmes and Area Development Programmes. Now in our country Swarnajayanthi Gram Swarozgar Yojana has been implementing since 1999. In the year 2001 the Government of India has introduced another Programme to create employment to the rural poor for 100 days in a year named as National Rural Employment Guarantee Programme(NREGP).

Anti-poverty policies focus on the well being of the people for the "Culture of Poverty". The chief weakness of the anti-poverty programmes today is that they are based on land. As it is not in the hands of poor, the poor has no power to come out of poverty. As emphasised by Gandhi we should wage war in the form of non-violent revolution for the eradication of poverty, by means of land distribution.

## Gender Inequality

Gandhiji's views on women often appear to be mere pronouncement and the solutions he proposed for removing of oppression of women often untenable. Even though he managed to draw many women into the mainstream of Indian Freedom

Struggle they never raised to the occasion. His views on women were out-dated in the sense that they flew from the pen of typical patriarch. Gandhiji had worked out a clear programme of action for the liberalisation of women. The tactics and strategy used by Gandhi had profound concern for women. Gandhiji was very much critical of the texts in smritis which affirm the subordination of the women to men. He pointed out that those texts are interpolation and suggested that an authoritative body should discard such text. Hence, Gandhi integrated the struggle for the equality of men and women in his broad frame work for Swaraj.

## Rediscovery on Gandhian Economy and Ecology

Many times Gandhi spoke about "Charkha" and written about Charkha. In the midst of the present crisis ridden socio-economic and cultural scenario it is indeed a pity that India is not looking at solution, for its problems. It is others who are trying to rediscover Gandhi in a desperate situation due to failure of capitalism, economists like E.F. Schumacher considered Gandhi as the "greatest innovative and original economic thinker of the 20th Century" Gandhiji's ideas and praxis are becoming more and more relevant as the existing system is suffering with economic crisis and erosion of values. Therefore, a time has to come to stop worshipping Gandhi in the ritual manner. The intellectuals in the country should turn to his writings with a sharp open mind to discover and retrieve social regeneration and sustainable economic development. The first step in this process of rediscovering Gandhi is to remove mythical elements.

## Non-violent Economics

The tragedy of modern India is that the important aspects of Gandhian philosophy are not given serious attention. The rulers and the administrators never realised that Gandhiji was much ahead of them, and that their psychological inability to keep pace with a great revolutionary is responsible for the present plight. The reappraisal of economic policies is being done now desperately by the political leadership. What happened two years ago in coastal areas of Andhra Pradesh, which is called the "Rice Bowl" of Andhra Pradesh, when the entire fish in that area died of a mysterious disease. This should be an eye-opener to the prophets of unlimited "Hitech" transfer. Several Dalit Bahujans were deprived of their livelihood. Such "Hitech" transfer should be opposed through non-violent Gandhian economics.

### The non-violent Gandhian economy: salient features

The non-violent economy which Gandhi envisioned would ensure.

- The widest possible dispersal of means and opportunity of employment and job.
- Non-concentration of wealth and means of living.
- Production with the help of locally available resources.
- Equitable distribution of wealth among the people.
- Co-operation and non-conflict among the people who are engaged in production.

It is true that changes take place in thoughts of humanity with passage of time. It is also true that there is a missing link between the Gandhian model of development, as it is so called, and the modern thinking of opening of the economy to market oriented globalised frame. But in so far as mass poverty, mass unemployment, inequality of income and wealth and self-sufficiency of village life of 68% of India's population are concerned, the best recourse is still to recast the plan strategy in line with Gandhian idea of making every village self-reliant through decentralised planning. One could only add here that as long as development of villages would mean development of India, the relevance of Gandhian economy will continue to survive.

## REFERENCES

1. M.K.Gandhi, (1947) *India of my Dreams;* Navajeevan Publishing House, Ahmadabad.
2. Ruskin (1944) *Unto This Last;* A parathrase by M.K.Gandhi – Translated from Gujarati by Valji, Govindji, Navajeevan Publishing House Ahmadabad.
3. Mathur, J.S.(ed), 1994, *Economic Thought Mahatma Gandhi,* Vol III, Arikant Publishing House Delhi.
4. R.A.Buchanan, *Technology and Social Progress.*

# 12

# Gandhian Economics: The Need of The Day

*P. Srinivas Subbarao, P. Suseela Rani* &
*G.V.L.Srikant*

Gandhiji first promulgated his radical economic theory in the book "*Hind Swaraj*" written on his journey from England to South Africa. The book was a powerful disparagement of the Industrial Revolution and its ill effects - written after a first hand experience in the home of the Industrial Revolution. His views on economics and how they have fared over the years is what I have sought to pen down here. Gandhiji held that machinery displaced labour and hence concentrated wealth in the hands of the few His ideas though met with constant change over the years from the time when he first published "*Hind Swaraj*" in 1912.

Gandhiji advocated the theory of Trusteeship which held the capitalists as trustees of wealth for the service of the society. Reliance in the mid-eighties and Infosys in contemporary times have amply demonstrated the true import of Gandhiji's teachings. Not only have these companies doubled and trebled the earnings of its shareholders but their promoters worked and strived for the shareholders, increasing their shares' worth, providing work to thousands of people and bringing prosperity to large parts of India.

Gandhiji believed that the key to the country's progress lay in the strengthening of the decentralized, self sufficient village economies. Lending power at the micro level ensures decrease in large scale corruption, clipping the wings of politicians and bureaucrats. Also the formation of decentralized, self-sufficient economies could ideally lead to a best of both worlds – by lending power to the people it creates a democracy and by preventing the "rich get richer, poor get poorer" cycle it ensures socialism.

## Gandhian Economics and Ethics

Gandhian economics do not draw a distinction between economics and ethics. Economics that hurts the moral well-being of an individual or a nation is immoral, and therefore sinful. The value of an industry should be gauged less by the dividends it pays to shareholders than by its effect on the bodies, soul and spirits of the people employed in it. In essence, supreme consideration is to be given to man than to money. In fact, the first basic principle of Gandhi's economic thought is a special emphasis on 'plain living' which helps in cutting down your wants and being self-reliant. Accordingly, increasing consumer appetite is likened to animal appetite which goes the end of earth in search of their satisfaction. Thus a distinction is to be made between 'Standard of Living' and 'Standard of Life', where the former merely states the material and physical standard of food, cloth and housing. A higher standard of life, on the other hand could be attained only if, along with material advancement, there was a serious attempt to imbibe cultural and spiritual values and qualities.

## Gandhian Economics and its Contemporary Relevance

"Gandhian Economics, and which has contemporary relevance, remarkable originality and the attributes of an analytical contribution of a high order. It is unfortunate that professional economists, with a few notable exceptions, have not given to Gandhian economics the scholarly attention it deserves. Nevertheless, Gandhi's economic ideas are widely known, in a general way, and have become associated in the popular and professional minds with certain definite conceptions. Among these, five seem to me, to have the widest currency. By and large, in the minds of most people, Gandhian Economics has come to be associated with the advocacy of the following:

### 1) Acceptance of poverty

The first of all Gandhi's advocacy is of the acceptance of poverty. In order to show his complete identification with the poor people of India, Gandhi adopted their dress and their simple ways of living at all times. Even when he went to see the British King George V, he wore just a loin cloth like the poor people of India, provoking an outraged Churchill to call him a "half naked fakir".

Nevertheless, Gandhi did not admire poverty, and most emphatically did not see in poverty the virtues that are sometimes claimed for it. He said "*No one has ever suggested that grinding pauperism can lead to anything else than moral degradation. Every human being has the right to live and therefore to find the wherewithal to feed himself and where necessary to clothe and house himself.*[1] Again he said "*If by advance you mean everyone having plenty to eat and drink and to clothe himself with, enough to keep his mind trained and educated, I should be satisfied.*[2]

No, Gandhi was not an admirer of poverty. He wanted India to develop herself economically, to make possible a satisfactory life for all. As early as 1928 he wrote "*According to me, the economic constitution of India and for that matter, the world, should be such that no one under it should suffer from want of food and clothing. In other words, everybody should be able to get sufficient work to enable him to make the two ends meet. And this ideal can be universally realized only if the means of production of the elementary necessities of life remain in the control of the masses.*"[3]

After thirty-five years of planned efforts, Indian economic development has not come anywhere close to fulfilling Gandhi's economic aspirations. In fact, even in the United States of America, universally regarded as the richest nation in the world, suffering from want of food and clothing is the lot of a substantial minority of her people. What Gandhi advocated was not poverty but sufficiency for all. He wanted enough development to enable all people to live in comfort and dignity. But, of course, he was opposed to extreme inequalities and to the pursuit of ever-rising material standards of living, because he realized that such a path would not lead to happiness.

As early as 1908, he wrote in his important book *Hind Swaraj* "*We notice that the mind is a restless bird; the more it gets the more it wants, and still remains unsatisfied. The more we indulge our passions the more unbridled they become. Our ancestors therefore set a limit to our indulgences. They saw happiness was largely a mental condition. A man is not necessarily happy because he is rich or unhappy because he is poor. The rich are often seen to be unhappy, the poor to be happy. Millions will always be poor. Observing all this, our ancestors dissuaded us from luxuries and pleasures.*[4]

Gandhi felt that the solution to the economic problem through continuous increase in material production was a false solution. Ever increasing wealth will not ensure happiness because of the tendency of wants to multiply even faster. This can be called Gandhi's first impossibility theorem. The experience of the rich nations and of rich people in poor nations testifies to its validity.

Gandhi, however, firmly believed that all human beings should have enough to satisfy their basic needs. In the planning efforts of India and other developing countries, economic growth is the central goal. Under a Gandhian scheme, reduction of inequalities, provision of full employment, and the eradication of poverty would be the dominant goals, and economic growth would not be a separate growth objective. In such a society, economic growth is likely to be the consequence of the pursuit of the other goals mentioned above.

### 2) Return to the simplicity of India's economic past

Many persons think that Gandhi advocated a return to India's economic past. For example, Dr Arthur Lewis, Nobel-laureate in economics, in an otherwise admirable book, observes "*Not all nationalist politicians favour economic development. Some like Gandhi have resisted Westernism and desire on the contrary to return to old ways.*"[5]

Gandhi called his ideal republic Ram Rajya, a throw-back to a mythical past where under the rule of God-King Rama perfect justice prevailed. Nevertheless, it is not correct to say that Gandhi advocated a return to India's past. To be sure, there were certain attributes of India's civilization, like the recognition of the dangers of the multiplication of human wants, and the need to exercise restraint, that Gandhi admired, and wished his countrymen not to forsake. But his face and feet were firmly turned toward the future and not toward the past. In an exchange of letters with Nehru, he drew a robust picture of the ideal village of his dreams.

*"My ideal village will contain intelligent beings. They will not live in dirt and darkness as animals. Men and women will be free and able to hold their own against anyone in the world. There will be neither plague nor cholera, nor small pox; no one will be idle; no one will wallow in luxury...It is possible to envisage railways, post and telegraph...and the like"*[6]

It is relevant to note that in that letter Gandhi describes the ideal village as his dream. Since at no time in India's past the village even remotely resembled the ideal portrayed by Gandhi, it would be hard to sustain the claim that he advocated a return to the past.

Untouchability, lack of freedom for women, and extreme inequalities has been part of village life in India from time immemorial to the present. Gandhi was uncompromisingly opposed to these. He said "*Today, there is gross inequality. The basis of socialism is economic equality. There can be no Ramarajya in the present state of iniquitous inequalities in which a few roll in riches and the masses do not get enough to eat.*[7] To his radical mind, the present which is a product of the past, was unsatisfactory and needed to be changed in fundamental ways. He was willing to borrow many bricks from the past, but the edifice itself was new and belonged to the future.

### 3) Elimination of machinery and large-scale production

On the subject of machinery and large-scale production, Gandhi's views are especially susceptible to misrepresentation because these views evolved over a period of time. As a rule, whenever there seem to be conflicting pronouncements of Gandhi on any subject, the chronologically latest one is the idea that should be attributed to him. Gandhi himself recommended this course to his followers. Another point that should be borne in mind is that Gandhi's economic ideas were evolved in the context of India's fight for independence. Some of the measures he recommended, such as hand-spinning and weaving were designed to weaken the hold of a foreign power over India. Since he died a revolutionary's death at the hands of a reactionary Hindu fanatic soon after independence, he did not have the opportunity to examine adequately the validity of many of his economic ideas to the problems of an independent India.

This underscores the need to pay special attention to the context in which his ideas were expressed in assessing their significance. Gandhi's attitude toward machinery changed considerably with the passage of time. In his book *Hind Swaraj*, written in 1908, he had said "*Machinery is the chief symbol of modern civilization; it represents a great sin. I cannot recall a single good point in connection with machinery. Books can be written to demonstrate its evils. It is necessary to realize that machinery is bad. We shall then be able gradually to do away with it.*"[8] Again in 1926 he wrote in *Young India* "*The fact is that this industrial civilization is a disease because it is all evil.*

*Let us not be deceived by catchwords and phrases. Our concern is therefore to destroy industrialism at any cost.*[9] from this uncompromising opposition to all machinery that he took in the early years, he gradually began to recognize the useful role that machinery can play under proper public control and in the appropriate conditions. Firstly, all machinery is permissible if it does not cause unemployment. In 1934 he wrote "*Mechanization is good when the hands are too few for the work intended to be accomplished. It is an evil when there are more hands than required for the work as in India. The problem with us is not how to find leisure for the teeming million inhabitants of our villages. The problem is how to utilize their idle hours, which areequal to the working days of six months in the year.*[10]

Increasingly he began to realize that it is not machinery as such that is an evil but the social conditions under which it is used. Four years later, we find him making a still stronger statement in support of machinery under appropriate conditions. He wrote "*If I could produce all my country's wants by means of 30,000 people instead of 30 million? I should not mind it, provided that the 30 million are not rendered idle and unemployed.*[11]

*But* even in his early years, he was in favour of simple tools and implements that improved the productivity of labour for he wrote "*I am uncompromisingly against all destructive machinery. But simple tools and instruments, and such instruments and machinery as save individual labour and lighten the burden of the millions of cottages I should welcome.*"[12] But Gandhi began more and more to see that under proper conditions of social control even large-scale machinery could be used in such a way as to serve the villages and their crafts and not destroy them as they did in the past in the absence of social control. He wrote in 1940 "*I do visualize electricity, ship-building, iron works, machine-making and the like existing side by side with village handicrafts. Hitherto industrialization has been so planned as to destroy the village and village crafts. In the state of the future, it will subserve the villages and their crafts.*[13] In other words, he wanted mass production to be replaced by production by the masses. Thus, the position that Gandhi came to hold on machinery was quite close to that of Marx. In the absence of social control machinery causes unemployment and leads to exploitation n of labour and the destruction of the artisan.

While the indiscriminate proliferation of machinery is harmful, under proper social control, machinery could confer many benefits on society. While Gandhi with the passage of time began to realize that machinery under proper conditions could be a valuable asset to man and society, the views advanced against large-scale industrialization very early in his life are valid to this day

He advances four reasons why it would be impossible for industrialization to provide a satisfactory solution to man's economic problem. This is Gandhi's second impossibility theorem and constitutes at the analytical level, an original and durable economic contribution.

1) First, he noted that industrialization involves exploitation of the underdeveloped countries by the industrializing nations. They require the poor countries as suppliers of raw materials and as buyers of their finished goods. Under these circumstances, if all countries attempted industrialization their efforts must surely fail. Stronger nations would try to prevent the weaker nations from embarking on independent paths of development. Competition and rivalries among the developed countries would lead to war and destruction of human life as well as material resources.

2) Secondly, the wide use of large-scale methods of production would lead to mass unemployment in many countries, especially in labour-abundant countries like India.

3) Thirdly, since industrialization involves a very high cost

of investment per worker, to provide employment for all unemployed human resources would involve capital accumulation on such a massive scale that it would be beyond the investment resource mobilization capacities of most of the poor countries.

4) Fourthly, the industrialized way of life when universally practiced would make such large demands on our non-renewable resources that simply cannot be met by our meager planet. Gandhi often said that there were enough resources for man's needs but not enough for his greed. Thus, long before all the countries could become industrialized, the process will be brought to a sudden halt by the barrier of resource depletion. [14] It is only in recent years that scientists and scholars in the rich nations are beginning to realize the validity of Gandhi's second impossibility theorem so presciently articulated by him half a century ago.

### 4) Adherence to the social and economic rules and regulations of orthodox Hinduism

The fourth myth that Gandhi was an orthodox Hindu who advocated strict adherence to the social and economic institutions and practices of Hinduism will also be shown on closer examination to be lacking in validity. Gandhi was a person with a strong religious motivation and found in each religion something of permanent value. What attracted him to Hinduism was its catholicity and freedom from doctrinal rigidity. It was the only religion which did not forbid him to be also a Muslim, a Christian and a Sikh. But there were many things about Hindu society he passionately disliked, and throughout his life, he carried on an active crusade against such established Hindu practices as untouchability, caste system and inferior status assigned to women. Even to this day in independent India, the caste system is rampant and the Harijans continue to suffer privations and persecutions of various kinds.

But Gandhi accepted the Harijans as his equals even at the beginning of the century and would not tolerate his wife washing the commode of a Harijan in their South African home with a sullen face. In the beginning, though always opposed to untouchability, Gandhi saw some merit in the caste system and the practice of hereditary occupations. But these positions he later abandoned, and, in fact, strongly opposed them. There was a time when he was opposed to inter-caste marriage. Later, he withdrew this opposition and would attend only inter-caste weddings. His fight against untouchability is well known, and no individual has done more for the welfare and uplift of the Harijans than Gandhi. For the cause of emancipation of women and their acceptance as equals, he fought a valiant fight against the citadels of Hindu orthodoxy. Gandhi was a Hindu heretic and a radical Hindu religious reformer whose message and achievements bear comparison with those of Martin Luther and the Buddha.

### 5) Rejection of communism and acceptance of a modified capitalism

Gandhi's attitude towards capitalism has also been subject to a great deal of misunderstanding. Marxists often portray him as an apologist for capitalism, and conservative Gandhians frequently invoke his name to oppose radical land reforms and other changes in society. Both of these positions are untenable and arise from misinterpretations of Gandhi's ideas and actions. When Gandhi was engaged in the fight for India's independence, the Indian capitalist class saw in that struggle an opportunity for its self-expansion and growth. It wanted to take the place of the foreign British capitalist class, and therefore gave its support to the independence struggle. Thus, the historical circumstances conferred on the Indian capitalist class a progressive role, and under these circumstances Gandhi saw no reason to oppose them. Indian capitalists like Birla were his followers, and Gandhi was often a guest in their homes. These were the circumstances that gave rise to the myth that Gandhi was an apologist for capitalism. Actually, Gandhi had a prescient understanding of the progressive role that the Indian capitalist class and the wealthy were playing during the struggle for independence. He knew that in an independent India there would be the need to oppose these people. So we find him as early as 1928 writing to Nehru "*I am quite of your opinion that some day we shall have to start a movement without the rich people and without the vocal educated class, but the time is not yet.*[15]

It is thus evident that Gandhi had an uncanny historical sense of the progressive role that the capitalists were playing during the independence struggle. But he had no great fondness for capitalism and nowhere in his writings or in his speeches can anyone find any support expressed for capitalism or for private property.

He was not only a firm believer in socialism, but his socialism is of a very radical kind. He sometimes referred to himself as a foremost communist. His disagreement with the Marxists and communists was not about the end to be sought about which he had no quarrel with them but about the means to be adopted for the attainment of the goals of communism. Gandhi felt that far from the end justifying the means, the means should justify the end. If communists were advocating violence for the attainment of socialism, Gandhi parted company with them at that point. He wanted socialism to be attained through the use of non-violence.

He clearly foresaw the need for change and did not use his dislike of violence to justify the status quo. He not only saw the need for fundamental change but even recognized its inevitability. In 1942 he wrote *"I see coming the day of the rule of the poor, whether that rule is through force of arms or of non-violence."*[16] He therefore urged his countrymen to establish socialism through peaceful means with the utmost dispatch. Gandhi saw with remarkable prescience that communism has not successfully dealt with the problem of power, either in theory or practice. Bringing all the means of production under public ownership creates enormous concentration of power, and the communists have not evolved a satisfactory method of dealing with this situation.

## Conclusion

The theory of socialism through trusteeship was Gandhi's answer to the problem of power. Unfortunately, his political preoccupations prevented him from elaborating on his theory. Soon after independence was won, his energies had to be given to the cause of the restoration of communal harmony, when his life was brought to an abrupt end by an assassin's bullet. But there is no doubt that Gandhi had great faith in the efficacy of trusteeship.

## REFERENCES

1. Quoted in J. B. Kripalani. *Gandhi –His Life and Thoughts,* p. 368.
2. *Ibid.*
3. *Young India* Nov. 15, 1928.
4. *Hind Swaraj,* Chapter XIII, p. 61.

5. W. Arthur Lewis. *Theory of Economic Growthm* p. 153.
6. Quoted in Nehru. *A Bunch of Old Letters,* pp. 505-506).
7. *Harijan,* June 1, 1947.
8. *Hind Swaraj*, Chapter XIX.
9. *Young India*, Oct. 7, 1926.
10. *Harijan,* Nov 16, 1934.
11. *Harijan*, Feb 12, 1938.
12. *Young India*, June 16, 1926.
13. *Harijan*, Jan. 27, 1940.
14. *Young India*, Aug. 6,1925, and Oct 7, 1926, *Harijan*, Nov 30, 1935, cf. also A. Das.
15. Hiren Mukerjee "Remembering Jawarharlal Nehru" in *Link*, Nov 16, 1980, p. 9.
16. *Harijan*, Feb 1, 1942

# 13

# Gandhi's Perception of Women: An Analysis

*K. Visweswara Rao & P. Sailaja*

Gandhi was completely opposed to many social customs, traditions, norms, and values and social events like child marriage/widowhood, the dowry system, the *purdah system, and prostitution which had/have* been oppressive of women in India. He also advocated equal legal rights for women. One of the main problems of society and more so in India, which drew Gandhi's attention was the social status of women. "His attitude to women's rights was uncompromising under all conditions". "He could visualize woman only as man's companion, gifted with equal mental capacities, possessing 'the right to participate in every minute detail in the activities of man' and an equal right of freedom and liberty". It would be relevant to state that Gandhi's *'Satyagraha'* movement was instrumental in releasing the countless inhibitions, social, emotional, political and physical, of the women in India.

## Status of Women in Pre-Independence India

Gandhi played a role for improving the position of women in society, it is essential to look at women's status, prevalent at that time. When Gandhi emerged on to the political scenario, social evils like child marriage and dowry system were rampant. Indian women had an average life span of only twenty seven years. Death of women in labour was a common phenomenon. The percentage of women with basic education was as low as two per cent. The patriarchal nature of the society confined women to the status of an inferior sex subordinate to their male counterparts. The purdah system was in full vogue in Northern India. Unless accompanied by their male guardians, the women were not permitted to venture out on their own. Only a handful few could avail of education and attend schools. It was in such a dismal milieu that Gandhi took the responsibility of shouldering a social crusade that led to a major reorientation of the common notion of women in the Indian society.

Accepting women's status within the family as an index of their own progress and modernity, the earlier reformers criticised particularly inhuman practices like widow immolation (sati), marriage of child brides to much older men, ban on remarriage of widows, and sought to promote some form of education for women. Orthodox criticism of such moves was countered by statements that such reforms would arrest conversions to Christianity or the drift of oppressed widows to prostitution, and strengthen the stability of the traditional (patriarchal) family. The changes that they sought to promote reflected fairly crudely the social, especially family ideology of the nineteenth century British middle class. They did so without examining its possible long-term impact on the gender role prescriptions—ideal or actual—within the indigenous cultures of the highly diverse Indian society.

The Committee on the Status of Women in India (CSWI) accused the government, the educational system, social analysts, the media, political parties, trade unions as well as women's organizations - i.e. most members of the intelligentsia of a failure to understand the implications of gender equality guaranteed by the Constitution. The Committee was especially struck by the total invisibility and neglect of the economic roles played by the "overwhelming majority" of women among the peasantry, in most rural industries and services, and among the urban poor in policies for agricultural, industrial and frastructural development. Despite the growing evidence of a decline in poor women's economic opportunities and consequent distress available from Census and a few other sources, official planners, social scientists and others continued to view women as economically inactive and dependent consumers, whose basic needs were confined to "education, health and welfare" not employment. Seeking an explanation for the wide gap between the reality of poor women's lives and official and academic beliefs that women were at the most "supplementary earners" for the family, whose contribution to the family's survival or improvement was "dispensable", the Committee attributed it to the class bias of the intelligentsia, which projected middle class experience as normal for all women. The development of women's studies in the post-1975 period, however, added other dimensions to this explanation. The theory of 'sanskritisation'-explaining a long-established pattern of social behaviour among upwardly mobile social groups-offered a handy framework for the social status of a family being linked to 'non-worker' status of women or their 'withdrawal' from the labour force, among families or groups (caste, community, class) seeking higher status within the social hierarchy.

The Committee on the Status of Women in India (CSWI) highlighted this continued ambivalence regarding the content of women's education within the educational system through the decades after independence. The mandate that the national education system as a whole had to play "a positive Interventionist role" in changing social (not merely women's) attitudes to one of acceptance of gender equality and 'empowerment' of women entered the Education Policy only on the demands of the women's movements.

## Gandhi's Voice against the Social Evils

According to the Mahatma, social reforms were essential for the restructuring of the societal values that had so far dominated the perception of Indian women. Although, he had great reverence for the traditions of the country, he also realized that certain customs and traditions of the Indian society were antithetical to the spirit of development of the women of the nation. To quote Gandhi, "It is good to swim in the waters of tradition, but to sink in them is suicide". The custom of child marriage became a target of his criticisms. In his opinion, child marriage is a source of physical degeneration as much as a moral evil. The system of dowry could not pass unnoticed from his critical eyes. He defined dowry marriages as 'heartless'. He opined that girls should never marry men who demand dowry, at the cost of their self respect and dignity. As Gandhi believed that the basis of marriage is mutual love and respect, he urged people to solemnize inter communal marriages between the Harijans and caste Hindus.

Gandhi was extremely perturbed by the plight of the widows, particularly child widows. He put forth an earnest appeal to the young generation of the country to marry the widows. He was also quite hopeful about the immense potentials of the widows in furthering national issues. The system of purdah also came under Gandhi's attacks and he questioned the very foundation of this practice. For him, the purdah system was no less than a "vicious, brutal and barbarous" practice. The predicaments of the devadasis, a part of the lower, untouchable segment of the society, had an indelible effect on the sensitive mind of the Mahatma. The pathetic conditions of the child prostitutes disturbed him immensely. He left no stone unturned for rehabilitating this segment of the society, as for him guarding the honor of women was no less than protecting cows. According to Gandhi, one of the first tasks that need to be accomplished as soon as the country won freedom was to abolish the system of devadasi s or temple women and brothels.

Some important aspects of Gandhian ideals on non-violence and ahimsa and their likes with women need mention Gandhi's non-violence embodied a stance of non-injury, or ahimsa, to the enemy. Destruction of the opponent merely perpetuates the injustice one tries to overcome. Instead, the goal is to win the opponent over to one's own side. Gandhi wrote, "We must try patiently to convert our opponents. If we wish to evolve the spirit of democracy out of slavery, we must be scrupulously exact in our dealings with opponents. We must concede to our opponents the freedom we claim for ourselves and for which we are fighting."(Mary Roadkowsky)

## Gandhi's Perception of Women

There was a marked departure of Gandhi's perception of women from that of other reformers. The stance taken by other social reformers and leaders, prior to Gandhi created a helpless image of the Indian women. With the emergence of Gandhi, a new conception of women gradually gained currency. For Gandhi, women were not mere toys in the hands of men, neither their competitors. Men and women are essentially endowed with the same spirit and therefore have similar problems. Women are at par with men, one complementing the other.

### Education for women

According to Gandhi, education for women was the need of the time that would ensure their moral development and make them capable of occupying the same platform as that of men.

### Purdah

Gandhi never approved of the system of purdah. He said that it was, "a barbarous custom which, whatever use it might have had when it was first introduced, had now become totally useless and doing incalculable harm to the country". He further said, "Chastity is not a hot-house growth. It cannot be superimposed. It cannot be protected by the surrounding wall of the purdah. It must grow from within, and to be worth anything, it must be capable of withstanding every unsought temptation... It must be a very poor thing that cannot stand the gaze of men. Men, to be men, must be able to trust their womenfolk, even as the latter are compelled to trust them... By seeking to-day to interfere with the free growth of womanhood of India, we are interfering with the growth of free and independent-spirited men... It partly accounts for our weakness, indecision, narrowness and helplessness".

Gandhi stated that "Chastity is not a hot –house growth. It cannot be superimposed. It cannot be protected by the surrounding wall of the purdah. It must grow from within, and to be worth anything it must be capable of withstanding every unsought temptation... It must be a very poor thing that cannot stand the gaze of men. Men, to be men, must be able to trust their womenfolk, even as the latter are compelled to trust them... Let us then tear down the purdah with one mighty effort." Lastly, he believed that – The real *purdah* was of the heart. A women who peeped through the *purdah* and contemplated a male on whom her gaze fell violated the spirit behind it. If a woman observed it in spirit, she was truly carrying out what the great Prophet had said.

Gandhi, also notes that the latter had been in favour of the complete abolition of purdah at the earliest possible moment.

### Women's peace movements the world over

In Gandhi's views, women can never be considered to be the weaker sex. In fact, women for Gandhi were embodiments of virtues like knowledge, humility, tolerance, sacrifice and faith. These qualities were essential prerequisites for imbibing the virtue of satyagraha. The capability of enduring endless suffering can be witnessed only in the women, according to the Mahatma. The doctrine of ahimsa as preached by Gandhi incorporates the virtue of suffering as is evident in the women. Therefore, Gandhi envisaged a critical role for women in establishing non-violence. Gandhi invoked the instances of ancient role models who were epitomes of Indian womanhood, like Draupadi, Savitri, Sita and Damayanti, to show that Indian women could never be feeble. Women have equal mental abilities as that of men an equal right to freedom.

Gandhi began to suggest various options to women, options that might include being centred in the home or in the nationalist movement: Women who had familial responsibilities such as the care of children and the aged were to fulfil only their primary duties which were not to be given up for the sake of the national movement. Yet a second group included women from whom he expected a sacrifice of the pleasures of housekeeping and child bearing. If already married, these women were expected to remain celibate for the sake of the nation. He advised Vijaylakshmi Pandit and her husband, for instance, to practise celibacy after having blessed their marriage... Thirdly, full-time workers were expected to stay single and dedicate themselves entirely to the struggle for independence. Gandhi is known to have opposed the marriage of the Kripalanis because he was afraid of losing a devoted worker. Thus, while he was trying to safeguard traditional images of women, he could not always avoid rupturing this mode.

**Rights of Women**

Gandhi does not need to be a girl to be wild over man's atrocities towards women. He counts the law of inheritance among the least in the list. The Sarda Bill deals with an evil far greater than the one which the law of inheritance connotes. But he is uncompromising in the matter of woman's rights. In may opinion, she should labour under no legal disability not suffered by man. He should treat the daughters and sons on a footing of perfect equality. As women begin to realize their strength, as they must in proportion to the education they receive, they will naturally resent the glaring inequalities to which they are subjected. (page. 71 Gandhi 21st century)

## Devadasis and Prostitutes

The women of India, like those of many other countries, have been brutally abused under the heinous system of prostitution. Gandhi's denunciation of this system was absolute and categorical. As said earlier, Gandhi considered a situation in all its aspects and so when he was keen to raise the status of women in India to its rightful place, he took into. account the question of the prostitutes and Devadasis. He felt very pained at the problem of Devadas is, because he felt that it was deceiving God to use young girls for the priests' carnal pleasures under the guise of service to God. Similarly, he considered the existence of the institution of prostitutes a shame on society and more so a shame on men. In connection with the problem of Devadasis, Gandhi considered the name 'Devadasi' a euphemism for prostitutes. He considered it in the same light as that of prostitution. And to him this crime of man against woman was much more serious than that of a hungry man stealing a banana or that of a needy youngster picking a pocket. Gandhi believed that this vice was prevalent in cities and the majority of villages were more or less free of it.

Gandhi talking to some women trapped in prostitution, he advised them how to get rid of this evil. The remedy he suggested was spinning and weaving which all could adopt without overcrowding. For the large majority of them there was no need to think of marriage. He stated "They must therefore become the true *Sannyasinis* (women ascetics) of India. Having no cares of life but of service, they can spin and weave to their hearts' content." If such women, he believed, gave up their vile occupation and turned over a new leaf, respectable men would marry some of them. In his opinion, "once a prostitute, always a prostitute-is not a sound proposition."

## Role of Women as Envisaged by Gandhi

According to Gandhi, the role of women in the political, economic and social emancipation of the country was of overriding importance. Gandhi had immense faith in the capability of women to carry on a non violent crusade. Under his guidance and leadership, women shouldered critical responsibilities in India's struggle for freedom. Women held public meetings, organized picketing of shops selling foreign alcohol and articles, sold Khadi and actively participated in National Movements. They bravely faced the baton of the police and even went behind the bars. Gandhi's urge to women to join India's struggle for independence was instrumental in transforming the outlook of women. Swaraj uprooted age old taboos and restrictive customs. Through their participation in Indian struggle for freedom, women of India broke down the shackles of oppression that had relegated them to a secondary position from time immemorial. As far as the economic emancipation of women was concerned, Gandhi felt that men and women had different spheres of work. In his opinion, women could take to economic activities to supplement the income of her families like spinning, which he believed to be a good option available to the women. In the social realm, Gandhi envisaged a critical role for women in doing away with the forces of communalism, caste system and untouchability. It can be said without an iota of doubt that Mahatma Gandhi was indeed one of the greatest advocates of women's liberty and all throughout his life toiled relentlessly to improve the status of women in his country. His faith in their immense capabilities found expression in his decisions to bestow leadership to them in various nationalistic endeavors.

Gandhi advised particularly the poor women to take up spinning and weaving of Khadi clothes which had the potential of offering productive work to a large number of them. He suggested the people to busy the products of their hands lest they could not progress. Every year of Khaddar purchased meant some money in the hands of these women.

### The Dowry System

The dowry System was contributed to gender discrimination at the very birth of child. According to Gandhi, he suggested certain measures to end the dowry system. To start with, a strong public opinion had to be "created in condemnation of the degrading practice of dowry. "The young men who soiled their fingers with such ill-gotten gold had to be excommunicated from society. Parents had to stop getting dazzled by English degrees and need not hesitate to go beyond their little castes and provinces to secure true gallant young men for their daughters. Gandhi believed that the system was closely connected with caste. And as long as the choice for marriage was restricted to a few hundred young men or young women of particular caste, the system would persist despite its condemnation. So he affirmed: "The girls or boys or their parents will have to break the bonds of caste, if the evil is to be eradicated."

## Child Marriage/Widowhood

Gandhi criticized several social customs and practices which degraded women in India. Here comes the practice of child marriages which he strongly detested. According to Gandhi, a girl widow was not a widow in a real sense of the term. The word "widow" had, he said, "a sacred odour about it. "He was "a worshipper of a true widow." In case of adult widows, especially those having children, he would have like them to remain true to their marriage vows and to their first love. He believed: "God created nothing finer than the Hindu widow. " Self-control reached perfection in a widow's life. She found happiness in her self-denial. Her duty was to serve others- family members and guests. She was never weary. She only prayed for strength to enable her to serve better. Gandhi opined: "If this holy life lived by widows becomes a thing of the past, if this living image of service is destroyed through ignorance or pride, incalculable harm will be done to Hinduism. " To him, adult widowhood was "not an undesirable state." Rather, it was good. It was good. It was "Hinduism at its best." He regarded the widow's life as "an ornament to know what widowhood means.

Gandhi strongly stated remarriage, rather proper marriage, of the girl widow. He laid down certain rules to be followed in this mater "necessary for preserving Hinduism and for order in Hindu society. " The rules are:

- No father should get a daughter under the age of 15 married.
- If a girl below this age has already been married and has become a widow, it is the father's duty to get her married again.
- If a fifteen –year-old girl becomes widow within a year of her marriage, her parents should encourage her to marry again.
- Every member of the family should look upon the widow with the utmost respect. Parents or parents-in-law must provide her with the means of improving her knowledge."

## Quotes of Gandhi on Women

The impatience of some sisters to join the good fight is to me a healthy sign. It has led to the discovery that however attractive the campaign against the salt tax may be, for them to confine themselves to it would be to change a pound for a penny. They will be lost in the crowd, there will be in it no suffering for which they are thirsting. In this non-violent warfare, their contribution should be much greater than men's. To call women the weaker sex is a libel; it is man's injustice to woman. If by strength is meant brute strength, then indeed is woman less brute than man. If by strength is meant moral power, then woman is immeasurably man's superior. Has she not greater intuition, is she not more self-sacrificing, has she not greater powers of endurance, has she not greater intuition, is she not more self-sacrificing, has she not greater powers of endurance, has she not greater courage? Without her man could not be. If non-violence is the law of our being, the future is with woman. He has nursed this thought now for years. When the women of the Ashram insisted on being taken along with men something within me and told me that they were destined to do greater work in this struggle than merely breading salt laws. He feels that he has now found that work. The picketing of liquor shops and foreign cloth shops by men, though if succeeded beyond expectations up to a point for a time in 1921, failed because violence crept in. If a real impression is to be created, picketing must be resumed. If it remains peaceful to the end, it will be the quickest way of educating the people concerned. It must never be a matter of coercion but conversion, moral suasion. Who can make a more effective appeal to the heart than woman? Prohibitions of intoxicating liquors and drugs and boycott of foreign cloth have ultimately to be by law. But the law will not come till pressure from below is felt in no uncertain manner. That both are vitally necessary for the nation, nobody will dispute. Drink and drugs sap the moral well-being of those who are given to the habit. Foreign cloth undermines the economic foundations of the nation and throws millions out of employment. The distress in each case is their husbands know what havoc the drink devil works in homes that once were orderly and peace-giving. Today the Charkha Sangh covers over one hundred thousand women against less than 10000 men. (S.N. 6785)

To sum up in Gandhi's words; "The wife is not the husband's slave but his companion and his help-mate and an equal partner in all his joys and sorrows - as free as the husband to choose her own path."

The women of India have a rare opportunity of serving the country. The Salt Campaign brought out tens of thousands from their seclusion, and showed that they could serve the country on equal terms with men. It gave the village women a dignity which she had never enjoyed before. The restoration of spinning to be central place in India's peaceful campaign for deliverance from the imperial yoke, gives her women a special status. In spinning, they have a natural advantage over men. Since the beginning of time, there has been a division of labour between men and women. Adam wove and Eve span. The distinction persists to the present day. Men spinners are an exception. Experience shows that spinning will remain women's speciality. He believes there is a good reason behind the experience. Spinning is essentially a slow and comparatively silent process. Women is the embodiment of sacrifice and, therefore, non-violence. Her occupations must, therefore, be, as they are, more conducive to peace than war. That she is now being dragged down for purposes of violent war, is no credit to modern civilization. He has no doubt that violence so ill becomes women that presently she will rebel against the violence of her fundamental nature. He heel that man, too, will repent of his folly Equality of the sexes does not mean equality of occupations. There may be no legal bar against a woman hunting or wielding a lance. But she instinctively recoils from a function that belongs to man. Nature has created sexes as complements to each other. Their functions are defined as are their forms. (*Harijan*: Dec. 2. 1939)

The correspondent's faith in his ability to stir the women heart flatters him. But he is humble enough to recognize his limitations. It seems to me that the days of my touring are over. Whatever he can do by writing he must continue. But his faith is increasing in the efficacy of silent prayer. It is by itself an art – perhaps the highest art requiring the most refined diligence. He does believe that it is women's mission to exhibit ahimsa at its highest and best. But why should it be a man to move the woman heart? If the appeal is addressed exclusively to me not as man but as the (supposed to be) best exponent of ahimsa to be practiced on a mass scale, he has no urge in him to go about preaching the doctrine to the women of India. He can assure his correspondent that there is no want of will in his that deters him from responding to her appeal. His feeling is that if men of the Congress can retain their faith in ahimas and prosecute the non-violence programme faithfully and fully, the women would be automatically converted. And it may be that there shall arise one among them who will be able to go much farther than he can ever hop to do. For woman is more fitted than man to make explorations and take bolder action in ahimsa. For the courage of self-sacrifice woman is any day superior to man as he believe man is to woman for the courage of the brute (*Harijan*, 5-11-1938)

Discussing the constructive programme, Gandhiji said that besides the charkha there were several other items in his fifteen fold programme and women could take to any of them as they liked. Women could take a large share in the freedom movement of the country as they always had done specially in Maidnapore and other places of India during the Salt Satyagraha. So he thought that it was needless to question what share the women could take in national movement. (*Amrita Bazar Patrika*, 3-1-1946)

Thus, in the question of uplifting the status of women, as in other questions, Gandhi looked at it from the totality and believed that the change should start at the root of social thinking. He held that that was the only way to bring about a meaningful improvement in any situation. Gandhi's method of combating an evil in society did not vary in its fundamental principle of social reconstruction from within and synthesis of the old and the new

The All India Women's Conference (AIWC) was formed in 1927. In this conference, originally convened only to discuss women's education, became a permanent body which succeeded in developing branches all over India. It called itself a political body; its constitution included a clause that declared that it would not engage in party politics. Its emphasis was on unity and women's uplift through education, and social and legal reform. It also emphasised women's contribution to national development. By 1932, however, the AIWC had become involved with women's political rights and all questions which affected women and children as well as with social problems such as untouchability. Although its major focus and priority remained the women's question and the elimination of women's backwardness, and stress was laid on the well-being of women and the family the future of India gradually became an important concern.

Gandhi is preparing a message to the women of India. He becoming increasingly certain that in the struggle for securing swaraj, the women of this country could contribute a greater share than the men. He felt that women well be able to explain the meaning of non-violence to the country more effectively than men. Not because men, out of vanity, regard them as weak but because they possess real courage in a greater proportion and an immeasurable sense of dedication, (*Prajabandhu*, 13-4-1930).

The entire khadi movement depends on the women. This movement would collapse today if the women were to refuse to extend their cooperation to it. Calling khadi essentially a women's movement served many purposes. It brought the women an income basic for their survival forced men to acknowledge women's higher skills in this activity, and unleashed women's aspirations to break through purdah and other barriers of inequality. It also enabled Gandhi to challenge the dominant upper caste and middle class value that equated the family status with women's non-involvement in productive work. He exhorted well-to-do women to support the movement in their dual capacity as consumers and producers, by criticising their lifestyles. It was their duty to help their poorer sisters who had lost their livelihood on account of the import of foreign cloth. Why had they given up spinning, which "even queens used to do", and become idle dependents? Why had they abandoned a skill which brought them so much pride and happiness? Why should they not spin to earn something for themselves, contribute to the family's income, or at least gift it to the poor weavers? Such involvement in productive work would also contribute to the nation's wealth. You have two or three hours in which you do nothing. You spend them in temples. Telling the beads in temples is dharma, but at the present time real bhakti consists in this work for cloth. For women to provide leadership in the movement, feeling virtuous by wearing khadi was not enough. They had to understand the dignity that came from being productive and independent. Such an understanding would help them to identify with poor women, emancipate themselves and achieve the new identity necessary for nation-building. Gandhi believed that only women could influence the growth of that new identity, and better values in the next generations. in 1917 he stated that "woman ... (is) ... mother to the Nation..." The economic and the moral salvation of India thus rests mainly with you. The future of India lies on your knees, for you will nurture the future generation... The destiny of India to far safer in your hands than in the hands of a Government that has so exploited India's resources that she has lost faith in herself.

Women alone can emancipate themselves not men. If women will, they can help in the fulfillment of ahimsa. Through the charkha, they can serve the cause of their poor sisters. By wearing khaddar, they can bring help to the homes of the poor. They can bring about Hindu-Muslim unity. They can abolish the purdah and drive away the ghost of untouchability. (C.W. 10362)

Remember that the beauty of a woman does not consist in the beauty of her clothes and jewellery but in the purity of her heart. Whether you give me your jewellery or not, is a minor matter. But I do want you to hear the truths that he has just told you, in mind. And I tell you from my experience that the desire for wearing much jewellery does no good. Husbands often ask me to advise you to revise your notions of jewellery and finery. I am free to tell you that there are husbands who have assured me that the wives who came to be influenced by my teachings, themselves rejoiced for such influence. (*The Hindu*, 19-10-1927)

He suggests that the spinning-wheel because of the deep poverty of the Indian masses. Some of us know that in this country, at any rate among the masses, women have to earn side by side with the men. This is perhaps one of the few countries in the world where women do the hard task also. I am coming from a part of India where women take up even a shovel or a pickaxe. They do the work on the roads and break stones. One hundred years age, they did not do this. Whenever social workers go to work among the masses, women surround them and ask for the spinning-wheel so that they might get a few price. This may mean nothing to you but they mean a fortune to them. I wish that your Principal will one day take you to the surrounding villages so that you might have an ovular demonstration of what the women of

India are doing. You will not then need that I should press this message home to you. You will have to take up the spinning-wheel, which is the bond that will tie you indissolubly to the masses. Let it be for ever a reminder to you. After your education is finished you will not disappear from public life, you will have to take up the spinning-wheel, which is the bond that will tie you indissolubly to the masses. Let it be for ever a reminder to you. After your education is finished you will not disappear from public life; you will not disappear in the household simply doing the household work but your will extend your helping hand to the poor and reedy, who need all the help that can be given to them. I hope this will serve as an inestimable instrument in your hands to bring cheer into those unhappy homes where extreme desolation prevails. The historians of India will tell us that about one-tenth of the population lives in semi-starvation (*The Hindu*, 25-3-1925).

## Conclusion

Gandhi viewed to be a women's special rôle in her life. He wanted the enlightened women of India to seek relentlessly the repeal of all legal disqualifications and removal of social discrimination against women in India. He considered legislation to remove the inequalities of women as essential... But at the same time, he did not favour women competing with men in -all vocations. He advocated selective education for women, not with any sense of women being inferior to men, but he did believe that they were not identical and that their fields of work were different.

Mahatma Gandhi brought the women out of their homes and made them equal participants in all walks of life-social as well as political. His entourage always consisted of several women and many of his closest associates were women. Under Gandhi's leadership thousands of women took leading roles in several movements. His politics give a new life not only to Indian women but women in many other countries who got the opportunity to search for new meanings in their life. Gandhi's writings and speeches suggest ample evidence to show that he head canvassed for women's active participation in public affairs. He suggested changes in the direction of gender equality and justice. Obviously, his thought in this matter was progressive. He was really a Hindu social reformer.

## REFERENCES


1. Gandhi, M.K (*1992*), *An Autobiography: Or the Story of My Experiment with Truth* (Ahmedabad: Navajivan Publishing House,), p. 4.
2. *Ibid.*, p. 33.
3. M.K. Gandhi, *An Autobiography: Or the Story of My Experiment with Truth*, p. 352.
4. Gangrade K.D. (2001), Gandhi and Empowerment of Women, *Gandhi Marg*, 22(4) 437-453
5. Kameshwar Choudhary, (1998)." Women's Oppression in India: The Gandhian View," *Gandhi Marg,* 19(4), 463-478
6. Lakshmi G, (2007), "Gandhi and Women's Peace Movements," *Gandhi Marg, 28(4)* 457-469
7. Mary Roadkowsky, "Feminism, Peace, and Power" in *The Class of Nonviolence"* op.cit.
8. Richard L. Johnson, (1999), "Gandhi's Soul Politics: The Liberation of Women and Men in India," *Gandhi Marg* 21(1) 5-19
9. Richard L. Johnson, (2000). "Gandhi and Feminisms: Towards Women-Affirming Cultures of Peace," *Gandhi Marg 22*(1), 37-56
10. Sandhya Chaudhri, (2000), "Gandhi as a Feminist," *Gandhi Marg,* 22(2) 155-164
11. Saxena Chandrakala Padia S.K. (2000), "Gandhi On Women and Liberty," *Gandhi Marg,* 22(3) 290-299 .
12. http://www.mapsofindia.com/personalities/gandhi/gandhi-and-women.htm.
13. http://www.gandhi-manibhavan.org/activities/essay_socialwelfare.htm

# 14

# Empowerment of Women: The Gandhian Model

*K.M. Kumar, P.M. Kumari & B.S. Rao*

Mohandas Karamchand Gandhi, who is affectionately called by the people of India as Mahatma Gandhi or Bapu, was a great practical philosopher who aimed at socio-economic development of the country, and for that the development of mankind. His key philosophical point was "Gram Swaraj" or the freedom at the level of villages. Even to-day one has to accept that about 70 per cent of the people are living in the villages, and without their development one cannot think of the overall development of the country. Mahatma was not a pure economist; his intention was to develop the society. For him, economics certainly is an important factor in this direction, but not the sole factor. Of course now it is accepted by the economists that the ultimate aim of economic development is social development, building-up a happy and healthy society.

A society which intends to develop rapidly has to take all sections of the people together into its fold, rich and poor, high society people and low caste people and both men and women. It was realised by Mahatma Gandhi and he sincerely experimented for a "free society". Of course he could not live to see it, as he was assassinated. Gandhi had his original vision and propagated a novel way of thinking in science of economics. He integrated economic aims and activities with mortality and non-violence. He synthesised our successful past experiences with the recent development process. He laid emphasis on labour force, livestocks and rural economy for the nation's smooth progress. He was the first man in the world who provided a practical alternative for the then economic system. The village based economy of China and Israel, the small-scale industry based economy of Japan are nearer to Gandhian concept of Sarvodaya or the welfare of all.

## The Concept of Sarvodaya

In a society all should have equal rights and also have equal duties towards it. But there are certain unprivileged classes in the society. The lower class people (Harijans) and the female folk in all the classes of society were considered as unprivileged. As the females are almost fifty per cent of the population and if they remained powerless and downtrodden in the society one cannot think of the development of the economy. Hence empowerment of women has to be the ultimate goal to improve the quality of the society and development of the economy. Gandhiji's vision for this Sarvodaya aims at welfare of all through co-operation and trusteeship in the economic sphere, equal participation in the political sphere and mutual aid in the social sphere without regard to caste, class and gender.

Since majority of people in the country live in the rural sector, Gandhiji specially emphasised the empowerment of village women. In the agricultural operations the women folk are equally engaged in the field with men apart from their household job. Mostly illiterate, they are the worst sufferers in the society as they have to bear and rear children many a time against their wish that enhances poverty for the family and the economy at large.

The three most important factors which promotes empowerment of women are as follows:

## 2. Education

In ancient India there were good lady scholars at par with the male scholars, but they were limited in number and belonged to rich royal or Brahmin families. Majority of the women folk remained illiterates because the higher community people were not allowing the lower class people to learn alphabets and read books. The law-givers defined the duties of the females to do household chores and upkeep the babies in the family and serve the husband.

Gandhi wanted the mass education to both men and women and emphasis was given to the female folk as he believed that the female is moulder of the family and the society. Once she is empowered with education she can fight for her rights in the family and in the society and can obtain equal status in the social life. Unless they are educated they cannot actively participate in the social, political or economic life as a citizen and cannot establish their status in the society. Even after about six decades of India's independence the combined rate of literacy according to Census of India, 2001 is 64.84 per cent and the female literacy is 54.16 per cent; in some parts of India in the remote adivasi areas the female literacy is as low as 6 per cent. One cannot think of empowerment of women without making them literate and educated.

Even today after more than seven decades after Gandhiji's concept of empowerment of women through education, the main obstacle to empowerment has been the dismal educational level among women. (Rao, 2001) Education that inculcates human values is of great significance for the empowerment of women. Poverty, education and income are interlinked. It is a vicious circle. Because they are poor they are not able to pursue education and because of lack of education, employment opportunities are limited consequently income is limited and they rot in poverty.

## 2. Employment

Participation in economic activity of the nation requires education. Since literacy and educational qualification of the females are low their employment opportunity is also limited. In the organised sector their participation is very low. Even though in all walks of life the females now entered into higher positions, but the majority of females are still working in the unorganized sector. Unless they are educated and employed the loud talk of empowerment of women is meaningless.

The problem of unemployment according to Gandhi can be tackled only by developing village and cottage industries. Moreover, they take the employment opportunities to the doors of unemployed and ideally fit in the rural conditions. Gandhiji advocated for the engagement of female folk in the cottage and small scale industries of the village such as gur, broom, basket and rope making and oil processing so that the rural women can supplement to the family income.

Gandhi was not a theoretical economist. He was a socio-economic applied economist. Gandhiji gave priority to khadi industry; according to him "khadi is the sun of the village system." It is the central industry on which all other village industries revolve. He not only advocated for women's employment but he practically started experiment of Charkha to produce cloth for the people at the same time employment at the family level. He proposed several measures to provide employment opportunities in the rural sector which would help both men and women of which the important ones are as follows:

## Empowerment of Women: The Gandhian Model

1. Cultivation of cotton in areas where it was not grown.
2. Organisation of weaving by the multi-purpose co-operative societies.
3. Compulsory introduction of spinning in all primary and secondary schools, so that the boys and girls can learn the technique.
4. Use of hand-spun cloth in all government and textile and weaving departments.

He was not opposed to heavy industries but he believed that heavy industries cannot provide employment to the people in the villages, both men and women; hence some form of family engagement has to be created to earn income by the family where women can also participate which in turn will empower them in the society.

## 3. Psychological trap

Education and employment are no doubt important factors for women empowerment, but the main obstacle is our traditional social system. The society has to change its social attitude with regard to the participation of females in all walks of life. No doubt in the urban sector the attitude is gradually changing but in the rural sector the female folk even the educated ones are not coming out of the social traditional trap, with regard to education, employment, household work, and public participation as well as participation in the political activities of the country.

Mahatma Gandhi was a ceaseless crusader of women's equality. He brought the women out of their homes and made them equal participants in all walks of life – social as well as political. Under Gandhi's leadership thousands of women took leading roles in national movement. Gandhi never considered women to be unfit for any position or task.

Because of Gandhi's support, women's groups were formed all over India and there was hardly a week when Gandhi did not address a women's group. Gandhi did not like Indian society's preference for a boy child. For this reason about four million woman risk their lives and get illegal abortions every year in the country. Gandhi was totally opposed to gender discrimination. He described women as "embodiment of sacrifice and ahimsa." He firmly believed that "women is weak in striking and strong in suffering." He advocated that daughter's share must be equal to that of a son. He opined that the slavery of women in the kitchen is a remnant of barbarism. In his policy of empowerment he advised men to participate in the household work and reduce the drudgery of woman's home work.

This is the most difficult part of empowerment. It is possible to expand educational institutions and establish small and cottage industries in the villages but to compel the females to go to school and for work leaving the household chore is not an easy task. Hence Gangarde believes that the goal of empowerment of women requires threefold revolution in the society.

1. Change of the people's heart; that is, change in the attitude of the people towards women to accept modern role for them in the family and in the society.
2. To create change in the lives of females in the family discarding to some extent the traditional duties of the female and accepting some other duties in addition to it performed by the male members of the society.
3. The traditional social structure is another factor that hinders empowerment of women. The society divided into several classes traditionally requires change. The class instead of classifying on the basis of caste and religion it should be classified according to the work performed by person.

As early as in 18th century with the coming of the British merchants, the social leaders in India thought of reforming the society on modern lines. Raja Rammohun Roy was pioneer in taking up social reforms with an aim of emancipating the Indian women from family slavery. Even though he was not succeeded fully during his lifetime but he started the social revolution and wanted radical changes in the Hindu society on the following aspects :

1. Abolition of child marriages
2. Abolition of Sati by the wife after the death of husband
3. Widow remarriage
4. Development of schools for the girl child

Mahatma Gandhi also stressed the above reforms and towards the end of nineteenth century he firmly advocated for social change of the traditional customs which are against the development of a healthy society. He never hesitated to criticize the evils which had griped the Indian society and tried to mobilize public opinion against such evils. He was against the deep-rooted customs like child marriage, not allowing widows for remarriage, atrocities on women and purdah system. He also advocated inter-caste marriage for better social integration.

Even today child marriage and Sati have not been completely abolished, though legally prohibited. Gandhiji has stressed all these and equal right for sons and daughters is yet to be successfully implemented in the country. Unless social attitude towards women changes, nothing can be done for the empowerment of women. And social changes require long time. After independence of India a silent social revolution is gradually coming up. The system operating for centuries in the country cannot be changed in few decades.

## The Gandhian Model

Mahatma Gandhi's approach for empowerment of women in India can be formulated into a logical triangular model. The three important components explained above are fitted into a graphical model and presented in Figure. The three important factors that promote women empowerment are : education, employment and change in social structure. All the three components are equally important and mutually related. Simply development of education of the women would not automatically empower them. The case in point is Kerala. The state has hundred per cent literacy but the women folk are not free from exploitation. This is because of the fact that the traditional Keralite society is yet to be reformed to provide equal rights to the women in de facto terms.

**The Gandhian Model**

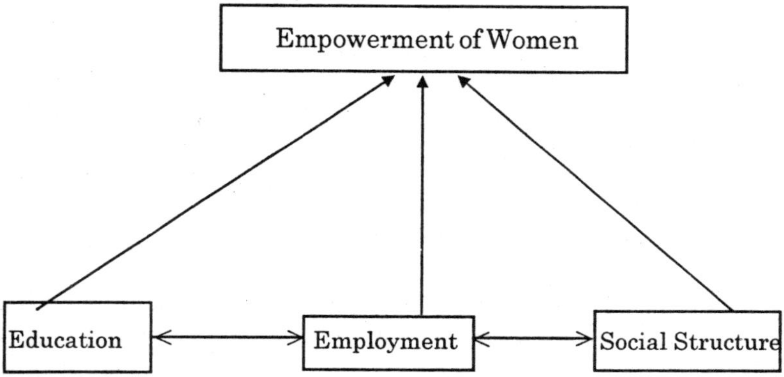


Employment of women is still restricted, even though not in legal terms, the females are not allowed to enter into certain jobs, beyond, doctors, nurses, teachers and clerical jobs. In the family and in the society the women are still treated inferior to men, even though they are now entering into some challenging jobs in a limited manner. The dignity of labour is still not given in proper perspective.

## Conclusion

The three important factors that influence the empowerment of women are education, employment and the changing of the social structure. They are interdependent and have to be promoted simultaneously to realise effective empowerment of women. Mahatma Gandhi experimented in all these three fields a century ago and shown the way for the empowerment of women. Even today at the beginning of the 21st Century his vision remains unfulfilled.

## REFERENCES

1. Bharati, K.S. (1998), *Political Thought of Mahatma Gandhi*, Concept Publishing Co., New Delhi.

2. Bharati, K.S. (2000), *Mahatma Gandhi, Man of the Millennium*, S. Chand & Co., New Delhi.

3. Bimani, Anil, *Relavance of M.K. Gandhi's Ideas of Self-sufficient Village Economy* (Internet : www.mkgandhi.org/articles.htm)

4. Chattopadhyay, Kamaladevi, *Woman the Comrade* (Internet : www.mkgandhi.org/articles.htm)

5. Chaturvedi, Usha and Arun Gandhi, *A Unique Practical Economist* (Internet : www.mkgandhi.org/articles.htm)

6. Gangrade, K.D. (2001), "Gandhi and Empowerment of Women-Miles to go", in *Empowering the Indian Women*, Promila Kapur (ed.). Publication Division, Government of India, Delhi.

7. Grover, Verinder (1997), (ed.) *Mohandas Karamchand Gandhi : A Biography of his Vision and Ideas*, Deep and Deep, New Delhi.

8. Jaitly, Jaya, *Gandhi and Women's Empowerment* (Retrieved from Internet).

9. Kaur, Rajkumari Amrit, *Gandhi and Women* (Retrived from Internet)

10. Paul, R.R. (1964), (ed.) *Gandhi : His Relevance for our Times*, Kalyani Publishers, Ludhiana,

11. Rao P.H. Sethumadhavan (2001), "Education for Women's Empowerment" in Promila Kapur (ed.) *Empowering the Indian Women*, Publication Division, Government of India, Delhi.

12. Saxena, Kiran, *Gandhi's Feminist Politics, Gender Equity and Pratriarchal Values* (Internet www.mkgandhi.org/articles/kiransaxena.htm)

13. Sinha, Shall, *Mahatma Gandhi : A Crusader of Women's Equality* (Internet : www.mkgandhi.org/articles/shallsinha.htm)

# 15

# Relevance of Gandhiji's Constructive Programme From Social Work Perspective

*M.Lakshmipathi Raju & V. Venkateswarlu*

Through constructive programme, Gandhi tried to attain unity of men without all distinction, social justice, self-reliance and sarvodaya samaj. Constructive programme is like preventive approach or preventive social work. Constructive programme is the mother of all developmental work including social work and they complement each other. The basic philosophy and thinking of social work is particularly relevant to enlist people's participation in their own development, and especially, rural development. Appreciation of the dignity and the value of the individual, his right to determine his own affairs, must surely be the bias of such endeavours because; villagers are after all individual human beings. According to Gandhiji's concept of village swaraj, every villager has to think that he is the make of his own destiny. He is his own legislator. If social work is taken to include such work as leading to desirable social change, then professional social work discipline and training are invaluable and are essential requirements for enlisting people's participation. The country cannot have a better ideal than that provided by Gandhiji to work with people. This ideal has to be emulated by constructive workers as well as professional social workers.

While Gandhi had struggled for awakening, enlightenment, freedom and so cio-economic justice for one and all, his utmost priority had been to serve the weakest of the weak. He tirelessly worked to strengthen the "weakest link", the poorest of the poor. This professional social workers.

## Gandhi's Constructive Programme

Gandhiji's constructive programme is a comprehensive instrument of reconstruction which specially included the needs of non-persons, the outcastes, the half persons, the castaways and the lowliest and the poorest section of human population. Gandhiji's constructive programmes included abolition of untouchability, promoting community amity, prohibition, development of rural industries, basic education, emancipation of women, organization of peasantry, village sanitation, uplift of the adivasis, improvement of cattle, charka and khadi. He initiated constructive social welfare programmes designed to remove the evils that had crept into society. His constructive programmes found ready acceptance among people.

The social worker would find these programmes enriching Indian society in general and rural society in particular constructive work is not merely for producing things; it is the means of 'educating and spiritualizing man. It means developing self-discipline and "self-control". When material manifestation is overemphasized, work is missing. The main reason for our downfall and decline is neglect of constructive work programme as evolved by Gandhi. This should become the beacon light for the twenty-first century. Gandhi included raising the status of women in his constructive programmes. He made all efforts to bring them in the mainstream of the Indian Society. Gandhi felt that the constructive programme is to enable masses to emerge out of unfreedom into freedom and out of economic and social deprivation into self-reliance and out of state of alienation into cooperative living.

As Ved Mehta asserts: "Between 1924 and 1940, Gandhi had devoted himself mostly to the social, economic and spiritual regeneration of the country which he came to believe, would be achieved not by constitutional concessions and reforms, political debates and resolutions, but by the efforts of the people themselves. For Gandhi, constructive programme was really another form of satyagraha, which was the only road to economic development for a peor country like India. The constructive programme was conceived as a means as well as an end for the creation of new civilization. The core of the programme is the synthesis between the material and moral advancement of human society. Through this programme, he explored the possibility of building up a power free, non-authoritarian, non-exploitative society by changing the preset setup.

The objective of constructive programme was to bring about socio-economic changes and reconstruction of social order based on freedom, equality and respect for individual personality. The ultimate purpose was to build a non-violent, non-exploitative social and economic order for a society based on the ideas of sarvodaya. The present and future crisis can be reduced by adopting fully constructive programme on evolved by Gandhi. Constructive work should become both a lamp and a mirror; it will show us what we are.

## Discrepancies in Development

Development has become a key word for social work educators and practitioners. But the gap between the haves and have nots has not been reduced many poor people. The task appears to be formidable for social workers to tackle the challenge of poverty. Social workers should aim at "No-poverty society" in an iniquitous world. Since serious distortions exist in the global economy, the words "growth" and "development" acquired different connotations of growing injustice. This kind of growth leads to wider disparities among the people.

Gandhi in the context of India had aptly said; "If India is not to perish, we have to begin with lower rung of ladder. If that was rotten, all work done at the top or at the intermediate rungs is bound to fall". (Harijan, 13 April, 1935). The affluent nations being basically urban and the poor nations rural, rural development is a critical factor to be tackled which bring about a less exploitative society and more satisfactory system of all round or total development or Sarvodaya.

## Sarvodaya

The term Sarvodaya means "the rise or welfare of all". It consists of two Sanskrit words, sarva and udaya which mean "all and rise" respectively. It aims at a complete transformation of the present social structure through constructive social work carried on primarily at the village level and in slum area. It looks upon service to society as the raison d' etre of man's life on earth. In this sense, Sarvodaya is all social work. Sarvodaya emphasizes truth and non-violence and the basic goodness of man; social work while upholding the values of dignity of man emphasises also acceptance of individual's right to self determination.

## Social Work Intervention with Dalits

The constructive programme evolved by Gandhi, included among others, uplift of Dalits and Adivasis. Salvation of social work profession lies in moving towards rural and tribal areas and giving Dalits a top priority in their work. This is because, the man belonging to the Fourth State (or poor) or the common man of India or for that matter of the third world of today as well as tomorrow and day after belong to rural and tribal India. To restore vitality to the Indian society and build up the future prosperity of the common man, it is necessary to strengthen and develop Dalits. Only then and in that process, the well being of the Indian people will be realised. Gandhi said that he will work for an India in which, the poorest shall feel that it is their country and they have voice in its making; there shall be no high class and low class of people; All communities shall live in perfect harmony; There is no room for the curse of untouchability; There is no exploitation of the weaker sections by the affluent sections and people in power; All interests of the society are not in conflict with the interests of dumb millions; there will be neither pampers, nor beggars, nor high nor low.

## Gandhi's Connection of Swaraj

The Swaraj of Gandhi's dream recognizes no race or religious distinction; nor it is the monopoly of the lettered persons nor yet of moneyed men. Swaraj is to be for all including the farmer, the maimed, the blind the starving toiling millions. According to Gandhi's conception of Swaraj, the contrast between places of New Delhi and miserable hovels of the poor, cannot last one day in a free India in which the poor will enjoy the same power as the richest in the land. Swaraj loses its meaning when there are millions of starving persons and the lowliest and the poorest section of human population who are deprived basic needs and amenities of life. The institutions and organisations or alternative structures have to emerge to meet the needs of poor people. The constructive programme was conceived as a means as well as an end for the creation of new civilization. The core of the programme is the synthesis between the material and moral advancement of human society.

## Gandhi's Constructive Programme from Social Work Perspective

Social work is both palthiative as well as responsible for changing institutions. It helps individuals in the framework of existing conditions as well as to help change social institutions. It recognizes the multiple causation of problems and realizes that the cause lies neither exclusively in the individual nor in the societal structure. It becomes clear that profession which works towards social justice in a wide sense must feel responsible for amelioration and social change. The change should begin. The change should begin from within to influence the policies at various levels to change from within to influence the policies at various levels to change the plight of Dalits and disadvantaged sections of the population.

Social workers must create conditions which would help the people to be self-reliant and realize the ideals of justice and equality. The basic philosophy of social work is to enlist the people's participation in their development, especially rural development. Gandhi's ideals and experiments provided much needed strength and inspiration to professional social workers.

Gandhi's work, teachings and his thought have greater relevance. Gandhi's constructive programme is the key to the construction of poorna swaraj or complete independence by truthful and honest means and it has greater relevance today. We have to remember the relevance of his thought in our life today. The relevance of Gandhian thought is as old as the constructive programme. There are some concepts of Mahatma Gandhi; they are truth, non-violence (Ahimsa), ends and means, non-possession, trusteeship, vows, and gram swaraj. All these concepts are found to gain greater relevance and currency. Based on the two basic principles of truth and non-violence, Gandhi developed the concept of constructive programme. Mahatma Gandhi helped in setting up the Harijan Sevak Sangh in Delhi, and the All-Inda Village Industries Association on etc. at Sevagram, Wardha, as part of constructive work; it was a movement for economic betterment and improvement in the social life of the people.

## Gandhian Social Work

Gandhian Social work is concerned with the reconstruction of society based on truth and non-violence and with welfare of the entire last and the lowliest. Hence it cannot ignore the problems relating to social adjustment and maladjustment, to social welfare needs of the people, and also the problems relating to social injustice, and economic exploitation. The objective of Gandhian social work would naturally be to find out the basic causes and conditions out of which arise all suit problems. The laws which are considered bad and obedience to which would be inconsistent with the self-respect of the individual or human dignity will have to be opposed or disobeyed if necessary which is the ultimate value of the profession of social work. Whenever collective energies are directed towards combating certain problems for obtaining long term results, we have social action.

The Gandhian model envisaged that development and governance should be bottom –up and not be top-down; goal should be self defined and not stranger defined; production should be aimed at basic goods to fulfil basic needs with useful vale and not at non-basic and greed-oriented luxury goods; the process of production should be by the masses and not through mass production and whole model in the words of J.C.Kumarappa leads to decentralized economic planning and actually 'Economics of permanence', while in the model of industrial economy there is the danger that the rich becomes richer. The need of the hour is that leaders and people of the country be inspired by the ideals and teachings of Mahatma Gandhi.

The principal element of Gandhi's significance lies in his constructive programme which aimed at changing the very basics of the whole social and economic order. Social work has been recently developed to help in solving social problems of modern society. It is something like a curative approach, whereas the constructive programme acts as a preventive approach in social behaviour. The constructive programme is based on non-violence, eliminating violence, domination, and inequality which are the causes for all the fundamental problems of mankind.

Ammu M. Mazumdar says: "In the course of many of his activities of a social welfare nature, Gandhi had developed certain principles, practices and procedures which harmonize remarkably with the principles and techniques of pre-professional social work as it has developed in the western world – settlement houses, social group work, social case work, community welfare organisation, social legislation, social action". Gandhi was not a social worker in the street sense of the term as it is understood by professional social workers. A social worker is one who enables the individuals in distress, singly or in groups, to adjust to their situation by helping them to help themselves, to overcome their difficulties through the well-defined techniques of case work, group work, and community organisation. But Gandhi never practised the techniques of social work in this spirit. But he combined the social work spirit with his activities in the field of politics, social reform and social welfare.

Dr. Frances M. Yasr studied critically the compatibaility of the professional social work values with Gandhian values. In this context, S.K. Khinduka says: "She (Fraces Yasar) finds that Gandhi's work is something of a reaffirmation of the basic tenet of social work philosophy that 'man is an object of infinite worth: Dr. Yasr does not lose sight of the few dissimilarities that exist between Gandhian values and social work values, but, .... She shows the essential compatibility and hence, the similarity between the philosophy of Mahatma Gandhi and the values underlying social work.

Social work today is something more than a method. It is a "social institution", as Witner calls it. It should be social and cultural forces of the society. Gandhi left an indelible impact on the thoughts and actions of the people. It is therefore necessary to examine the contribution to the theory and practice of social work. Frances M. Yasr also says: "Indian students could learn the basic values of professional social work more easily, if they could see them as different ways of saying some of the things that have been taught by their philosophers, saints, social thinkers, and social reformers, especially a person the stature of Mahatma Gandhi".

## Implications for social work intervention

In the present scenario of the problems confronting the society and in view of the Gandhiji's constructive programme, the role of the social worker is essentially to work with the community as a whole. The role can be divided into two types, manifest and latent. Manifest roles can be easily identified by the worker and the community alike such as facilitator. The latent roles are interwoven in the manifest roles which guide the worker's intervention. The social worker's role is basically two-fold; as catalyst he sets ideas is motion; as facilitator he helps to structure the development process. The role of the worker is to help people from their own organization in order to be able to tackle their problems.

The role involves various tasks, first, worker should positively discriminate to work amongst those who have been benefited least, or not at all from Government programmes. That is, worker should work with the poor and oppressed who have least access to aid. Secondly it is important that the worker works with groups as opposed to individuals because it is only as groups that people can have the bargaining power, necessary to achieve their goals. Thirdly the task of the worker is to initiate the process of conscientization - of critical awareness - by getting people to formulate and articulate their desires about issues important to them. It is most important that these are their issues and not those preconceived by the worker. The worker should encourage people to analyse the situation, thus activating some of their innate critical abilities.

## To revamp social work

To revamp and change programme of social work education to suit to the contemporary needs of the society. The following areas of intervention need emphasis in social work education.

1. Peace movements.
2. Resolution of conflicts.
3. Social legislation and social action.
4. Policies and programmer for development of SCs, STs and BCs.

5. Anti-poverty programmes.
6. Sarvodaya (Gandhian model) Vs Western model of development.
7. To build participating democracy from grassroots upward through Panchayat Raj System.
8. Communication and its effective use in educating people.

Constructive work is the mother of all the development works including social work and they complement each other. The more we do Gandhian constructive work and social work, the more prosperous will be the community at large. Both constructive work and social work are the noble works which can be carried out by the individuals and organizations wedded to the welfare of all which means the creation of a Sarvodaya Society and a Sarvodaya social order.

## REFERENCES

1. Choudary, G.P, *Relevance of Gandhism*, Capital Publishing House, Delhi
2. Gandhi, M.K, *Economic and Industrial life and Relations*, Ahmedabad: Navajivan Publishing House, 1957.
3. Gandhi, M.K, *Hind Swaraj*, Ahmedabad: Navajivan Publishing House, 1962)
4. Gangrde, K.D, *Gandhian Approach to Development and Social Work*, Concept Publishing House, New Delhi
5. Khinduka, S.K, *Social Work in India*, Allahabad: Kitab Mahal Pvt. Ltd, 1965
6. Muzumdar, Ammu, H., *Social Welfare in India: Mahatma Gandhi's Contribution*, Bombay: Asia Publishing House.
7. Narayana Swamy, S. , Gandhian Concepts of Social Work, *Gandhi Marg*, July-September, 2000.
8. Singh, R.R., *Social Development*, Association of Schools of Social Work in India, Delhi School of Social Work, Delhi, 1995

# 16

# Gandhi and Rural Development

*M.Gopi, T.Sreenu & D.Syamala Devi*

"India Lives in its villages." Mahatma Gandhi

Indian society is heterogeneous in nature. There are urban areas where people are living sophisticated life with all modern facilities and rural areas without having basic amenities. Majority of the people in India are living in rural areas. So mahatma Gandhi, the father of nation stressed the need of developing rural areas. In this context the concept of rural development was gaining popularity. The aim of this article is to express the views of Gandhi on rural development and suggest ways to improve the present rural development programmes in the light of his views.

## Evolution of Rural Development

Independent India has pledged to establish a "socialistic pattern of society" through planned development. Rural development, therefore occupies priority in the agenda for national development in India for more reasons than one. Rural development is the main thrust of national development efforts. It is advocated as a basic strategy for economic development. Copp has defined it, as a process through collective efforts, aimed at improving the well-being and self-realization of rural people. Specialists on rural development have defined the term 'Rural Development' in many ways. According to one of them, rural development involves the development of rural economy so as to raise the standard of living of those rural people who are poor and require upliftment.

Rural development in India has a long history in terms of

period and also a variety of efforts under different historical circumstances. The villages in India have well-established traditions, conventions, service institutions and customs of co-operative action of their own. Historical, sociological, political and economic factors, the structure, organization and ethos of the village communities began to be influenced in many ways.

In pre-independent India also several rural developmental programmes were conducted. In this connection a resolution was passed by Lord Rippon in 1882. He extended the principles of self-government to rural areas also. Thus the rural areas, too by this system, were able to effect their upliftment to some extent. Because of the above said resolution, Rippon has come to be known as "The father of the Local Self-Government". During Lord Curzon's period the department of agriculture owe their existence to the foresight and energy. Rural development received a powerful fillip in 1921, when "Dyarchy" was introduced in the provinces under the Government of India Act 1919. According to the Government of India Act 1935, a few notable happenings in rural sphere had taken place. They are improvement in village industries, improvement of village communication, rural sanitation, medical facilities etc. India emerged as an independent state in 1947, though the concern of the government towards rural development was by no means entirely absent under colonial rule, it was only after the country's independence, that rural development programmes acquired high level of priority. In post-Independence period, government, voluntary organizations and financial institutions have implemented a large number of rural development programmes for the upliftment of rural mass. Now let us observe the view of Gandhiji on rural development.

## About Gandhiji

Mohandas Karamchand Gandhi was a major political and spiritual leader of India and the Indian Independence movement. He was the pioneer of Satyagraha showed resistance to tyranny through mass civil disobedience, firmly founded upon Ahimsa or total non-violence which led India to independence and inspired movements for civil rights and freedom across the world. He was commonly known around the world as Mahatma Gandhi and in India as Bapu. His greatest contribution to the billions of the world population 'conquest of violence by love and goodwill'; many of the political bigwigs better acquainted with Gandhi observed that the sense of values, the sensitivity that Gandhi, displayed may be what the world needs today. Gandhiji's thoughts are based on four principles; they are Truth, Non-violence, Dignity of Labour and Simplicity. It is a combination of idealism, individualism and socialism. Socialism paved the way for improvement of the condition of the people living below poverty line, especially in rural areas.

## Gandhiji and Rural Development

Gandhiji's approach to India's rural development was holistic and people-centred. He was influenced by Tolstoy, Ruskin and the teaching of Gita, he placed more emphasis on moral and spiritual values than economic motives as a means of overall development. Gandhiji concentrated his entire attention on the development of rural areas. The goals of development are:

1. Satisfaction of basic needs and not greed since Earth provides enough to satisfy every man's need, but not for every man's greed.
2. Full employment, since work is not a disutility but is part of the living process.
3. Modes of employment which satisfy man's urge for fulfillment of personality through work.
4. Decentralization in government.
5. A development of technology which serves social needs.

He further says that 'Developing the knowledge, skills and attitudes of officials, functionaries and representatives involves in rural development so as to introduce them to the newest concepts, techniques and information to enable them to act as catalysts for qualitative development. Identifying possibilities and exploring potentials for integrated development through research and study of on going rural development programmes and schemes to ensure the harnessing of resources towards the achievement of development's goal'.

The Gandhian model of rural development is based on the following values and premises:

1. Real India is found not in its cities, but in its villages.
2. The revival of villages is possible only when the villagers are exploited no more.

3. Exploitation of villagers by city dwellers was 'violence', in Gandhiji's opinion.
4. Simple living and high thinking, implying voluntary reduction of materialistic wants, and pursuit of moral and spiritual principles of life.
5. Dignity of labour: everyone must earn his bread by physical labour, and one who labours must necessarily get his substance.
6. Preference to the use of indigenous (swadeshi) products, services and institutions.
7. Balance between the ends and the means: Gandhiji believed that non-violence and truth could not be sustained unless a balance between the ends and the means was maintained.

His ideas on rural reconstruction had two main aims to make the Indian villages self sufficient and independent of government to the possible extent. Gandhiji's political work and struggle against the British Raj was an extension of his mission to uplift the rural poor from poverty and flight. Gandhiji also advocate the importance of agriculture, cattle forming, dairying, etc., He believed that the home industries like canning dairy, bullock-oil pressing, paper-making, hand-pounding of rice, home made bread and jam, soap making, making of match boxes etc. are to be revived and encouraged because rural reconstruction will be incomplete without these industries.

Gandhiji emphasized that people under decentralized economic and political system will be quite competent to run and manage their Panchayats and other social self-governing institutions. He strongly pleaded for decentralization through the organization of village Panchayats. He was of the view that 'Panchayat system in India, if worked on scientific lines, could not only build up the social and economic strength of the country side but also strengthen the forces of national defense against the risk of foreign invasion. Gandhiji believed that 'an ideal Indian village will be so constructed as to lend itself to perfect sanitation. It will have cottages with sufficient light and ventilation built from a material obtainable within a radius of five miles of it. The cottages will have courtyards enabling households to plant vegetables for domestic use and to house their cattle. The village lanes and streets will be free of all avoidable dust. It will have wells according to its needs and accessible to all. It will have houses of workshop for all, also a common meeting place, a village common for grazing its cattle, a co-operative dairy, primary and secondary schools in which industrial education will be the central factor, and it will have Panchayats for settling disputes. It will produce its own grains, vegetables and fruit, and its own khadi.

Gandhiji observed that in our villages, there are inexhaustible resources not for commercial purposes in every case but certainly for local purposes in almost every case. The greatest tragedy is the hopeless unwillingness of the villagers to better their lot. He advocated village-oriented economy, free from violence and exploitation. In his words; 'Rural economy, as I have conceived it, eschews exploitation altogether, and exploitation is the essence of violence. You have, therefore, to be rural-minded before you can be non-violent, and to be rural-minded you have to have faith in the spinning wheel'.

As part of a larger non-cooperation movement to reject British control over India, Mohandas Gandhi launched the khadi movement in 1915. Gandhi encouraged all Indians to wear khadi, and abolish foreign cloth. Mahatma Gandhi used to refer to khadi as 'the livery of freedom'. Khadi rendered an opportunity to every man, woman and child to cultivate self-discipline and self-sacrifice as a part of the non co-operation movement.

Khadi, based on decentralized production and distribution, plays an important role in the village economy. According to Gandhiji, khadi alone can solve a number of economic and other problems of India, viz., the poor villagers can supplement their meager resources, spinning wheels can give employment opportunities to village carpenters blacksmiths, weavers, etc. For the upliftment of women it provides an honorable and leisurely occupation; even for poor and uneducated people spinning is easy to learn and requires no outlay of capital; it is such a type of industry which can absorb the largest number of people and can provide employment to the unemployed at any time of the year without much difficulty. Moreover, it is an insurance against the adversity of famine conditions. However, critics say that the spinning wheel does not pay, but Gandhiji positively answered that the spinning wheel is an attempt to produce something out of nothing. Khadi, not only adds to the national income but also this additional income is equally distributed among the poor strata of the society.

He opposed 'the big machines of industry' which make many Indian laborers as jobless person. He viewed the self-sufficient community as the best matrices for the holistic development of human beings allowing them to realize their full support for Gandhi; khadi symbolized these ideals and served as a uniform for the larger non-cooperation movement. The biggest success of the khadi movement was the psychological impact that it had on the Indian people, especially those who were wholly or partially unemployed.

## Rural Development Programmes: Gandhian Perspective

The present rural developmental programmes are more or less in the tune with views of Gandhiji. It is concerned with economic growth and social justice; improvement in the living standards of the rural people by providing adequate and quality social services and minimum basic needs becomes essential. The present strategy of rural development now mainly focuses on poverty alleviation, better livelihood opportunities, provision of basic amenities and infrastructure facilities through innovative programmes of wage and self-employment. In this connection government is carrying out several rural development programmes like; Intensive Agricultural District Programme, High Yielding Variety Programme, Drought Prone Area Programme, Crash Scheme for Rural Employment, Minimum Needs Programme, Command Area Development Scheme, Desert Development Programme, Food for Work Programme, Integrated Rural Development Programme, Training of Rural Youth for Self Employment, National Rural Employment Programme, Development of Women and Children in Rural Areas, Rural Landless Employment Guarantee Programme, Twenty Point Programme, Jawahar Rozgar Yojana, Prime Minister Rozgar Yojana etc. Recently programmes like JRY, SJRY, and PMRY were merged under National Rural Employment Generation Programme.

The above goals will be achieved by various programmes support being implemented creating partnership with communities, non-governmental organizations, community based organizations, institutions, PRIs and industrial establishments, while the Department of Rural Development will provide logistic support both on technical and administrative side for programme implementation. Other aspects that will ultimately lead to transformation of rural life are also being emphasized simultaneously.

## Suggestions to Improve Rural Developmental Programmes in India

The following suggestions may be followed to implement rural development programmes effectively by taking some of the views of Gandhiji into consideration.

1. Honesty and sincerity as said by Gandhiji should be there among the officials who are concerned in the implementation of rural development programmes.
2. Development of village and khadi industries should be developed in order to provide more employment to the villagers.
3. Strengthening of village Panchayats by giving more legislative, administrative and judicial powers.
4. Besides all the above said measures people's participation is more essential in rural developmental programmes.
5. Proper monitoring should be there at each level in the process of implementation in order to check corruption among officials.
6. To create awareness among the rural masses, publicity about rural programmes should be intensified.
7. Proper market facilities should be provided in order to sell the products that are produced by the villagers.

In conclusion we can say that what the rural poor today expecting not the gold and silver, but basic amenities like food, water, shelter, housing, health services and education for their children. If the Government is going to provide all these facilities to the rural people, then definitely the aspirations of our Father of the Nation are fulfilled successfully. Gandhiji believed "If the village perishes India will perish too." So there is greater need to improve the condition of people living in rural areas.

## REFERENCES

1. Durgesh Nandini (1992) *Rural Development in India*, Rawat Publications, New Delhi.
2. Bhatnagar and Chib (1987) *Rural Development in India, A strategy for socio-economic changes*, ESS Publications, New Delhi.
3. Patwari B.Prabhudas (1978) *Some Reflections Gandhi's Relevance Today*, Gandhi Darshan Samithi – Calcutta.
4. Mathew. T (1981) *Rural Development in India*, Agricole Publishing Academy, New Delhi.
5. Mohsin, Nadeem (1985) , *Rural Development through Government Programmes*, Mittal Publications, New Delhi.

# 17

# Gandhian Approach to Rural Development and Village Planning

*Mande Ramesh & B. Lilly Grace Eunice*

> "The man had no equal in our time that one who treated all men as equals"
>
> - *Vincent Sheean*

Gandhiji as we understood him was a revolutionary and a most active idealist. During his effective lifespan he had established social institutions involving masses for overall development of the society. India being a vast land inhabited by diversified population groups, Gandhiji's approach of self-help and natural trust is of greater relevance. His approach of rural development may be divided into three parts viz. 1) City civilization and rationale for separate attention to the village, 2) Model of an ideal village community, and 3) the measure for revitalization of the existing villages.

When Gandhiji entered the Indian scene, he could see the poverty of Indian villages very closely. He read the analysis of Indian Economy written by R.C. Dutt and concluded, "that villages in India were being exploited by foreign government and city dwellers as well". As late as in 1944 he observed, "there are two schools of thought current in the world. One wants to divide the world into cities and other into villages. The village civilization as the city civilization is totally different things."[1] Acquisition of money seems to be the main aim of life for the city dwellers. Huge profits and high wages in cities were possible by exploitation of cheap labour and raw materials mostly contributed by villages. The prosperity of the urban world in India could be possible because it drained off lifeblood of the village by dumping cheap and shoddy goods from foreign land. "With their insolent torts city dwellers are a constant menace to the life and liberty of the villagers". Thus according to Gandhiji, the basis of rural and urban relationship was conspiracy and exploitation of the former by the latter.

According to Gandhiji villages have to fend for themselves by becoming self-sufficient and self-sustaining. In Gandhiji words "My idea of self-sufficiency is that villages must be self-sustaining in regard to food, cloth and other basic necessaries."[2] With the significance and permanence of the village system in India Gandhiji stated "if villages perished India will perish."

Gandhiji has given a model of ideal village community. It is organized community of persons, active, educated, healthy, intelligent, self-reliant and morally of a very strong fibre. Its population shall be engaged in farming and allied activities and industries based on handicraft, self-sufficient in vital needs, undertaking dignified occupations and enjoying a close contact with nature, sharing non-violently equal duties, rights and opportunities of a really democratic society.

The ideal village provides diversified and flexible opportunities to earn and enjoying on par with the cities of today. It must maintain its own theatre, school, dispensary, public hall, water works, recreation and playground for adults and children, hall for worship and lanes and streets with free of dust. Railways, post and telegraphs and electricity should be provided by the state. Every individual in the village should be able to obtain a balanced diet, a decent house to live in with clean and hygienic surroundings. Adequate medical relief needs to be provided. Educationally, every adult must have cleared of final basic course. All possible activities in such a community should be organized on the co-operative basis. Collective cattle rearing should be the order of the day. Small scale, individual intensive cattle based farming should produce foodgrains, fiber, fruits and vegetables to meet the basic needs of the community. The balanced growth of animal, plant and human life for mutual benefit is stressed. Industries based on handicraft, employing local resources and simple labour intensive techniques should grow. The "law of return to the giver" [3] is to be flowed scrupulously.

Land utilization must conform to the needs of the village to produce foodgrains, pulses, vegetables, and fibres useful non-harmful cash crops for non-exploitative exchanges. As an ideal, each one should own land to earn breed through family labour, land shall be reserved for cattle grazing, play grounds, public places, residential accommodations etc. Market must be local, in essence, consumption being guided, not by imitation but by the felt needs of the community; ownership of land should necessarily belong to those who till and on the principles of Swadeshi.

Transport may be needed to clear cash crops and surplus of the village industrial goods. Wage must be adequate enough to provide a decent living. A worker should neither be exploited nor should the worker exploit his/her employer.

As regards the practicability of the ideal village, Gandhiji wrote in 1940, "the work to shape an ideal village was difficult,"[4] but if only one ideal village is produced, out of such effort will emerge a new wholesome, harmonious world of life worth imitating by the whole world. At present the Indian village life is far away from the village life of Gandhiji's dream. Our modern villages are the examples of exploitation and decay. The chronic poverty, illiteracy, inertia, insanitation, indifferences and inadequate employment opportunities are the symptoms of our decaying villages. How to prevent this decay is a big issue.

Since most of the elite live in cities, Gandhiji suggested, to the city dwellers to pay their attention to the village's upliftment. Once their hearts are rooted in the villages, all other resources required for the village upliftment would follow automatically.

Operationally, it suggests cities to refrain from exploiting village's commercially and culturally and further to offer their monetary resources, human talents, etc., for developing the villages. The cities should serve as clearing houses of surplus village production. Thus the Gandhi and concept of village enlistment does not mean urbanization of the rural area but to retain, develop, strengthen, stabilize and vitalize the village communities.

Finally, the scheme of basic education provides the villager with all ideas and arts to equip themselves with the necessary foundations of self-reliance, prosperous life, dignified interdependence through a selfless Satyagrahi worker and well-informed basic school organization.

Gandhiji developed a well organized and all embracing village reconstruction programme by conforming to his concept of an ideal village. As it is broadly adopted, it includes corporate sanitation, basic education, adult education, women and child welfare, propagation of principles of health, economic quality, self-sufficiency, agricultural development, Khadi and village industries, handicrafts etc. This can be achieved only by activating the most inherent talents of the community. This is a huge task as it requires restructuring of all organizations, socioeconomic and political, so that the shortcomings and inabilities of the individuals and groups are removed.

The railings of Ruskin against the accepted cannons of political economy prompted Gandhiji to evolve his own scheme of economics to have human salvation on the triple principle of i)self regulation ii) Trusteeship and iii) Productive systems evolved for the uplift of those that were at the lowest strata of the society.

With these cardinal principles as guidelines, Gandhiji formulated a programme consisting of 18 items of work for the emancipation of seven lakhs of villages viz., promotion of village industries such as paddy husking, gur-making, oil crushing, weaving, manufacture of hand-made paper, woolen blankets etc. basic and adult education, rural sanitation, uplift of backward tribes, uplift of women, education, public health and hygiene, propagation of Rashtrabhasha (National Language), love for the mother tongue, organization of kisans, use of reforms through the extra income made available to them.

Gandhiji said "Khadi is the sun of the village Solar System, the planets are the various industries which can support khadi in return for the heat and the subsistence they derive from it."[5] He wanted to spin his way to Swaraj and his ideas are portrayed in the sentence "I saw in a flash that without the spinning wheel there was no Swaraj".

Gandhiji condemned machinery from two angles. 1) it atrophied man reduced him to be a cog in the machine, 2) The heavy machinery was contributed much for the growing unemployment. So he stood against industrialization, keeping in view of the social and economic conditions of India. He said,

"Mechanization is good when hands are too few, it is evil when there are more hands than required for the work."[6] The most urgent problem in India is the under employment of the peasant.

## Decentralized Planning

Planning is a continuous movement towards desired goals, whereas development is the process of growth of man gaining self-confidence and becoming self-reliant and self-sufficient. In India planning has largely been sectoral with macro approach and hence highly centralized and importance was given to prepare sectoral plans for agriculture, industry, transportation, communication, health, education etc. in this context, the formulation and implementation of plans deserve keen analysis as it has bearing on the regional planning process, which again is to grow from concept into a practical proposition. Both at the State and National levels sector planning has dominated all these years and a very limited importance is given to spatial planning and village planning.

The theoretical justification for village level planning are:

a) Planning in order to be effective must be related to local resources and needs.

b) Better use can be made of local resources.[7]

c) Village level plan is considered as an effective means of reducing disparities and removing absolute poverty at the Village level by encouraging people's participation.[8]

The rationale for village level planning for rural development may be stated to be four fold:

i) "Better perception of the basic issues at the village level with the specific attention to the rural poor and formulation and executive of programmes and productivity and increasing production;

ii) Better exploitation of growth potentials of an area for improving productivity and increasing production;

iii) Opportunities for direct participation by the local population, particularly the poor majority in development decision-making at the lowest (homogeneous groups, hamlet villages) level and between representatives at higher sub-district, district level, also opportunities for participation of target groups concerned as an end in itself, and

iv) Also opportunities of local resources mainly surplus labour".

"Real planning" wrote Gandhiji, "consists in the best utilisation of entire manpower of India[7]. This is in quite consonance with the ideal of full employment as economists call it. In such a structure of society a decentralized state power is needed. The people will be the core of state power in such a society. Gandhiji interprets people's powers and supremacy in a democratic form of government. He expressed his strong disapproval of centralization of authority and power by a small coterie or oligarchy in a democratic state.

That would be a negation of democracy. "True Democracy" he pointed out, can not be worked by 20 sitting at the center; it has to be worked out from below by the people of the village [10].

## Village Planning

During the struggle for Independence, Mahatma Gandhi pleaded for a decentralized administration system with village as basic unit.[11] Mokshagundam Visweswarayya, the Dewan of the then Mysore State suggested a four-tier planning in the state[12]. The first five year plan launched in 1951, envisaged that planning would be done at the National Level, States, Districts and Local Community Levels.[13]

As of today, the political parties, the State and Central government departments are not really interested in organizing people at village level to shoulder their own responsibilities. Most of the voluntary organizations working in the rural development are also not interested in organizing people in the villages and helping them to govern by themselves. Governmental departments and most of the voluntary organizations as an important means to plan and implement development programmes do not think of organizing Gram Sabhas or village assemblies and constituting planning and executive committees at the village level.

The success of village level planning depends upon the availability of necessary infrastructural facilities such as credit, agriculture, inputs extension, roads, market facilities, communication, education, health, recreation and cultural etc., and effective and full use at this level. Although many of the anti-poverty programmes are beneficiary oriented, the real poor are missing in that beneficiary list. The reality as experienced by the poor living on the margin of existence is often different from the assumption made by the administrators. It is difficult for us to understand fears, the hesitancy, the pain and the labour with which poor live and which, therefore, separates the project from its implementation, from what is possible and impossible, or what is easy or difficult for the rural poor. It requires village level basic planning to comprehend such basic issues in Rural Development.

## REFERENCES


1. Press Report: December, 6th 1944.
2. Harijan, January, 9th 1937.
3. Mahatma; D.G. Tendulkar, Vol.6. Publications Division, Government of India, p.66.
4. *Harijan*, 25th August, 1940.
5. M.K. Gandhi, *Khadi and Spinning in Villages*, Navjivan, 1969, p.138.Khadi – How and Why (1955 Ed.) p. 19.
6. T.Thimmaiah, G. *District as a Unit of Sub-regional Planning*, Allied Publications, New Delhi, 1978.
7. Thimmaiah, G. "District Level Planning: Lessons from experiencing, Rural Development in India – A Multi Dimensional Analysis (Ed). T.K. Publishing House, Bombay, 1984.
8. *Harijan*, 23rd March, 1947, p.79.
9. *Harijan*, 18th January, 1948.
10. Planning for Sarvodaya Varanasi, A.B.Sarva Seva Sangh Publications, 1957.
11. Viswesvarayya, M. *District Development Scheme Economic Progress by Forced Marches*, Bangalore, 1942.
12. Planning Commission, GOI, *Draft for First Five Year Plan*, 1951.

# 18

# Gandhi on Rural Development

*K. Hari Babu & A.S. Acharyulu*

The term 'Rural Development' connotes overall development of rural areas with a view to improving the quality of life of the rural people. In this sense, it is a comprehensive and Multi-dimensional concept which encompasses also the development of agriculture and allied activities, village and cottage industries and crafts, socio-economic infrastructure, community service and facilities and, above all human resources in rural areas. As a phenomena, rural development is the end result of interactions between various physical, technological economic, social, cultural and institutional factors (Katarsing, 1999).

About 70 per cent of Indians live in villages. In other words any planning for the development of India could not be complete without embracing the rural chapter of India in its fold. Over the years, rural development has emerged as "a strategy designed to improve the economic and social life of a specific group of people, the rural poor. It involves extending the benefits of development to the poorest among those who seek a livelihood in rural areas." (International Labour Organisation, 1968:56).

Gandhiji underlined the importance of rural India by saying that 'India lives in villages'. Since then successive governments have been trying to develop the rural India. In the various five year plans, development of rural areas has been one of the most abiding concerns. The Government of India started its plan for the planned growth soon after the Independence. After 50 years of Indian independence, it is worthwhile to assess how far how much distance is covered in respect of the rural development and the milestones laid down by the martyrs who sacrified their lives to make the nation independent from British rule, more specifically of the father of nation Mahatma Gandhiji.

Gandhi in his various speeches and articles written throughout the freedom struggle spoke highly of democratic decentralization and rural development. In the 22 July 1946 issue of Harijan, Gandhiji stated that "Independence must begin at the bottom" (Anil Dutta Mishra, 2002: 1). Gandhiji wrote in Harijan (29 August, 1936) : "I would say that if the village perishes India will perish too . It will be no more India. Her own vision in the world will get lost. The revival of the village life is possible only when it is no more exploited" (*Indian Farming*, 1978 : 2 and 31).

## Conceptual Analysis of Rural Development

The concept of rural development was born in the context of agriculture and it remained, for a long time, coterminus with agricultural development in India. Since the 1970s the concept of rural development has undergone a change and has become more comprehensive. The World Bank defines rural development as a strategy designed to improve the economic and social life of a specific group of people, that is, the rural poor. It involves the extending of the benefits of development to the poorest among those who are living in the rural areas. This group includes small-scale farmers, tenants, and landless. Rural development should include a mix of activities including projects to raise agricultural output, create new employment, improve health and education, expand communication, and improve housing (World Bank, 1975 : 28 – 29). Thus the World Bank defines rural development in terms of an improvement of the economic and social life of the rural poor (S.R. Maheswari, 1995 : 18).

Besides the above concepts, various other concepts of rural development have been propounded by various authors. The former Union Finance Minister, C. Subramanian, who put forward the thesis of rural development at the All India Science Congress, Waltair 1976, viewed it as a "systematic and scientific use of all our natural resources and as a part of this process enabling every person to engage himself in a productive and socially useful occupation and earn an income that would meet at least the basic needs" (K.R. Dasguptha, 1997, 25). Uma Lele defines rural development as "improving living standards of the masses of the low-income population residing in rural areas and making the process of rural development self-sustaining" (Ibid).

Thus rural development is, of late, viewed as a strategy to bring about improvement in the economic and social life of the rural poor. It implies both economic betterment of people as well as greater social transformation. It encompasses a spectrum of activities and human mobilization to make people stand on their own feet and break away from all structural disabilities which claim them to condition in which they may live in (S.N. Mishra, 1983 : 34).

## Gandhian Views on Rural Development

### 1. Relationship between City and Villages

It was Gandhiji who first understood the importance, role and place of Indian villages in the whole country. His objective assessment of villages in overall Indian economic and political sphere was the key which helped him to bring them to the main stream and ultimately win the freedom.

The rural character of the economy and the need for regeneration of rural life was stressed by Mahatma Gandhi. He wrote in *Harijan* (4, April, 1936). "India is to be found not in few cities but in its 700,000 villages. But we town dwellers have believed that India is to be found in its towns and the villages were created to minister to our needs. We have hardly paused to inquire if those poor get sufficient to eat and clothe themselves with and whether they have a roof to shelter themselves from sun and rain". He was thus critical of the role of the urban setups as they did not share proportionate resources with their counterparts living in villages. He considered urbanisation as an evil insofar as (1) it is based on the exploitation of the countryside, and (2) is totally divorced from the rural way of life rooted in nature. *He said* (in 1946), "I regard the growth of the cities as an evil thing unfortunate for mankind and the world, unfortunate for England and certainly unfortunate for India. The British have exploited India through its cities. The latter have exploited the villages. The blood of the villages is the cement with which the edifice of the cities is built". He has asked whether it was possible to retrace the steps and, if this was possible, whether this would not be incompatible with progress. Gandhi gave a remarkably balanced answer to this question in the form of the following propositions: (1) "I want the blood that is inflating the arteries of the cities to run once again in the blood-vessels of the villages": (2) "I do not want to depopulate the cities and send the city folk back to the villages. All I want is that they should re-adjust their lives so as to cease to sponge upon the poor village folk and make to the latter what reparation is possible, even at this late hour, by helping to resuscitate their ruined economy"; (3) "In my picture of the rural economy the cities would take their natural place and not appear as unnatural, congested spots or boils on the body-politic, as they are today." (Ganguli, B.N., 1973 : 187).

The views of Gandhiji on urbanisation and its relationship with that of the villages are still evading us as we find the ballooning of the cities as population due to migration is increasing day by day, pollution, famines, shortage of safe drinking water etc., as ringing problems to day. In addition, as the size is increasing their share in the proportion of the total funds at disposal is also increasing disproportionately.

## 2. Co-operative Form of Enterprise

In the East man has relied on his group – family, clan, caste, guild or the village community. Gandhi thought that if the Indian economy as well as the Indian policy, if it has to be restructured from the bottom outwards (rather than upwards in a phyramidal structure) it would be necessary to refashion the village communities as an 'ideal type' and readapt them to the modern methods of "cooperative" operations (*Ibid.* 147).

Gandhi did not think that the village communities in future India would be a replica of the old village communities. In answer to Louid Fisher's suggestion on the nature of the new order in India after British left, Gandhi said in 1942 : "I admit that the future society of India is largely beyond my grasp." But he took care to explain (1) that power concentrated now in New Delhi or in Calcutta and Bombay, in the cities, would have to be distributed among the 7,00,000 villages of India; and (2) the "voluntary cooperation will produce real freedom and a new order" (*Ibid*: 148).

Gandhiji's conception of a new economic order in the villages included a programme of cooperative farming in agriculture. Many raised their eyebrows when Gandhi declared in 1942: "I firmly believe that we shall not derive the full benefits of agriculture until we take to cooperative farming. Does it not stand to reason that it is far better for a hundred families in a village to cultivate their lands collectively and divide the income there from than to divide the land anyhow into a hundred portions? He thought in terms of wind-mills, power-generation by village communities and rural electrification. He favoured the use of electricity for operating rural tools and implements. In 1941 he explained his own conception of rural industrialisation. He wished to revolutionise the 'Khadi mentality' which had by then become part of a strange cult. This he explained that this mentality "means a wholesale swadeshi mentaility, a determination to find all the necessaries of life in India and that through the labour and intellect of the villagers.... it means the decentralisation of the production and distribution of the necessaries of life... Every village is to produce and use all its necessaries and, in addition, to produce a certain percentage as its contribution to the requirements of the cities. Hereby industries will necessarily be centralised and nationalised. But they will occupy the least part of the vast national activity in the villages." (*Ibid*: 156). The present co-operative movement in India, except a few exceptions has gone to threads. It is marked by corruption, instability, nepotism etc., to name a few evils.

## 3. An Ideal Village

In 1919 Gandhi wrote for the *navjivan* a series of articles on the condition of Indian peasants and the means of ameliorating it. The English translation appeared in the *Young India*. Gandhi said: "Mr. Lionel Curstis' description of an Indian village as a collection of insanitary dwellings constructed in a dunghill is not much exaggerated. There should be some system about the structure of a well ordered village, there should be some order about the village lanes, and the roads should be so scrupulously clean in this and of crores of barefooted pedestrians that nobody need not hesitate in walking or even sleeping in the streets. The lanes should be mechanised and have gutters for letting out water. The temples and mosques should be kept so beautifully clean that the visitors should feel an air of tranquil holiness about them. The village should, as far as possible, be full of shade giving trees and fruit bearing trees in and around them. It should have a *dharmsahala*, a school and a small dispensary. Washing and privy arrangement should be such as may not contaminate the air, water and roads of the village. There was time when the Indian village satisfied most of these conditions. Every village should be self-sufficient, so far as its needs of foods and clothing are concerned and should be capable of defending itself against robbers or wild animals. An ideal village should approximate to the description I have given for. Only such village could be called self governing, and if all Indian villages could come up to that ideal, India should be free from most of its worries... It is my firm belief that these small units are easily capable of being well ordered and organised." (*Ibid*: 150).

Gandhiji thought of a casteless egalitarian rural society against the stark background of a caste-ridden village community. This was a contradiction. He not only faced it, but also tried to resolve it by means of a progressive interpretation of the ancient differentiation of social functions, which, in the course of social decay, and in his view, degenerated into a hide-bound, caste ridden social order." (*Ibid*: 150 – 151).

## 4. "Village Republic:" A Vision of Gandhiji

This picture of a new India which Gandhi presented in Harijan article must be delineated in his own words as follows. Only the paragraphs have been re-arranged for convenience of analysis.

1. "Indian independence must begin at the bottom. Thus every village will be a republic or panchayat having powers. It follows, therefore, that every village has to be self-sustained and capable of managing its own affairs, even to the extent of defending itself against the whole world. It will be trained and prepared to perish in the attempt to defend itself against any onslaught from without.

2. "Ultimately, it is the individual who is the unit. But this does not exclude dependence on the willing help from neighbours or from the world. It will be free and voluntary play of mutual forces".

Gandhi was thus thinking of village republics, completely free to manage their own affairs, and united by mutual aid even to the extent of joint defence against any external aggression. A village panchayat, if it has to be a republic, must be an egalitarian organisation in which "ultimately it is the individual who is the unit". The relations between individual must rest upon equality, mutual aid and willing cooperation. Their relations with the outside world will be governed by the same principles of solidarity. But such solidarity can neither be established nor sustained, unless consumption is maintained at a level that every individual, however humble, can reach. In other words, if there is poverty that also has to be shared equally. Gandhi, therefore, said:

3. "Such a society is necessarily highly cultured in which every man or woman knows what he or she wants, and what is more, knows that no one should want anything that the others cannot have with equal labour".

In Gandhi's view the essence of culture lies in knowing what one really wants. Also, if one wants anything that cannot be had with equal labour, there is an element of exploitation which means violence as well as inequality that violence helps to sustain.

4. "In this structure composed of innumerable villages there will be ever-widening, never-ascending circles. Life will not be a pyramid with the apex sustained by the bottom. But it will be an oceanic circle whose centre will be the individual always ready to perish for the village, the latter ready to perish for the circle of villages till at last the whole becomes one life composed of individuals, never aggressive in their arrogance, but ever humble, sharing the majesty of the oceanic circle of which they are integral units. Therefore, the outermost circumference will not wield power to crush the inner circle, but will give strength to all within and will derive its own strength from it".

5. "In it there is no room for machines that would displace human labour and that would concentrate power in a few hands. Labour has its unique place in a cultured human family. Every machine that helps every individual has a place".

A "village republic" is not designed to revert to crude and primitive communism. Labour will be dignified and not degraded into drudgery. Electricity and Machinery will save labour, but they will save labour for all and will not be a means of enriching, the few and "concentrating power in a few hands".

Gandhi was aware that by presenting a picture of republican village India he was exposing himself to ridicule in a political atmosphere in which politicians of the urban classes were dreaming of power-politics and power-structure of the usual run of democracies, while reflecting on the content of independence in conventional terms".

Gandhi's conception of an "oceanic circle" as opposed to a pyramidal structure of society, and his almost mystical idea of ever-ending, but never ascending, concentric circles that signify interdependence, mutual support, and solidarity, without there being any relation of coercion, on the one hand, and dependence, on the other, as between the periphery and the inner circles."

## Conclusion

The views of Gandhiji on rural development have been classified as Utopian by some thinkers. But as we realize that some of these are fully successful and some are partly successful i.e., co-operative movement in giving right direction to rural development. The ideas are of the same relevance as they were at the time of presentation. The rural development of India leaves a lot to be fulfilled in respect to the vision of Gandhiji. His meticulous and indepth understanding of social stratification and structure of Indian society could help a lot in designing an appropriate rural development programme.

## REFERENCES

1. Anil Dutta, Mishra(2002), *Panchayati Raj: Gandhian Perspective* New Delhi: Mittal Publications, 2002, p. 1.
2. K.R. Dasgupta(1997), "Rural Development Programmes in India : Concepts and Strategies, "*Kurukshetra,* Vol. 45, No. 11, August 1997, p. 29.
3. World Bank(1975), *Rural Development and Sector Policy Paper*, 1975, Washington D.C., pp. 28 – 29.
4. S.R. Maheswari(1985), *Rural Development in India,* New Delhi : Sage Publications. p. 18.
5. *Ibid.*
6. S.N. Mishra and Sweta Mishra, *Decentralized Governance,* p. 66.
7. International Labour Organisation (1965), *Human Resources*

*Development, Objectives Problems and Policies*, Geneva, 1968, p. 56.

8. "Mahatma Gandhi on Rural Development" *Indian Farming*, October–November, 1978, p. 2 and p. 31.

9. Ganguli, B.N.(1973), *Gandhi's Social Philosophy: Perspective and Relevance*. Council for Social Development, Vikas Publishing House Pvt. Ltd., 1973, p. 187.

10. *Ibid*, p. 147; 6. *Ibid*, p. 148; 7. *Ibid*, p. 156; 8 *Ibid*, p. 150;9, *Ibid*, p. 150-151; 10, *Ibid*, p. 156-157; 11. *Ibid*, p. 156-157; 12. *Ibid*, p. 159; 13. *Ibid*, p. 160.

11. Katar Sing (1999), *Rural Development : Principles Policies and Management*, Sage Publications, New Delhi, 1999.

# 19

# Gandhian Approach to Rural Development

*N. Sreerama Murty*

Gandhiji said, "India lives in villages". According to 2001 Census, 72.3 per cent of India's population inhabits in rural areas. The rural people in India are living in conditions of extreme poverty, illiteracy and ill-health and lack the knowledge and access to resources for improving these conditions. Mahatma Gandhi once said that "every single person will admit that 80 per cent of the people (in his times) is almost the whole of the people that what affects them will affect the whole nation, and that what does not touch them is of little consequence". No programme in our country can become national programme if it is not a rural community programme. It is believed that India would flourish only when its villages progress.

Gandhiji's primary concern was the development of the human being. Man who would be raised in his own estimate and in the estimate of others. Gandhi relied on the conscience of individuals for all his movements. His programme was identified with the needs of home. He wanted that the movements of the people should be self-inspiring and self-generating. People were to be the pivot around which the programme had to revolve.

He believed that programmes produced through people's initiative are something much more living and integrated, something in which there is a sense of intimate partnership.

The importance of rural development was recognized long back and the origins of rural development in India may be traced to the several isolated experiments in rural reconstruction pioneered by different individuals and organizations. The early pioneering efforts included the village uplift work of Mahatma Gandhi; the rural reconstruction at Sriniketan of Rabindranath Tagore; Martandam Experiment by Spencer Hatch; the Gurgaon district development work of F.L Brayne; the rural reconstruction programme in Baroda; the Firka Development Scheme of Tanguturi Prakasam; the Pilot Project of Albert Mayer in Etawah; and the Nilokheri Experiment by S.K. Dey (Venkatareddy, 2001).

Among the early pioneers of rural reconstruction schemes, Mahatma Gandhi occupies a significant place. He conceptualizes rural development in its totality, consistent with the Indian situation. His concept of rural development was not mere economic prosperity for few at the cost of many; it was the participation of the entire population in production as well as consumption "unto the least of all."

The pathetic condition of villages pained him. He agreed with Lionel Curtis's description of an Indian village as "a collection of unsanitary dwellings constructed in a dunghill" and added that he could give more details about the neglect of the villages. The exploitation of the villagers by the town dwellers, the condition of poverty due to insufficient marketing facilities for their products, lack of supplementary occupation and inadequacy of medical attention, were only some of the many evils that existed. But he maintained that Indian villages were not originally like this and that the deplorable condition was brought about by foreign rule and continuous neglect. He stressed the great importance of the village in the Indian social system, and, in order to drive home this truth he even went to the extent of declaring that "if the villages perish, India will perish too" (*Harijan*, 1936).

## Definition of Rural Development

The Rural Development Sector Policy Paper of the World Bank (1975) observed, "Rural development as a strategy designed to improve the economic and social life of a specific group of people-the rural poor. It involves in extending the benefits of development to the poorest among those who seek a livelihood in the rural areas. The group includes small farmers, tenants and the landless. Lele Uma (1975) defines rural development as "improving the living standards of the masses of the low-income population residing in rural areas and making the process of rural development self sustaining."

Parthasarathy (1981) opines that 'the critical element in the rural development is improvement of living standards of the poor through opportunities for better utilization of their physical and human resources; in the absence of this, utilization of rural resources has no functional significance. Making the process of rural development self-sustaining not only implies the mobilization of capital and use of technology for the benefit of the poor but their active involvement in the building up of institutions as well as in functioning of these."

Michael P. Todaro (1977), views that "Rural Development encompasses: 1) improvement in levels of living, including employment, education, health, nutrition, housing and a variety of social services; 2) decreasing inequality in the distribution of rural incomes and in rural-urban imbalances in incomes and economic opportunities, and 3) increasing the capacity of the rural sector to sustain and accelerate the pace of these improvements."

Krishnaswamy (1985) rightly views that rural development involves integration of spatial aspects (integration between areas), different sectors of the rural economy, agriculture, off-farm activities, industry, etc., with forward and backward linkages; integration of economic development with social development, integration of total area approach and target group approach; integration of credit with technical services; integration of human resource development with anticipated manpower needs and integration of income-generating schemes with the minimum needs programme of education, rural health, water supply, nutrition, etc.

## Challenges of Rural Development

Rural development is a critical factor to be tackled which would bring about a less exploitative and more satisfying system of all-round development. Gandhi in the context of India aptly said, "If India is not to perish, we have to begin with the lower rung of ladder. If that was rotten, all work done at the top or at the intermediate rungs are bound to ultimately fall" (*Harijan*, 1935:68). Gandhi in his writings further dramatized the problems of city-village antagonism. He said: "The blood of the villages is the cement with which the edifice of the city is built. I want this blood that is today inflating the arteries of the cities to run once again in the blood vessels of the villages" (*Harijan*, 1946: 198). Gandhi did not talk simply in terms of city-village dichotomy. In addition to referring to the village exploitation and role of the city, he spoke of alienation of city dweller. He referred to village as a 'community' rather than a socially and culturally structured unit. (Gangrade, 2005).

Throughout his life he worked for the reformation of the Indian villages where the majority of the Indian population lived under appalling conditions. It was his deep-rooted conviction that prosperity of a permanent and fair nature can be secured through the proper development of villages and cottage industries. He prescribed the following conditions for the ideal Indian village (*Harijan*, 1942).

1) There should be orderliness in the structure of the village.
2) The lanes and the roads should be orderly and must be kept absolutely clean so that "in the land of barefooted pedestrians" nobody need hesitate to walk or even sleep in the streets.
3) The lanes should be macadamized and have gutters for draining off water.
4) Temples and mosques must be kept beautifully clean so that visitors feel an air of tranquil holiness about them.
5) The villages should be filled with shade and fruit trees.
6) They should have a *Dharmasala*, and a small dispensary.
7) Washing and privy arrangements should be such as not to contaminate the air, water and roads of the village.
8) Every village should be self-sufficient so far as its food and clothing requirements are concerned.
9) Every village should be capable of defending itself from robbers or wild animals.
10) It should have recreation facilities and a playground for adults and children and a reserve for its cattle.
11) If space is left over, the village should grow money crops except tobacco, opium, etc.
12) The village should maintain a village theatre, school and public hall.

13) It should have its own water-works, ensuring a clean water supply.
14) Education should be made compulsory up to the final basic course.
15) Caste, with its graded untouchability, should not be practiced.
16) As far as possible, all activities should be conducted on a cooperative basis.
17) Non-violence, with its technique of Satyagraha and non-cooperation, should be the sanction of the village community.
18) There should be a compulsory service of village guards, to be selected by rotation from the register maintained by the village.
19) The Government of the village should be conducted by a *Panchayat* of five persons, annually elected by adult villagers possessing the minimum qualifications.
20) Since there should be no system of punishment in the accepted sense of the term, the *village Panchayat* would be the legislature, judiciary and executive combined.
21) Two *Panchayats* should jointly elect one leader, and they should form a working party. Fifty such working parties should elect a second grade leader. Parallel groups of two hundred Panchayats should continue to be formed till they cover the whole of India, each succeeding group of Panchayats electing a second-grade leader. All second-grade leaders should jointly serve the whole of India and severally for their respective areas. The second-grade leaders might elect a chief, whenever they deem necessary, to regulate and command all the groups.
22) He wanted to present the model of real village government, to depict his ideal of a perfect democracy based upon individual freedom and at the same time upon collective and cooperative action. Gandhi admitted that the conditions he prescribed apply to the ideal village of his conception, and that it might take a life-time to model such a village. He asked any lover of true democracy and village life to take up such work and to start by being the village scavenger, spinner, watchman, medicine man and schoolmaster simultaneously. He was convinced that "if all Indian villages could come up to the ideal, India would be free from most of its worries" (Unnithan, 1979).

## Constructive Programme

Gandhi from 1915 to 1945 was able to formulate a compact programme of total transformation of society. This programme has been described as the constructive programme. In its final form in 1945, it covered the following items:

1. Communal Harmony
2. Removal of Untouchability
3. Prohibition
4. Khadi
5. Village Industries
6. Village Sanitation
7. Basic Education
8. Adult Education
9. Women uplift
10. Education in Health and Hygiene
11. Provincial Language
12. National Language
13. Economic Equality
14. *Kisan* (Peasants)
15. Labour
16. Adivasis (Tribals)
17. Leprosy
18. Students
19. Improving of Cattle
20. Nature Cure.

Gandhiji felt the constructive programme in its entirety is to enable masses to emerge out of unfreedom into freedom and out of economic and social deprivation into self-reliance and out of state of alienation into cooperative living. Through this programme, he explored the possibility of building up a power free, non-authoritarian, non-exploitative society by changing the present set up. In 1948, there were ten national level constructive work organisations having about 2,500 cadre workers and lakhs of ordinary workers all over India. There had come into existence a body of experience and experiments in the field of education, social action and community building and techniques. After his passing away, the constructive programme was taken up by his followers through two agencies Sarva Seva Sangh (SSS) and Gandhi Smarak Nidhi (or Gandhi Memorial Trust)... After Gandhi's death on 30th January 1948, the followers of his constructive work met at Sevagram in March 1948. The meeting was ended with the formation of (i) Sarvodaya Samaj and (ii) Sarva Seva Sangh for continuation of all the constructive work with which Gandhi himself had been conducting experiments (Narayanaswamy, 1996).

We have to teach the village folk to economize time, health and money. Since the economic reorganization of villages has been commenced with food reform, it is necessary to find out the simplest and cheapest foods that would enable villagers to regain lost health. The addition of green leaves to their meals will enable villagers to avoid many diseases from which they are now suffering. The villager's food is deficient in vitamins; many of them can be supplied with fresh green leaves (*Harijan*, 1935.). The village sanitation covers attending to cleaning tanks and wells and keeping them clean, getting rid of dung heaps in the villages.

The purpose of the constructive program is to bring the economic and political destiny of the common people within their own control through determined cooperative effort. Gandhiji fully realized that the process of rural reconstruction was a tremendous undertaking, requiring infinite patience, considerable understanding, and a thorough grasp of the many problems involved.

Since Independence, constructive work has been undertaken not only by those who were directly influenced by Gandhi's thought but also by a large number of agencies, groups and individuals. There are thousands of constructive work organisations having lakhs of workers spread all over India. Gandhi wanted the cadre of workers composing the institutions to take for themselves minimum means for their own sustenance.

## Impact of Constructive Workers on Policies

It is a pity that the constructive workers at present are not pulling their full weight either in shaping or the implementation of national policies and programmes. It is the Central and State Governments, little influenced by constructive workers, which are shaping national policies. These policies and programmes are rarely in conformity with those laid down in the Gandhian Constructive Programme (Narayanaswamy, 1996: 306).

Constructive workers are not yet able to affect the situation for the reason that they have not fully realized their own unity of purpose and organization. So long as Gandhi lived, he was the point of unity and among all constructive workers and he was the authoritative link between them and political leaders. After Gandhi, the constructive workers have had to discover some other effective points of unity. They have not yet succeeded in doing this (Radhakrishnan, 1996: 69-81)

The Gandhian constructive workers who could have acted like a watchdog and catalyst must equally share the responsibility for the state of affairs obtaining in the country today. The Gandhian constructive workers who were the symbols of idealism, dedication and in- corruptive lifestyle in the 50s and 60s have now allowed themselves to be marginalized because of their own weakness for power. It is history now how many of them strayed into the practical field which proved to be a fatal blow to the Gandhian movement in this country (Radhakrishnan, 1999).

Gopinath Dhawan felt that everything is not lost, for the Gandhian constructive workers. There is still tremendous goodwill for many of them and probably they should consider the following:

> They should stop politicking and singly and jointly undertake extensive tour of the country spreading the message of peace and non-violence as Mahatma Gandhi would have done had he been in our midst today. The Gandhian constructive workers have to realize that the enemy within is to be fought vigorously and seriously. The threat from this is far more serious, for if we can fight this enemy all extraneous problems will get resolved on their own.

## Social Work Practice in Rural Development

Community organisation as method of social work would be of help in organising villages by identifying the needs of the people (defining their needs and problems), order or rank them (prioritize their needs), identifying the resources within and outside the community, make individual and collective plans to meet these needs and problems, execute these plans with maximum reliance on the community resources and supplement these resources when necessary from outside the community through cooperative and collaborative attitudes and practices. Though community organisation method is identified with the development of urban slums but it would be more effective in rural areas since the people have intimate relations and with the involvement of local leaders issues can be solved amicably. Today we have village local self-governments on the constitutional basis. Village communities are provided with funds and they have their own administrative set-up. While working with the villages the professionally trained community organizers have to guide the local functionaries in the preparation of micro plans, help motivate people's participation and plan for collaborative activities with the non-governmental organisation and financial institutions for all-round development of villages. Village youth have to be organised on the lines of Gandhian philosophy.

While social action as a method social work is of much help in bringing mass movement on various social problems that affect the life of rural people. The methods we use to tackle the village problems include education, persuasion, awareness building, capacity building through training and updating skills of the rural people. Imparting people about non-violent methods of expressing resentment against the policies of the government such as Special Economic Zones (SEZs) and of projects involving mass displacement and cause environmental degradation. Persuading government to take up policies and programmes that promote sustainable development in villages. Develop pressure groups to bring village and environmentally friendly programmes at the national and state levels. Enacting legislations to deter individuals resorting to antisocial activities. Take measures to bring a thorough change in the mental outlook of the people. Advocacy as a method may be used in protecting the interest of the village people. Seminars, symposiums, conferences, processions or marches, satyagrahas, debates, essay writing competitions and discussion may be organised to protect rural environment and encourage village people to use biofertilisers, vermiculture, withdrawal of excessive use of pesticides, genetically harmful seeds and undertake mass rodent control measures to ensure sustainable agriculture and prevent threat to the nature.

## Conclusion

The future of India is inextricably connected with the future of villages. There are increasing problems. With courage and conviction and with abiding faith in the teachings of Gandhi, we have to tackle the problems of poverty, ignorance, malnutrition, insanitary conditions, population explosion, and the caste system. In every village, there should be a body of workers (not servants) of the nation engaged in constructive work to achieve social, moral and economic freedom. It should be organised democratically from the bottom upwards. (Narayanaswamy, 1996: 306). Gandhiji wanted to make each village a "complete republic independent of its neighbours for its vital wants, and yet interdependent for many others in which dependence is a necessity." (Venkatareddy, 2001). Fulfilling the dreams of Gandhiji, the successive governments have made efforts to strengthen village local self-government by bringing amendment to constitution. Gandhian way of village life still has its relevance in the wake of urbanizing populations.

Policies promoting globalization, privatization and liberalization may land villages in problems. Social action as a method of social work can be of use to bring modification in the policies and programmes to be suitable to the life of the villages. Village youth may be trained and involved in community building programmes on Gandhian lines.

## REFERENCES

1. Gandhi, M.K. 1947. *India of My Dreams*, Bombay: Hind Kitabs Ltd.
2. Gangrade, K.D. 2005. *Gandhian Approach to Development and Social Work*, New Delhi: Concept Publishing Company.
3. *Harijan*, 1935. February 15.
4. *Harijan*, 1936. August29.
5. *Harijan*, 1942. India of My Dreams, July 26.
6. *Harijan*, 23April 1946, p.198.
7. Krishnaswamy (1985)
8. Lele Uma (1975) *Design of Rural Development: Lessons from Africa*, The Johns Hopkins University Press, Baltimore and London, p.20.
9. Michael P. Todaro (1977) *Economics for Developing World*, London: Longmans Group Ltd., p.249.
10. Muzumdar, A.M. 1964. *Social Welfare in India: Mahatma Gandhi's Contributions*, Bombay: Asia Publishing House.

11. Narayanaswamy, S. 1996. "Relevance of Gandhian Constructive Programmes Today," *Gandhi Marg*, No.3, October-December, p. 306.
12. Parthasarathi, G. (1981) "Integrated Rural Development: Concept, theoretical Base and Contradictions", In T.Mathew (Ed.), *Rural Development in India*, New Delhi: Agricole Publishing Academy, p. 25.
13. Radhakrishnan, N. 1996. The Linkage between Education and Constructive Work Towards a Culture of Peace, *Journal of Gandhi Smriti and Darshan Sam*iti, Vol.2, No.2&3, July, pp. 69-81
14. Unnithan, T.K.N. 1979. *Gandhi and Social Change*, Jaipur: Rawat Publications.
15. Venkatareddy, K. 2001. *Agriculture and Rural Development (A Gandhian Perspective)*, Mumbai: Himalaya Publishing House.
16. World Bank, (1975). *The Assault on World Poverty*, Baltimore: Johns Hopkins University Press, p. 3.

# 20

# Gandhi and Rural Development: With Reference to Khadi

*D. Syamala Devi, K.A.P. Lakshmi & M. Sandhya*

"India Lives in its Villages" —Mahatma Gandhi

Mohandas Karamchand Gandhi, better known as Mahatma Gandhi is not only the Father of nation, but also the Father of modern 'Khadi'. Gandhiji concentrated his entire attention to the development of rural areas. These "thoughts" significantly are relevant to the present scenario, though not implemented with true spirit. The aim of this paper is to present the thought of Gandhiji towards rural development with particular reference to khadi and suggested measures to improve the state of khadi.

## About Gandhiji

Mohandas Karamchand Gandhi, respectfully known as "MAHATMA GANDHI," is undeniably one of the greatest and most interesting personalities of the world. Millions of people who had never seen him, or have heard him the remember him for these principles that targeted at the welfare of a "common man" in fact a "Common Indian". His greatest contribution to the billions of the world population-- 'Conquest of violence by love and goodwill' many of the political bigwigs were inked out others more patient being and those who were better acquainted with Gandhi observed "The sense of values, the sensitivity that Gandhiji displayed may be what the world needs today. Gandhiji thought are based on four principles these: Truth, non-violence, dignity of labour and simplicity. It is a combination of idealism, individualism and socialism. Socialism is based upon 'rural Development'

## Gandhiji and Rural Development

Gandhiji concentrated his entire attention on the development of rural areas. The goals of development are:

1. Satisfaction of basic needs and not greed since Earth provides enough to satisfy every man's need, but not for every man's greed.
2. Full employment, since work is not a disutility but is part of the living process,
3. Modes of employment which satisfy man's urge for fulfillment of personality through work,
4. Decentralization in government, and.
5. A development of technology which serves social needs.

His ideas on rural reconstruction had two main aims to make the Indian villages self-sufficient and to make them independent of government to the possible extent. Gandhiji's political work and struggle against the British Raj was an extension of his mission to uplift the rural poor from poverty and plight. He was convinced that "if the village perishes India will perish too".

Gandhiji believed that "an ideal Indian village will be so constructed as to lend itself to perfect sanitation. It will have cottages with sufficient light and ventilation built from a material obtainable within a radius of five miles of it. The cottages will have courtyards enabling households to plant vegetables for domestic use and to house their cattle. The village lanes and streets will be free of all avoidable dust. It will have wells according to its needs and accessible to all. It will have houses of worship for all, also a common meeting place, a village common for grazing its cattle, a cooperative dairy, primary and secondary schools in which industrial education will be the central fact, and it will have panchayats for setting disputes. It will produce its own grains, vegetables and fruit, and its own Khadi (Gandhi, 1959, 13).

Gandhij observed that "there are, in our villages, inexhaustible resources not for commercial purposes in every case but certainly for local purposes in almost every case. The greatest tragedy is the hopeless unwillingness of the villagers to better their lot. He advocated village-oriented economy, free from violence and exploitation. In his works: "Rural economy, as I have conceived it, eschews exploitation altogether, and exploitation is the essence of violence. You have, therefore, to be rural-minded before you can be non-violent, and to be rural-minded you have to have faith in the spinning wheel.

Gandhiji also advocated the importance of agriculture, cattle farming, dairying, etc. He believed that the home industries like canning, dairy, bullock-oil pressing paper-making, hand-pounding of rice, home-made bread and jam, soap- making, making of match-boxes etc., are to be revived and encouraged because rural reconstruction is incomplete without these industries. Gandhiji emphasized that people under decentralized economic and political system will be quite competent to run and manage their panchayats and other local self-governing institutions. He strongly pleaded for decentralization through the organization of village panchayats. He was of the view that "panchayat system in India, if worked on scientific lines, could not only build up the social and economic strength of the country side but also strengthen the forces of national defense against the risk of foreign invasion.

To sum up, much of the rural development effort in India has drawn its inspiration from Gandhian ideas of rural upliftment. However, technology adaptation and the use of science for rural development are the products of recent times.

## Gandhian Khadi Movement

As part of a larger non-cooperation movement to reject British control over India, Mohandas Gandhi launched the khadi movement (alternatively called the swadeshi movement) in 1915. Gandhi encouraged all Indians to wear khadi, and abolish foreign cloth. Indian handspun and woven cloth wrapped loosely around the body, instead of British-style suits with ties and stiff-collared shirts. The idea was unusual, considering the international movement towards industrialization and modernization.

In his 1908 book *Hind Swaraj*, Gandhi described the hand loom and the spinning wheel as" the panacea for the growing pauperism in India. Gandhi came to believe "that every organic community, from the village to the nation, should strive to be self-sufficient in basic necessities, as competition for natural resources can lead to conflict and war. He opposed "the big machines of industry" which had led to a concentration of power and the displacement of many Indian laborers. He viewed" "the self-sufficient community as the best matrix for the holistic development of human beings, allowing them to realize their full potentialities, physical, intellectual, emotional and spiritual. For Gandhi, Khadi symbolized these ideals and served as a uniform for the larger non-cooperation movement.

When he returned to India from his travels in 1915, Gandhi decided that he and his family and friends would live in a self-sustaining community, in an "atmosphere of renunciation and service". One of the many rules of the community was that everyone was to wear and use Khadi, and to refuse foreign made cloth. Beyond his commune, Gandhi encouraged women to make Khadi, and fellow Indian to wear it. As Gandhi wrote, "My idea is to get these [semi-starved, semi-employed] women to spin yarn, and to clothe the people of India with Khadi woven out of it."

Therefore his thoughts become the main source to understand properly the genesis and the background of Khadi inevitably; therefore, he would have to be quoted profusely in this chapter for authoritative exposition and clarity of his thoughts regarding Khadi. He discovered 'charkha '(spinning where) in London in 1908 during discussions with fellow Indian regarding the conditions in India. "I saw as in a flash that without the spinning wheel there was no 'swaraj" (Self-rule). I knew at once that everyone had to spin. But I did not then know the distinction between the loom and the wheel". He had a clear vision of his programme of reviving the ancient industry of hand-spinning and making charkha the focal point of economic regeneration of pauperized villages, as well as political awakening amongst the Indian masses, when he finally came to India in 1915, Boycott of foreign goods, specially cloth and swadeshi movement was going on and he claimed that his Khadi programme gave a concrete and positive meaning to swadeshi. "In my opinion, it is Khadi alone that has made such boycott a practical position "he said. In 1919 he formally launched the khadi programme in the country, but clearly differentiating between the charkha of medieval times and that of his vision, in so far as the former was symbol of exploitation and helplessness of spinners, while the latter was a symbol of revolution in thought and action, as well as an embodiment of non-violence. The Indian National Congress decided in its Nagpur session held in 1920 to encourage khadi. The first khadi production centre was established in Kathiawad, Gujarat. In 1921, khadhi found a formal place in the Congress programme and charkha its proud place on the naional flag. However, the Congress formed an independent autonomous specialized body called All India Spinners Association (AISA) or charkha sangh in 1925 for implementing Khadhi programme vigorously throughout the country. Gandhiji firmly believed that charkha was his best gift to the nation, contributing to its all - sided development - economic, political, social and moral. "I may deserve the curse of posterity for many mistakes of omission and commission, but I am confident of earning its blessings for suggesting a revival of the Charkha. I stake my all on it. For, every revolution of the wheel spins peace, good will and love.

The biggest success of the Khadi movement was the psychological impact that it had on the Indian people, especially those who were wholly or partially unemployed.

## The Khadi Movement

When we have become village-minded, we will not want imitations of the West or machine-made products. – Gandhi.

- One of the most vivid elements of Gandhi's struggle for people's self- reliance can be seen in the Khadi movement.
- To Gandhi, economic equality between India's people was the key to non--violent independence for the country. In order to achieve a new social reality based in economic equality for the villages, he created a constructive program, made up of 17 key areas for action.
- A critical element of the constructive program was the promotion of Khadi, or home-spun cloth.
- Gandhi advocated that village people produce Khadi rather than rely on foreign goods. This would give people control over economic production, as well as create an awareness of their own productivity and self-worth.
- Instead of mass production, Gandhi advocated production by the masses.
- The handloom and spinning wheel thus became a symbol

of self-respect and self-reliance gained by the poor.

- Even today, Khadi and village industries are supported by the India government, and Khadi continues to be worn by India's highest politicians.
- The Khadi and Village Industries sector in India employed nearly 6 million people in 1996-7.

## Advantages of Khadi

Khadi, based on decentralized production and distribution, plays an important role in the village economy. According to Gandhiji, Khadi alone can solve a number of economic and other problems of India, viz , the poor villagers can supplement their meager resources, spinning wheels can give employment opportunities to village carpenters, blacksmiths, weavers, etc., For the upliftment of women; it provides an honorable and leisurely occupation; even for poor and uneducated people spinning is easy to learn and requires no outlay of capital; it is such a type of industry which can absorb the largest number of people and can provide employment to the unemployed at any time of the year without much difficulty. Moreover, it is an insurance against the adversity of a famine conditions. However, critics say that the spinning wheel thus not pays, but Gandhiji positively answered that the spinning wheel is an attempt to produce something out of nothing. Khadi, not only adds to the national income but also this additional income is equally distributed among the poor state of the society.

## Suggestions to improve Khadi

1. Khadi cloth should be used to make contemporary designs that attract everyone to use.
2. "Fashion week" like other big shows should be conducted to attract fashion designers to make new designs.
3. Pricing of the cloth should be changed according to seasonal demand. Discount during winter and rising of price during summer.
4. Khadi dress should be made compulsory in schools, colleges and government offices at least twice in a week.
5. Khadi cooperatives should be strengthened to promote khadi industry.

6. Export potential for khadi should be increased through identifying the needy countries.

## Conclusion

In conclusion we can say that Gandhian thought towards Rural development are perfectly implemented by our Indian Government irrespective of the political party in power. Nowaday's more and more concentration has been given by the Centre and State Government, towards the implementation of rural development programmers. But unfortunately Khadi Industry at present is not working up to the expectation of Gandhiji. There is greater need to improve the Khadi Industry if we want to fulfill the dream of our father of Nation.

## REFERENCES

1. Mohandas K. Gandhi, *Gandhi, An Autobiography: The story of my experiments with truth* 489 (2 ed. 1957)
2. Kamla Chowdhry, *Gandhi and Sustainble Development: Earth Summit and Agenda 21.*
3. Arora, R.C (1978), "Industry and Rural Development" S. Chand & Company, New Delhi
4. Bhatnagar, S, and SS. Chib (1987) *Rural Development in India, A Strategy for Socio- Economic Changes*, ESS Publications, New Delhi.
5. Youesh Chandra sharma, *Cotton Khadi in Indian Economy.*

Web sites: www.Indianchild.com egandhi@anc.org.za.

www.mkgandhi.org

# 21

# Gandhian Approach for Empowerment of the Rural Poor

*D. Pulla Rao*

## The Problem

Empowerment of the rural poor has become a major problem of rural India over the last 100 years. In 1930s when Mahatma Gandhi took the reigns of freedom movement, about 300 million rural poor were suffering from chronic poverty for 120 days during the lien period in agriculture and were relegated to subsistence living for the rest 245 days in a year. The situation of the rural poor over the last 70 years had further worsened in spite of our continuous efforts to alleviate rural poverty. At present also about 300 million rurai poor are in chronic poverty. Ironically, the seasons changed and the persons changed over the period but the magical number of 300 million rural poor did not change. Probably it may not change also in the near future because about 50 per cent of the chronic poor are from the Scheduled Tribes and about 40 per cent are from Scheduled Castes who are economically, socially and politically marginalized. Unless, we integrate this huge 'poverty batallian' from these 'marginalized sections' of the society with the main stream of India rural poverty will have its permanent settlement in India. Mere palletive efforts will not work. It needs a historic intervention on behalf of this poverty batallian to bring the dramatic change required on this front.Under these circumstances, a close look at the Gandhian approach for empowering the rural poor is highly essential.

## Gandhiji: A Great Participatory Rural Appraiser of All Times

The primary objective of Mahatma Gandhi was to achieve freedom for India from the British Raj. And this forced him to make extensive tour of the Indian sub-continent and mingle with the rural masses more frequently. His close association with the rural masses necessitated him to spend sufficient time, within the villages which enabled him to examine very closely the pathetic living conditions of the rural masses in general and the most vulnerable groups like the Scheduled Castes, Scheduled Tribes, Other Backward Communities, the rural artisans, the weavers etc., in particular. And, thus he obtained the first hand knowledge about the rural poverty pervading throughout the country. In his own words "the people are rooted to the soil, and the vast majority are living a hand to mouth life. Whatever may be said to the country, having traveled throughout the length and breadth of the land with eyes open and mixed with millions, there can be no doubt that pauperism is growing."

Gandhiji said again that "When all about me are dying for want of food, the only occupation permissible to me is to feed the hungry. It is my conviction that India is a house on fire because its manhood is being daily scorched, it is dying of hunger because it has no work to buy food with." (The Village Reconstruction)

This suggests the depth of knowledge, Gandhiji had gained about the living conditions of the rural poor. And there from onwards Gandhiji added an equally important agenda for his mass movement, I.e., freedom from hunger for the rural masses. All through in his speeches, press meetings and writings in the young India and the Harijan, as well as his private letters to various friends in India and outside Gandhiji always mentioned the rural poverty, the reasons and the solutions there off and urged every body to fight against rural poverty also.

## Gandhian Philosophy of Truth and Non-violence

Mahatma Gandhi took up the philosophy of truth as his personal living experimentation and adopted the method of non-violence, whenever and wherever he has to overcome the obstacles in the pursuit of truth. For Mahatma Gandhi facts speak of the truth and the personal observation and involvement is a method of knowing the facts. According to Mahatma Gandhi truth and peace are two sides of the same coin. For cross checking himself the path of the truth, he was always dependent on religious guidance particularly, the Gita and the exhortations of Jesus Christ on 'love thy neighbour as thyself'.

## Serving the Suffering was Serving God

Mahatma Gandhi always looked into the man to find out Krishna or Rama or Jesus Christ. For him neither the name of the religion nor the name of god was that important as much as serving the suffering man. In Gandhiji's own words "I cannot starve my neighbour and claim to serve my distant cousin in the North Pole. This is the basic principle of all religions and we will find it is also of true and humane economics" (Village Reconstruction). Therefore, whenever any person that be a woman or a man; a child or an aged; a Hindu or a Christian or a Muslim; a single person or a group of persons complained any suffering he took up the cause and acted immediately to mitigate the suffering in the best way he could through his twin philosophies of truth and non-violence. Gandhiji had neither friends nor foes at large. He treated all persons equally as his brothers and sisters that was why he was rightly called Mahatma.

## Analysis of Rural Poverty

Mahatma Gandhi who went round the entire country several times had got the opportunity to meet the rural masses personally, stayed with them for sufficient time and observed their living conditions and understood the causes for their poverty more than any researcher had ever done before him. He was a great participatory rural appraiser of all times.

Mahatma Gandhi identified 'the period of no work' (unemployed days) as the reason de' etre for rural poverty in India. According to him the rural masses were unemployed for about 4 months or 120 days in a year. And he considered that about 85 per cent of the rural masses were faminished during that period of unemployment. As agriculture had no scope to provide extra-employment required during its lien period, an alternative was to be chalked out. This necessitated the creation of about 3600 crores of mandays of extra employment (30 crores of rural unemployed x 120 unemployed days).

## The Wheel of Truth and Non-Violence

For Mahatma Gandhi the spinning wheel was not just the one that spine yam for the production of khadi only. It was the wheel of Truth and non-violence. Mahatma Gandhi proposed the spinning wheel as the tool for the unemployed rural masses to earn their bread during the lien period in agriculture. Gandhiji proposed the spinning wheel keeping two basic constraints; he had observed in rural India.

The first and the foremost constraint he observed was that agriculture was staturated and could not be improved further to provide extra-employment for the unemployed labour force. He categorically stated that the Indian peasant required a supplementary industry. (*Young India*: April 6, 1922)

The second constraint he observed in rural India of his times was the limited and acceptable non-agricultural rural occupations for the common masses. Among the then existing rural non-agricultural occupations, spinning and khadi was the chief village handicraft that could absorb any number of persons (*Harijan*: January 20, 1940). Besides, it was the most decent, acceptable and easily adoptable with out much financial investment. Above all it was highly labour oriented occupation that answered the employment and income needs of the teeming millions of rural India. Therefore, Gandhiji proposed spinning wheel programme for the entire rural India. It was his undaunted faith in his philosophy of truth and non-violence that led Mahatma Gandhi to propose the spinning wheel as the mass rural employment programme. In his own words "Spin me, and you can find a crust of bread for yourself' (*Young India*: December 8, 1927).

Gandhiji visualized 3 messages in the spinning wheel. They are: (a) the economical message, (b) the cultural message and (c) the humane message. For him the spinning wheel supplies bread, brings people together and makes man to live a simple life with high thinking (*Young India*: December 8, 1927). In fact, spinning and khadi production was a decent occupation, it was a non-caste, colour and creed based occupation. Unfortunately, most of the then leaders in India and abroad failed to see the virtues of the spinning wheel as Gandhiji did see. In his days who ever sought even a small favour from him like an autograph, Gandhiji put forward the condition of taking up the spinning wheel quid pro quo.

## Gandhiji was as practical as philosophical

Any body with some basic knowledge about the social and cultural setting up of rural India could not but appreciate the spinning wheel movement of Gandhiji as the most practical one. Till the time of Gandhiji more than ~ne third of the rural population in India were socially and culturally treated as untouchables or semi-untouchables or second-rate citizens. These people were not allowed to pursue such occupations the products and services of which are prohibited in the caste ridden India. Had Gandhiji asked such socially and culturally marginalized masses to take up the occupations of the upper castes that could not have been allowed at all. Here was the spinning wheel any person without any bar can take up. The yam and the khadi produced by any body and every body could be acquired and pooled together and sold in the market by any government sponsored organization like the Khadi and Village Industries Commission or any voluntary organization. Thus, yarn and khadi had got readymade outlet. Any body can participate in this programme and earn his/her bread though the networking of all the people engaged in spinning and khadi cloth production. A kind of brotherhood was supposed to be brought in across various castes, communities, and regions of India. Gandhiji wanted to look for a smile on every face and a sigh of relief in every household. In addition, the khadi cloth was supposed to gain more market by replacing the banished mill cloth from England through Gandhi ji's sponsored 'banishment of foreign goods movement'.

## Minimum Clothing to the Rural Poor

Food, clothing and shelter are the three basic needs of Indian daridranarayana (The name given to the poor by Gandhiji). Agriculture was providing food, sufficient or insufficient whatever it may be all through the ages. But most of the Indians at the time of Gandhi were either naked with just a 6 inches piece of cloth to cover their shame or half naked with a dhoti of 3 feet length.

Therefore, Gandhiji wanted to provide a reasonable clothing to the daridra narayana of rural India. The spinning wheel came handy to fulfill his dream. Mass mobilization of the people through his programme after the banishment of foreign made mill cloths totally from India was supposed to achieve 'Swadeshi' (self-reliance) objective of Gandhiji. And he wanted to achieve through non-violence method.

## A Retrospect

Many scholars, even today, failed to understand as most of the leaders of the Gandhian days, the basic philosophy behind the spinning wheel. Now the rural society changed a lot. The two basic constraints Mahatma Gandhi observed at his time may not be tenable nowadays. Agriculture is no more saturated. It is expanding and it got great scope for further expansion. The green revolution that brought technological changes on various fronts in agriculture had expanded income and employment opportunities for the rural masses. The modernization and globalization of the economy all around the world have further widened the scope of income and employment opportunities for many including the rural masses in India.

Similarly, several types of handicrafts are helping the rural masses through gainful employment and substantial additional income. And many more handicrafts are in the pipelines which are fast spreading into the rural areas. Undoubtedly, the Information Technology sector is also spreading into the rural areas.. The barriers between the traditionalism and modernism are also vanishing away fast.

However, the need for extra employment for the unemployed rural labour force is also increasing simultaneously due to high growth of rural population. Still about 40 per cent of the rural population in India are living below the poverty line and the peasant community is suffering from unemployment for about 100 days in a year. This suggests that the two basic observations Gandhiji had made 70 years ago remained as they are.

And when we multiply the number of the rural unemployed persons with the number of their unemployed days, the total number of man days needed to fill the gap with extra employment will be more than double now than it was at the time of Gandhiji. And hence, the issue of employment of the rural masses through massive rural employment programmes outside agriculture is more serious now than at the time of Gandhiji.

Therefore Gandhian prescription of empowerment of the rural masses through creation of extra employment outside agriculture is highly valid at present than before. At that time Gandhiji prescribed only spinning wheel, where as now we are expanding our basket by undertaking several supplementary occupations for the rural masses. We are only expanding and extending his philosophy further and further to cover several other areas to tackle the same basic issue that is elimination of rural poverty (upliftment of the daridra narayana) in a changed setting. The rural poor in India are still looking up towards the sky for a deliverer to come down, may be another Mahatma Gandhi.

In the modern world, as also in India Information Technology sector is the biggest, fast growing, more labour absorbing one. Therefore, picking up the thread from Mahatma Gandhi it is time to induct the rural youth belonging to Scheduled Castes, Scheduled Tribes and Other Backward Class communities in large numbers and thus dig a whole into the hardcore poverty group in rural India.

## REFERENCES


1. Anand T. Hingorani. (ed). (1998): *The Village Reconstruction*, Bharatiya Bhavan, Mumbai.
2. Gandhi, M.K. (1927): *An Autobiography*, Navajivan Publishing House, Ahmedabad.
3. ————. (1959): *Panchayat Raj*, Navajivan Publishing House, Ahmedabad.
4. ———— (1960): *Village Industries*, Navajivan Publishing House, Ahmedabad.
5. ———— (1962): *Village Swaraj*, Navajivan Publishing House, Ahmedabad.
6. IF AD. (2007): *Rural Poverty Portal*, 2nd April, Rome.
7. Shashi Prabha Sharma. (1992): *Gandhian Holistic Economics*, Concept Publishing Company, New Delhi.
8. Nayar, D.P. (1955), 'Gandhi View of life and its educational imperatives, Naitalim, *IASSI*, Vol.13, No.3.

22

# Gandhian Vision for Harijan Upliftment

*Y. Ashok Kumar*

The disease of untouchability is fairly old in our society; it generated social hatred and discriminatory feeling of high and low and as a result the later category suffered for centuries in the hands of the former. Untouchability in India, as the race and colour problems in the west, rested upon the idea of the superiority of one section of people over another on account of their birth. Gandhi called these so called religious sanctions as a serious stigma on the fair name of a society which have a deep rooted culture and historical traditions to support its identity (S.R. Bakshi: 1987). Gandhi believed that the so called Caste Hindu had a personal obligation to fulfill towards the Harijans which they must do unconditionally and it was to be their atonement. 'Whether in this world or the next, it is for each one to free oneself from bondage by one's own effort. Harijans should not look upon themselves as lowly, weak or crippled' (*The Collected Works of Mahatma Gandhi*).

Gandhi called Harijan as men of God and believed that all the religions of the world describe God pre-eminently as the friend of this privileged, help of the helpless and protection of the weak. He stated that rest of the world apart, in India who could be more friendless, helpless or weaker than the forty millions or mere Hindu of India who were classified as untouchables.

He opined, 'when Caste Hindus have of their own inner conviction and therefore voluntarily, got rid of the present day untouchability, we shall all be called Harijans, for according to my humble opinion, Caste Hindus, will then have found favour with god and may, therefore fitly described his men' (Haijan: 1993). Gandhi believed Hinduism will die if untouchability lives and untouchability has to die if Hinduism is to live (Yogesh Chandra: 1997). Through his speeches in public and writings in young India and Harijan, he emphasized the problems of untouchability and its removal from its roots. He hated untouchability with his entire soul. Gandhi was quite Sure in his mind that untouchability would not be removed by the force, even of law. It could only be removed, he opined, when the majority of Hindus realized that it was a crime against the god and man and were ashamed of it. In other words, it was a process of conversion, i.e. purification of Hindu heart. The aid of law had invoked when it hindered or interfered with the progress of the reform as when, in spite of the willingness of the trustees and the temple going public, the law prohibited the opening of a particular temple. (*Harijan*: 1934)

He assessed the social position of untouchables as follows: 'socially they are lepers. Economically they were worse than slaves. Religiously, they are denied entrance to places we miscall 'houses of God'. They are denied the use on the same terms as caste Hindus of public roads, public schools, public hospitals, public wells, public taps, public parks and the like.... The wonder is that they are at all able to eke out an existence or that they still remain within the Hindu fold. They are too downtrodden to rise in revolt against their suppressors. ...It is only ceaseless effort that can raise these down trodden fellow beings from degradation, purify Hinduism and raise the whole Hindu society and with it the whole of India'. (*Harijan*: 1933).

He always preached to the Harijans, cleanliness, abstention from carrion eating and intoxicating drinks and drugs, necessity of taking education themselves and giving it to the children also abstention also from eating the leavings from Caste Hindu's plates. He stated, on the contrary, I suggest to caste Hindus that the shortcomings are not inherent to Harijans but that they are due to our criminal neglect of even deliberate suppression of these brethren of ours.... we must approach Harijans as penitents or debtors, not as their patrons or creditors extending generosity to the undeserving.

Besides Gandhi has recommended, that common schools and wells should be opened where the existing ones were not available for Harijans either owing to the violent and successful opposition of the neighbors or some other unavoidable cause. Gandhi wrote in 1931, 'Untouchability cannot long endure. Some years ago we obstinately clung to it, today we are different. It will be a thing of the past only when the indifference is translated into a conscious, deliberate awakening to a sense of the duty of self purification. Even the indifference on sufferance would have been impossible fifteen years ago'. (*Harijan*:1946)

## Upliftment of Harijans

The steps for the upliftment of Harijans, taken by Gandhi were unique in our History along with numerous other issues—political, social, economical, cultural, and other. He ardently identified himself with numerous causes which had deep connection with the daily life of a downtrodden member of our society. He always wished to give the Harijan a place of honour and respect in our society which was denied to him since centuries. In this task what he preached, he professed. He spoke much in their favour by undertaking strenuous tours of all the regions of India He castigated caste Hindus and criticized their behavior towards the untouchables. By doing so, he demanded their financial and social co-operation for upliftment of this neglected community. At Mahatma's persuasion, numerous affluent persons came forward and funded his schemes of reform. The money thus raised was spent on their educational, moral, social economic and religious development. Undoubtedly much progress was visible in this regard with the passage of time. The Hindu orthodoxy in many areas had to bow down before Mahatma's humanitarian gestures. Gandhi used to spend some time with the Harijans by living himself with them. This kind of personal identification of the Mahatma made the Harijans realize their sense of importance in our society. He taught them the sense of cleanliness and advised them to raise their economic and social standards by hard work and honest means. He raised their colonies and advised them to raise their economic conditions to devise schemes of their upliftment.

## Harijan Sevak Sangh

Gandhi's constructive programme was devoted to social reform and development of the backward communities. His aim was to regenerate a new spirit, a new thinking and self reliance amongst the Harijans. This kind of feeling, he believed, would greatly enhance their prestige and self respect. They could raise their heads by becoming economically stronger by hard work and incessant labour (J.B.Kripalani: 1970).

To boost up the work for the upliftment of Harijans, Gandhi laid the foundation of the *'Harijan sevak sangh'*, It's main function was the removal of all such disabilities which hampered the progress and development of Harijans. As it consisted of dedicated workers it did remarkable work; so Gandhi brought a Harijan family in the Ashram and he adopted their daughter as his own. He also offered his blessings on the eve of marriages which were celebrated between Harijans and Caste Hindus. A few such marriages were celebrated in his own Ashram. The Mahatma recommended a *'Harijan Day'* to be fixed under the auspices of the Harijan Sevak Sangh. It should be a day of sanitation and cleanliness. The poorest could do this by denying themselves a meal or a position there of House to house collection was to be made by the members. The literature should be sold or given away as the exigency of the time might require.

Gandhi fought against these social practices and advised the status-conscious people to behave in a decent way toward untouchables. They are also *'men of God'* was Mahatma's constant refrain. He opened schools for them afforded them an honorable place in his Ashram fought for their temple entry at numerous places, lived amongst them and participated in their social and religious functions.

In this social exercise, Gandhiji sought the support of the numerous elements, social organizations, prominent individuals and the congress organization. He greatly succeeded in his mission by devising novel ways and means for the social upliftment of Harijans. Some constitutional safeguards were afforded to Harijans under the category of scheduled castes which were offered a sizeable percentage of jobs in different departments under the central and state government (S.R.Bakshi: 1987).

B.R. Ambedkar was greatly influenced by Gandhi. It is proved by the fact that he made efforts to cooperate with him in the removal of untouchability programme in 1924. He got the

Satyagraha technique from Gandhi. This influence was more marked during the early phase of his life. The Chowdar Tank Satygarha, Kalaram Temple Satyagraha and Mukhed Village Satyagraha can be cited as example (K.S. Bharathi: 1990).

Gandhiji has recognized that Muslims had much to answer for, with respect of their past-war like attitudes, and dominion over much of India. However, he argued that Hindus also needed to acknowledge that there had been evil in their past, especially with respect to the practice of untouchability and to be ready to reform themselves. Gandhiji analysis was that the basic teachings of each tradition were good and should be respected. Believers in both cases needed to affirm the good from their respective pasts, but they should also be ready to reform and change elements of their traditions (Sheila McDonough:1994). Gandhi's long struggle against untouchability in Hinduism was motivated by the conviction that its practice was a falsification of basic human values.

## Gandhian View on Basic Education

Gandhi strongly believed through education the practice of untouchability can be reformed. Gandhiji insisted on the Basic Education; it deserves mention here, as Gandhiji conceived it, the primary school was to have organized its work and curriculum in such a manner that the social and natural environment of the child and some productive activity would occupy a central place. The learning or reading. writing Social Studies and general knowledge would be centered round these. This emphasis is similar to what happened to primary education to all countries with industrialization and democracy when (a) greater training of senses and skills and greater participation of all individuals were demanded and (b) Schooling was extended to children of previously non-literate social groups.

During the past 20 years, the excessive stress on spinning and weaving, as the major centre of basic education has been given up, as has been in a larger context, the Gandhian perspective of a decentralized society consisting mainly of small villages. On other hand, it has unfortunately also been a case of throwing away the baby with the bath water. A more realistic rather than a bookish tendency in school programmes has been promoted to great extent, as was initially hoped for. One reason for his difficulty has been able to adjust their entrance requirements and education to the needs of the children.

## *Gandhian View towards Conversions*

The conversion of untouchables to Islam or Christianity was criticized by Gandhiji. He favored religious bonds as it were; a 'matter of the heart', others should not take advantage of the helplessness of untouchables. A remedy suggested to 'untouchables' is rejection of Hinduism and whole sale conversion to Islam or Christianity. And if a change of religion could be justified for worldly betterment; If the inhuman treatment of the *panchamas* were a part of Hinduism, its rejection would be a paramount duty both for them and for those like me who would not make a fetish even of religion and condone every evil in its sacred name. Untouchability is no part of Hinduism, rather its excrescence to be removed by every effort. And there is quite an army of Hindu reformers that have set their heart upon riding Hinduism of this blot.

Those who use the threat (of conversion) do not, in any humble opinion, know the meaning of religion. Religion is a matter of life and death. A man does not change religion as he changes his garments. He takes it with him beyond the grave. Nor does a man profess his religion to oblige others. He professes a religion because he cannot do otherwise. A faithful husband loves his wife as he would love no another woman. Even her faithlessness would not wean him from his faith. The bond is more than blood relationship.

Gandhi's first interview to the press since entering prison spoke of himself as touchable by birth and untouchable by choice. It was his ambition to represent and identify himself with people of the lowest rung of the society. 'What I want, and what I am living for, and what I should delight in dying for, is the eradication of untouchability root and branch'. I believe that if untouchability is really rooted out, it will not only purge Hinduism of a terrible blot but its repercussions will be worldwide. My fight against the untouchability is fight against the impure in humanity. Commenting on the movement of anti-untouchability Mahatma Gandhi says, "if this preference for quality is good, it is specially so, for an essentially religious movement that of anti untouchability. In religion indifference to quality may even lead to a disaster Mahatma does not believe in external sanctions which enforce obedience to the moral law by external law. He cherished an ideal of *Swaraj* that was attainable through accent on non-political realities-spinning, ruralism, basic education, anti communalism Etc.(Brown, Jucith:1980).

## Rural Development for Harijan Upliftment

Gandhiji gave an idea and a programme of rural development and then a practical shape to his thoughts and this inspired a large number of his followers for the welfare of the villages where the great majority of people lives. Even today, the large scale rural welfare programmes that are presently under execution in India, aiming at revolutionizing the conditions of life and ameliorating the standards of living of the rural population, steeped for ages in the mine of neglect, poverty, and disease can be regarded as the direct outcome of the primary importance which Gandhiji accorded to rural areas. The village industries, Khadi development work in rural areas, basic education, Harijan uplift, eradication of untouchability and many other programmes, which he prescribed for unremitting adoption for village reconstruction and the momentum they received during his time on his behest, has provided a powerful propelling force for the country-wide rural welfare schemes.

Gandhi gave us a vision of Indian living in largely self sufficient villages, purges of the scourge of untouchability which people of all religions did not merely tolerate but respected each other's traditions, customs, thought and feelings.

## REFERENCES

1. AK. Gorpade, (1959) Babasaheb Ambedkar, Vol-I, Bharat Bhusan Printing Press, Bombay, p.80.
2. Brown, Judith M.: "Mahatma Gandhi" in History Today; Vol.30, London May 1980, p. 18
3. Encyclopedia of Social Work in India, the Planning Commission of India, Publication Division, Government of India.
4. J.B. Kripalani, (1970) *Gandhi: His Life and Thought*, Delhi p. 383.
5. KS.Bharathi (1990) Foundations of Ambedkar Thought, Dattsons

Publisher & Distributors, Sadar, Nagpur.

6. Sheila McDonough (1994) Gandhi's Response to Islam, D.K Print World(p) ltd., New Delhi.
7. S.R. Bakshi (1987) *Gandhi and Status of Harijans*, Deep & Deep Publications, New Delhi.
8. *The Collected Works of Mahatma Gandhi*, Vol. LV, p. 364. Publication Division, Government of India
9. Why the Construction Programme", *Selected writing and Utterances by Ghandiji*, Indian Congress Publications, New Delhi, p. 21.
10. Yogesh Chandra (1997), *Rediscovering Gandhi*, Century Publications, London, p. 326.

# 23

# Gandhi and Eradication of Untouchability

*M. Gopi & T. Sreenu*

"I do not want to be reborn, but if I have to reborn, I should be born as an untouchable"—*Mahatma Gandhi.*

India is a caste based society, caste plays a predominant role in Indian society and its importance is growing day by day. Manu divided the society into four varnas – Brahmins, Kshtriyas, Vaishyas and Shudras. The panchama varna was named as untouchables. Untouchability is a buy-product of caste system in India. The untouchables were the poorest section of Indian society. Their avenues of employment were strictly limited. They lived apart, unhygienic surroundings on the out skirts of villages and cities. Though they were Hindus and believed in Hinduism and worshipped Hindu gods and goddeses. They were not allowed to enter Hindu temples, Public institutions like schools, hostels etc, were closed to them, it always violated human dignity by compelling untouchables to do work which was unclean and degrading. It was opened that Untouchability against the spirit of democracy. The aim of this article is to present the views of Gandhiji on Untouchability and the measures he has taken to eradicate it from the society.

## About Gandhiji

Mohandas Karamchand Gandhi was a major political and spiritual leader of India and the Indian Independence movement. He was the pioneer of Satyagraha, resistance to tyranny through mass civil disobedience, firmly founded upon ahimsa or total non violence which led India to Independence and inspired movements for civil rights and freedom across the world. He commonly knew around the world as Mahatma Gandhi and in India as Bapu. He officially had known as the Father of the Nation.

Gandhiji was a caste Hindu, the father of independence who is said to have spoken and written more on Untouchability than on any other subject. He belongs to the Bania caste as Bania family and his fore father did not practiced the caste occupation, but served as Prime Ministers in several princely states of the Kathiwad peninsula (Gujarat). This was, and is an essentially conservative region in its adherence was to traditional patterns of social relations.

Vaishya or Bania castes are third in the traditional four fold division of Hindu society included with Brahmin and Kshtriya among the twice born. However in Gujarat probably more than in any other part of India, Banias are without peer in wealth influence and piety. They tend toward orthodoxy.

Gandhi publicly put the abolition of Untouchability along with hindu-muslim unity as the essential pure quite for India's true independence. He also made popular the form "Harijan" (children of God) for the untouchables.

Gandhi selected the Bhangi, a scavenger caste of north India, to represent the problem of Untouchability. Gandhi's abhorrence of Untouchability and his association of such practices with the sweeper caste appear rooted in childhood experience. Although not mentioned in his autobiography Gandhi's reactions to his family's sweeper at the age of twelve and recorded in an article that he wrote in young India 27th April, 1921.

Gandhiji said that, a scavenger named uka an 'untouchable' used to attend his house for cleaning latrines—often he would ask my mother why it was wrong to touch him. If he accidentally touched uka, he was asked to perform abolitions and though he naturally obeyed. Gandhi wrote in his article that he was a very dutiful and obedient child, and so far as it was consistent with respect for parents, he often had tussles with then on this matter. He told to his mother that she was entirely wrong in considering contact with uka as sinful.

Uka remained the symbol for untouchables in Gandhi's mind. Scavenging and the Bangi figure prominently in many of Gandhi pronouncements and actions. He himself cleaned a dirty latrine at the Calcutta congress of 1901. He often used the metaphor of the mothers cleaning work for her child as a counter part to the Bhangis work for society. Sanitation work of Gandhi's ashram was done by all members as a means for demonstrating the honorable nature of these essential duties.

Gandhi opened that the colour prejudice in South Africa was nothing but a form of Untouchability. He however felt that Indians Untouchability was far worse than the colour prejudice in South Africa. In this context, he observed: "If is, however worth nothing the distinction between the two untouchabilities. In South Africa, it is based upon color prejudice and has no sanction either in religion or in Law. In India, unfortunately it is claimed by a large number of Hindus to have religious sanction to law. The Indian Untouchability is therefore much worse than the South Africa. Both are no doubt equally his achieves so far as the victim is concerned. Both deserve equal condemnation only in India, it seems that the fight is likely to be much more harder than in south Africa. Gandhi described untouchability at various times as a curse, an excrescence on Hinduism, a position, a snake, a canker, a hydra-headed worster, a great blot, a device of satan, a hideous un truth, dyresim and 'O' dwyerism and the Barsinister.

At the time of his assumption of leadership of the Indian national congress in 1920, Gandhi made what seemed to be his first strong public statement on Untouchability. They reflect his dual role as mahatma and politician in Indian life, already apparent at that time, as politician, Gandhi said, "Swaraj is as un attainable with out the removal of the sin of Untouchability. In Dalton words, 'Indian society saw Gandhi and Gandhi regarded himself, as occupying the peculiar position of a figure above the discord around him and capable of harmonizing it'.

Gandhi wrote in 1931, Untouchability cannot long endure some years ago we obstinately clung to it, to day we are indifferent. It will be a thing of the past only when the indifference is translated into a conscious, deliberate awakening to a sense of the duty of self participation even the indifferences of sufferance would have impossible fifteen years ago. He was the firm conviction that it Untouchability was an integral part of Hinduism, the latter was a spent bullet. But Untouchability, he states was hideous on truth, what he was aiming at was not every hindu touching an untouchable, but ever touchable hindu driving out Untouchability from his heart, going through a complete change of heart. In fact inter dining or inter marrying was not the main point. Twenty six years later, he said, "If I had my way I would persuade all caste hindu girls coming under my influence to select harijan husbands".

Although Gandhi was not the first to cry out against Untouchability, he was the most prominent caste Hindu to proclaim than it was harmful to Hinduism, to make its removal a personal responsibility of the caste hindu, to keep it before the public eye with passionate oratory and vivid imagery and to found an organization for service to untouchables perhaps as important as his ideology and his pronouncements was his personal example, from the beginning of touching the untouchable.

**Measures taken to eradicating Untouchability**

***Temple Entry:*** Gandhi was of firm belief that when the untouchables were permitted to enter the temples, the blot of Untouchability would vanish. It was this belief which prompted Gandhi to incorporate temple entry as a part of his anti-untouchability campaign which was intensified during the post-poona pact period.

After his release from the Yeravada prison, Gandhi made prevent appeals to the orthodox the Sanatana caste Hindu to open up their hearts and treat the untouchables as their brothers and sisters. He decided to under take an all India tour to create awareness amongst the caste hindu about the urgent need for such a social reform. Accordingly he undertook the tour which is commonly referred to as the harijan tour during the period from November 1933 to August 1934; he addressed the people at 161 places and covered at distance of 12,650 miles.

The burden of song of Gandhi at all these places was that the hindu temples shall be thrown open to the untouchables precisely on the some terms that were applicable to the caste hindus. In his view, one single act of opening temples would open up the hearts of caste Hindus and untouchables and consequently purify Hinduism.

## Harijan Sevak Sangh

Gandhi established Harijan Sevak Sangh, to improve the condition of harijans. He said that the objective of sangh shall be the eradication, by truthful and non-violent means of untouchability in Hindu society with all its incidental evils and disabilities, suffered by the so called untouchables here in after described as harijans in all walk of life and to scene for them absolute equality of status with the rest of hindus.

The main function of Harijan Sevak Sangh was the removal of disabilities which hampered the progress and development of harijans; Gandhi brought harijan family in the ashram and adopted their daughters as his own. He also offered his blessing on the eve of marriages which were celebrated between harijans and caste Hindus. A few such marriages were celebrated in his own ashram. Harijan Sevak Sangh was not only having central office but different branches also. Two or three reformers had collected a cores if rupees and with it established branches all over India to cover it with schools and hostels for harijan boys and girls. It would not have hastened the day of the doom of untouchability. The Mahatma Gandhi recommended 'Harijan Day' to be fixed under the auspices of the harijan sevak sangh, it should be a day of sanction and cleanliness.

Gandhi always advised the harijan workers to work for the promotion of cleanliness and hygiene among the harijans, improve methods of carrying on what were known as unclean occupations, ex., scavenging and tanning, giving up carrion and beef eating if not meat altogether, giving up of intoxicating liquors and inducing parents to send their children to day schools wherever they were available and parents themselves to attend night schools wherever such were opened.

Gandhi advised the caste Hindus to remove untouchability in order to save Hinduism from the danger of it being perished. In this connection he remarked 'untouchability is a gangrenous limb of Hindu society and if measures are not taken to remove it, the society would become crippled and a crippled society cannot go on like that, so that it will ultimately perish.

Gandhi advised the untouchables to get rid of their inferiority complex. According to him, this inferiority complex was taken advantage by the caste Hindus and induced untouchables themselves to accept the 'Humiliating and Absolutely irrational status assigned to the harijans in society by laying down'. To fulfill the desires of Gandhiji the constituent assembly, of independent India passed a provision legally abolishing untouchability on 29th November 1948. In our Constitution articles 15 and 17 deals with abolishing of the untouchability. Inspite of all the above measures taken by Gandhiji untouchability is still remained in Indian society, especially in rural areas.

## Suggestions to Eradicate Untouchability

1. The attitude of savarnas towards the untouchables should be changed.
2. Since the childhood parents must inculcate the concept of equality to their children by indicating that all are equal with out any discrimination.
3. Teachers must develop a sort of harmony and friendly atmosphere among the students free from caste and religious differences.
4. People must come out of their traditional attitudes and customs and treat all as equal along with them.
5. Untouchables should not have inferiority complex in their minds and try to compete along with other caste people in all most all aspects.
6. Increase in literacy rate of people will automatically increase the rational thinking.

## Conclusion

In conclusion we can say that every individual in this society must try to fulfill the desire of our father of the nation by eradicating untouchability completely not only from the society, but also from their hearts. Gandhi said that "If I should die with any of my desires unfulfilled, with my service of the untouchables unfinished with my Hinduism unfulfilled, I may be born again amongst the untouchable to bring my Hinduism to fulfillment".

## REFERENCES


1. Bakshi, S.R, (1987), *Gandhi and Status of Harijans* , Vanity books, New Delhi.
2. Anil Bharadwaj (2002), *Welfare of Schedule Castes in India,* Deep and Deep Publications Private Limited, New Delhi.
3. Bakshi S.R. (1987), *Untouchables Gandhi,*
4. Freeman, Jamaes. M. *Untouchables in India.*

# 24

# Gandhi's Swaraj Through Panchayati Raj

*A. Srinivasacharyulu & K. Hari Babu*

The tragedy of modern India is that the important aspects of the Gandhian philosophy are not given serious attention. The politicians, policy makers and bureaucrats never realized that Gandhi was much ahead of them and their psychological inability to keep race with this great revolutionary is responsible for the present plight. The quest of humanity for social justice and sustainability will remain a dream until and unless humanity realizes what Gandhi meant when he said, that economics is untrue which ignores and degrades moral values(Anil Dutta Mishra, 2002:1). Mahatma Gandhi arrived from South Africa in January 1915. Mahatma Gandhi for the first time made mention of the Panchayats on February 14, 1946, in a Madras Missionary Conference; "Following the Swadeshi; I observe, the indigenous institutions and village Panchayats hold me. Congress concern for Swaraj (self-rule) and the non-enforcement of Decentralisation Commission's recommendation relegated the Panchayat to the background for some time (Mario D. Zamora, 1990:21, 22). The plea for greater autonomy to rural local bodies received conceptual strength with the advent of Mahatma Gandhi on national scene and his enunciation of the doctrine of national development through autonomous rural organization which he desired to model on the lines of panchayat system as it prevailed in ancient India. Mahatma Gandhi was careful to state that his concept of "RamRajya" of which panchayat autonomy was an integral component, was not derived from any specific historical period but it was an ideal construct based on the best features of different periods of ancient Indian history (Iqbal Narain, *et al,* 1970: 4).

Gandhi claimed that India lived in it s villages and pleaded for the distribution of power among rural masses in India; he believed in the supremacy of the people and insisted in the people's democracy and sovereignty at the grass roots level which he called Panchayati Raj. For Gandhiji, Panchayati Raj was a kind of commonwealth of reformed and reconstructed village communities. He thought that decentralization was essential for ideal democracy, in which everyone can participate in the decision- making and implementation process. His concept of decentralization implies of the basic principle of self-sufficiency in respect of the basic needs of men and the absence of exploitation. In his vision village was a pivot in the Indian polity and future of India depend upon the future of its villages (Jhadhav, V.D. 1984: 108).

His emphasis on the uplift of the India masses though improvement of agriculture, village and cottage industries, khadi, handlooms ,etc., was ridiculed as out-moded and feudal minded people who were exposed to European industrial economy based on large scale production through machinery and culture of urban elites (Rajput R.S. and Meghe D.R., 1984:26). But Gandhi's dream of village republics visualized full literacy, employment, nutritious food, well ventilated dwellings and sufficient khadi for covering the body. He emphasized Swaraj from below saying "Independence must being at bottom thus every village will be a republic (Shakuntla Sharma, 1884:111).

Panchayati Raj is an Indian political institution and it is a part of our ancient civilization. A Panchayati Raj institution (PRIs) is the need of the hour. It will give 'voice to voiceless, power to power less', people irrespective of caste , creed, sex and religion living in six laks villages in India. And the new PRIs provide "power to the ". No doubt, PRIs in India can create history for the generations to come.

The Indian experiences with the PRIs shows that much has been achieved but much more remains to be done. The need now is to recognize that the main objective of the PRIs is to bring the government within the reach of the people. Gandhi held that by serving the villages, Swaraj could be established. The country's prosperity and progress depends upon the villages. He maintained that if the village perishes, India will perish too.

The importance of Panchayati Raj system should be obvious in the country where four of every five citizens live in the villages. Panchayati Raj systems are integral part of concerned system for social and economic development of the rural people. Panchayati Raj came to be established in parts of India as early as in 1959. It was felt that no speedy development in rural or otherwise backward areas was possible unless the people were involved in the programmes. The panchayati Raj was thus devised as a means for furthering his involvement.

Gandhiji was convinced about the efficacy and strength of these village bodies and to him every village was to be conceived as little republic. He was in favour of broad-based pyramidal structure of decentralized power- with numerous village panchayats at the bottom as the vibrating sources of power and a National Panchayat at the apex elected body by the intermediary levels of district and state panchayats with the ultimate control vesting in the hands of the village panchayats. Thus, he subscribed to village based government and self-sufficient, autonomous village economy. A panchayat of five persons-male-and female annually elected by villagers having the required authority and jurisdiction was his idea of the village government. The panchayat was to be of the legislature, judiciary, and executive – perfect village government where perfect democracy would be based on individual freedom.

It is clear that the age of old tradition of village government which was advocated by Gandhiji and was also embedded in our constitution by Gandhi's followers, ultimately found place in legislation. However it must be noted that the proper functioning of Panchayati Raj Institutions, pretend a bright ray of hope for our rural people. India will become powerful nation only when its rural masses achieve economic prosperity and self-reliance. It is high time that we now turn our face positively towards brethren in the countryside and strive towards its prosperity.

Gandhi was very clear about the governance of the villages, and had thought about every aspect of it and had given enough suggestions and plans for their full and all- round development. If we want to uphold peace and order, individual liberty and all-round development, empowerment of the people should begin at the gross-root level, particularly in the villages where the sole of India lives. India is a country of villages and they have the right first to enjoy the benefit of freedom and self-government. Only they can sustain our freedom and discipline, our politicians who badly need it now. They should possess the power and no politician should be able to have access to it, if he does not carry out his will into reality. At the same time it is also necessary that we should concentrate more upon organizing strong Gram Sabhas based on individual liberty and training people in the village to take up responsibilities (Anil Dutta Mishra, 2002:1-3).

## Gandhi's Concept of Panchayat

To Gandhi, panchayat symbollises the power of the people. This is his concept of Swaraj: "Every village will be republic or Panchayat having all powers... every village has to be self – sustained capable of managing its affairs ... This does not exclude dependence on and willing help from neighbours or from the world. In this structure composed of innumerable villages, there will be ever –widening, never ascending circles, "Life will not be a pyramid with the apex sustained by the bottom. But it will be an oceanic circle whose centre will be the individual". In short, by Swaraj he meant" Government by the consent of largest number of such voters; Gandhi was utopian and more practical. So he visualized the phases by which the weaker sections of the society could be organized and made effective through organized non- cooperation and Satyagraha. In this way, he advocated non- violent class – struggle. For example, he said "what can the poor zamindar do when they say that they will simply not work on the land unless they are paid enough to feed, cloth and educate themselves and their children in a decent manner (Ramjee Singh, 2002;11,12).

## *Meaning and purpose of Panchayati Raj*

Gandhi had the right perception of the Indian situation. At the instance of Gokhale when Gandhi traveled all over India after he came back from south Africa he realized the condition of India. And this perception helped him to workout his future plans for the Indians, Gandhi said "I have not pictured a poverty- sticken India containing ignorant millions. I have pictured to myself a

India continually progressing along the lines best suited to her genius. I do not; however picture it as a third class or even a first class copy of the dying civilization of the West.

Gandhi's concept of Panchayati Raj which is probably the only way to real village Swaraj is to be seen from the above background. He says "Panchayat has an ancient flavour; it is a good word it literally means an assembly of five, elected by villagers, it represents a system, by which the innumerable village republics of India were governed. "Therefore Panchayati Raj means governance by the elected five.

Gandhi wants to make every village a republic. Panchayati Raj is supposed to serve two main purposes:

- Economic, pontifical decentralization taking democracy to the grass roots
- Preparing every individual in the process of achieving real Swaraj .

Gandhi wanted to provide basic necessities to everyone and he thought it was possible through Panchayati Raj. It is not possible to achieve Swaraj with empty stomachs and naked bodies. Therefore first of all make every one at least a "man" (he must look like a man) and then let him become a proper human being.He said Independence must be at the bottom. Thus every village will be a republic or panchayat having full powers it follows, there fore, that every village has to be self –sustained and capable of managing its own affairs. In managing its own affairs every villager will find a place for himself and his involvement will create in him a sense of feeling that he is a part of his own republic and is responsible for its own, well being (Hedge V.S and Harijan M.B,2002:167-169)

## Swaraj

According to Gandhi, Panchayati Raj will open the flood gates to real Swaraj but his understanding of Swaraj is entirely different from its usual meaning; it is not merely, political independence. It includes economic and moral independence as well. Self – rule which is the product of self – control will make way for Sarvodaya and self realization. It is Swaraj for the individual and Swaraj for the nation. And Panchayats in their true spirit, Gandhi believed, will certainly lead to individual glory and collective happiness.

### Village Development and Panchayati Raj

To be able to fulfill the objectives of Panchayati Raj, Gandhi wants to prepare a band of good men who with an intention of social service could properly execute the work of Panchayats fairly and squarely. Social service is not a joke for Gandhi. Those who are not spirited with social service cannot and should not hold power. Power corrupts man unless one is morally upright and strong it is the real test of man. Abuse of power can be reduced and proper service can be extended to if holders of authority observe certain code of conduct.

Therefore he said:

They must be votaries of Truth and Ahimsa;

They must like a life of utter simplicity;

They must be "easily approachable";

They must be eager to know the true condition of their subjects;

They must belong to the common people, live like them;

They must be the genuine servants of the people;

They must read be the signs of the times and march with them;

They must be watchful of their own personal and public conduct;

They must take from the revenue the honest minimum necessary to support themselves as a commission for their labours on behalf of the ryots;

They must not break their promises;

They must not indulge in moral turpitude;

They must not pass most of their time outside their states;

They must not be the members of any communal organization and

They must not receive for their own personal use "addresses of value of costly floral tributes"(Ram Rattan 1972; 41-42).

Proper use of Panchayati Raj will certainly usher Gandhi's dream of Ram Rajya will not come unless every individual prepares himself to be proper and worthy citizen of Ram Rajya; it is a process which is difficult but not impossible. We have a tendency to think that whatever is difficult is almost impossible. Because of this tendency we hardly try; unless we try; how can we succeed?

### Functions of Panchayati Raj

Though according to Gandhi Panchayats are expected to do everything for the development of villages one can very briefly mention some of the important functions of every Panchayat. 1) Village administration 2) Education 3) Sanitation 4) Providing Medical needs 5) Service of the poor.

It is important to note that Gandhi wants villge disputes to be settled by village Panchayat. Approaching court for the settlement of dispute is not desirable according to Gandhi. His views on litigation are well known and his warning about lawyers and law courts are very important (Hedge V.S and Harijan, 2002:170-171).

## DEVELOPMENT THROUGH PANCHAYATI RAJ

Gandhi introduced Panchayati Raj for the all round development of villages. All round development means a congenial atmosphere which provides every individual with opportunities for the development of complete personality, i.e. the development of body, mind and soul. This type of development is not possible, if power is centralized. When Panchayati Raj is introduced then it creates situation where both the villagers and the Panchayats can work together for the upliftment of economic, social, educational moral-religious development of all concerned; we can with certainty say that Panchayati Raj system can pave the way for Ram Rajya if it is properly understood by every one of us. For, the development of one village is dependent not only upon surrounding villages but the nearest cities also.

### Panchayats, Governments and Gandhi

Many State Governments have introduced Panchayati Raj in their own way. The way these states introduced Panchayati Raj shows that they are not really interested in the decentralization of power. But at the same time they want to show people, that they have given sufficient respect and regard to the thought of Mahatma Gandhi. According to Gandhi people in the villages should get power and by getting power and participating in the administration, they realize their responsibility which creates desire of doing something for their village and which can affect every villager, including the administrators. This makes them work with dedication and devotion; whereas Panchayati Raj introduced by the States, is not really as per Gandhi ideology. They do not want to give power to the people. Real power is centralized in the States.

In the Gandhian approach to Panchayati Raj, failure to implement and execute the decision of panchayat, rests on the elected members. But the Panchayatis introduced by the States the failures are passed on sometimes to the States and sometimes to the Panchayats. It is natural that they blame each other, because responsibility is not fixed either on the State Government; or to the Panchayats. Even if they are fixed if anything goes wrong in the implementation of the programme, one can easily blame the other, thereby creating a feeling that we are not responsible for the failures.

Gandhi's concept of Panchayati Raj can properly work if and only if Gandhi's other concepts like Swadeshi, Swaraj and his views in other fields are implemented in toto. If we try to introduce Gandhi part by part it will be a grand failure everywhere. There cannot be Gandhian programmes without Gandhian objectives; there cannot be Gandhian objectives without Gandhian principles; Gandhi programmes, objectives and principles are invariably related.

It is necessary to consider why many of the Gandhian programmes are not adopted or even if they are adopted they are not successful; we have already motioned one of the important reasons being; (1) Gandhi's programmes taken up in piecemeal; second important reason is Gandhi programmes are rather difficult to follow and when we pursue difficult programmes we face many hardships. Especially in Gandhi it requires a lot of application from our part, and it demands from us many sacrifices. This kind of difficulty very few are ready to face and therefore we are hardly ready to take as well; Thirdly there is a need to make special efforts to understand Gandhi's view on any subject since Gandhi is a blend of theory and practice. It is not enough, if we understand theory alone; it is equally important to understand his practice in the light of the theory. Because of this sometimes we fail to grasp the hidden meaning in Gandhi's statements. The consequence is that we have distorted understanding of Gandhi.

In Hind Swaraj Gandhi criticizes modern civilization, because, it destroys our own civilization and cultures. It destroys every aspect of our civilization i.e. our education is destroyed ;our own medicine is destroyed; our own legal system and even Panchayati Raj System. In short today we are on the verge of losing everything of our own. That is the effect of modern civilization. That is why Gandhij opposes modern civilization lock, stock and barrel. Why we have failed? Owing to lack of proper education, we have not succeeded in grasping the importance of Panchayati Raj; our education, if at all it has done anything, has made us read and write. It has not succeeded in imparting knowledge and wisdom. Consequently, we have not proper human qualities. Education is to give us proper human qualities. It should prepare us to face day to day problems. It should help us distinguish between what is good and what is bad for us. It should make us understand the importance of our culture. Otherwise no amount oOf education will help us. Panchayats, if properly constituted and given proper power, are supposed to provide true education that we have described above. We have to prepare ourselves to follow Gandhian principles and programmes, it requires an awareness which helps both individual and society. If the villagers are good, the village panchayat will be good. If the village Panchayat is good it will make the villagers good, unless both are good we may not be able to achieve the desired goal. Gnadhi once said of democracy: "Democracy is not for the sleepy and the ignorant; it is for the enlightened". This Cleary shows that unless we are enlightened we are not going to make proper use of Panchayati Raj. Therefore it is necessary for us, to prepare ourselves not only to understand Gandhi but even to implement his programmes.

## Way to Swaraj

Swaraj both for the individual and society cannot be achieved without undergoing and adhering to a course of moral regeneration because self rule is not possible without self- control self-control; can only be the result of rigorous discipline in matters social political, economic, moral-religious. A decentralized power structure i.e. Panchayati Raj which is supposed to provide every individual in a village with opportunities leading to all round development; paves way for everyone concerned. Unless pursuit of power is checked by Dharma, power is likely to be misused. According to Gandhi power intoxicates man. Power whether it is of authority or of money can create problems for anyone. Therefore in the interest of the individual and society power should be regulated be dharma.

Politics, as it should not be mere greed for power, it should be combined with morality; as it is an aspect of life, its relationship with other aspects of life should make politics worth pursuing. Then and then only it can fulfill Gandhi's aspirations that politics can be converted into one of the ways of Social service.

If we understand the relationship between any two or among all aspects of life, then the view that Panchayati Raj is the way to achieve Swaraj may be seen in the proper perspective if life. If no aspect of life is to be neglected, then no aspect of life is to be lived, then no aspect of life is to be neglected. If no aspect of life is to be neglected, then, one should also know how it is to be lived. Panchayati Raj can create a sense of sharing responsibility in every individual by participating in its functions. Not only can this, it also teaches how to discharge our duties as administrators, as co-villagers. It can teach the importance of collective action. It can make you work for the benefit of society; one can hope for the self- realizations as the ultimate fruit of real Swaraj.

## REFERENCES

1. Mario D. Zamora (1990). *The Panchayati Tradition: A North India village Council in Transistion 1947-62*, Reliance Publishing House, New Delhi; 1990, pp. 21, 22.
2. Rajpat, R.S. and Meghe D.R (1984). "Decmocracy at the Grassroots an Indian experience", in, Rajput R.S and Meghe D.R. (eds), *Panchayati Raj in India: Democracy at Grass roots,* New Delhi, Deep and publications, 1984, p. 26.
3. Shakantla Sharma (1994)."Panchayati Raj Historical Perspective" in, Shakantla Sherma (ed), *Grassroot Politics and Panchayati Raj,* New Delhi, Deep and Deep Publications. 1994, p. 111.
4. Ramjee Singh (2002). "Panchayati Raj Grossroot of Democracy" in, Anil Duta Mishra, and Mahadev Shivappa Dadage (eds).

*Panchayati Raj,Gandhi Perspective,* New Delhi; Mittal Publications, 2002, pp. 11, 12 .

5. Hedge V.S and Harijin M.B (2002). "Swaraj through Panchayati Raj some consideration", in Anil Dutta Mishra and Mahadev Shivappa Dadage (eds), *Panchayati Raj: Gandhian Perspective,* New Delhi; Mittal publications, pp. 167-174.
6. Ram Rattan (1972). Gandhi's Concept of Political Obligation, New Delhi, The Minarva Associates, 1972, pp. 41, 42.
7. Jhadhav. V.D (1984). "Impediments in the Proper Functioning of the village Panchayats", in Rajput R.S and Meghe D.R. (eds), *Panchayati Raj in India: Democracy at Grass roots,* New Delhi, Deep and publications, 1984, p. 108.
8. Anil Dutta Mishra (1984). "Introduction", in Anil Dutta Mishra Mishra and Mahadev Shivappa Dadage (eds) *Panchayati Raj: Gandhian Perspective,* New Delhi, Mittal Publications, pp. 1-3.

# 25

# Gandhian Approach to Tribal Development

*Rama Rao Dharmana & Rajeswari Gulipilli*

India has the world's second largest concentration of tribal population next only to Africa. As per 2001 census, India has tribal population of 8,43,26,240 (8.20%) which accounts one-fourth of the world tribal population. According to people of India project, Anthropological Survey of India, there are 461 principle tribal groups, if we include the 174 Sub-tribes, then the total become 635. Tribal population in India is distributed in all states except Punjab and Haryana. Large chunk of tribal population is concentrated in the forest areas of Eastern ghats, Western ghats, Central, north-eastern and Himalayan mountains. The tribals are known as forest dwellers (*vanavasis*) or aboriginals (*Adivasis*) and they have developed symbiotic relationship with the forests since ages.

Adivasis are the original inhabitants, who still love relatively in isolation of hills and forests. They are excluded from the mainstream population. Gandhiji said that "Adivasis economic conditions are worst than that of Harijans who have long been victims of neglect on the part of the so called high classes." Even after India's Independence, the tribals are still struggling hard to eke out their livelihood and live in extreme poverty condition. Around 50% of tribal population stands below poverty line. Majority of the tribal population unable to meet their basic prime need of food and encountered with malnutrition, morbidity and mortality.

## Definition of Tribe

Several definitions were given to the concept of 'Tribe' by the scholars of Social Sciences. In anthropological view ' a tribe is a social group with territorial affiliations, endogamous, with no specialization of functions, ruled by tribal officers, hereditary or otherwise united in language or dialect, recognizing social distance from tribes or castes but without any stigma attached in the case of a caste structure, following tribal traditions, beliefs and customs, liberal of naturalization of ideas from alien sources, above all, conscious of a homogeneity of ethnic and territorial organization.

The tribals are different from the other communities. The Scheduled Tribes are considered to be primitive, isolated and backward when compared to the caste communities, these depend on their habitat, cultural customs, beliefs and way of living, dialect and socioeconomic conditions.

During the last two decades, a large number of activists have been viewing the tribals as communities whose livelihood i.e., the natural resources, is threatened by modern development, which is presented by the dominant classes as national interest. Thus while speaking about the tribals one refers to the communities that are waking upto the reality of their ongoing impoverishment and marginalization, to the communities that are demanding their right to be fully human and to be an integral part of the country. They realize that, together with other impoverished communities, they are paying the price of what is called national development, but do not get its benefits. They refuse to continue this situation.

Gandhiji mentioned that "respect the tribals as humans and show sympathy towards them and bring them on par with other communities." The tribals demand that they be recognized as communities with full rights. Decisions are taken about them without consulting them. Projects that displace them are planned, so are policies around their forests, education and development, without their knowledge. The assumption seems to be that they are not capable of taking decisions for themselves and that the dominant sections should tell them what is good for them and their communities.

They refuse to accept this situation. They are convinced that they have a right to be part of the decisions that affect their lives as individuals and as communities. They are not prepared to let the corporate sector or the forest department to have monopoly over the forest that is the centre of their culture of their social, political and economic life. Their land is not to be treated as state property that the government can take over without their being involved in decisions concerning its use.

The other area of their alienation is their culture. Most people seem to think of as the externals of dance and song. This gives the 'mainstream' the justification it needs to view them as communities of happy go lucky persons, who are not capable of developing themselves. To them their culture is a value system, whose externals may change but the core remains sacred. It is essentially a system based on the values of equity, renewability of the natural resources and respect for the whole community, past, present and future. The value system is the core of their identity. Many of them have been using it as a rally rallying point in mobilization against their exploitation.

Such a culture has been basic to their survival. It is built around the natural resources. Through the Centuries they have developed such as conservative culture that has helped them to view their life support system as a community resource inherited from their traditional culture is community based. It has equity and conservation of the resource, i.e. sustainable development and use of the resource as its basic principles.

The geographical distribution of the Indian tribes can be demarcated into those living in the North-eastern states where they constitute the majority and those living in other states where they are in minority. Accordingly their status identity and problems differ in the social, political and economic arenas. Geographical and socio-cultural isolation, subsistence economies ignorance and illiteracy are some of the distinctive features of these autochthonous groups, especially among those living outside the North-eastern states.

The tribes inhabiting the North-eastern states had a distinct historical advantage in view of their majority status and also due to their early exposure to Christianity that has helped in improving their quality of life especially in the fields of education and health.

Importantly they are spared from exploitation from outside non-tribal elements that has been the bane of the tribes living in other parts of the country. Independence along with democracy, decentralization of power, improvements in communications and infrastructure facilities have resulted in greater culture contact and the concomitant problems of exploitation for tribes living in other parts of the country. Large scale land alienation, indebtedness, loss of identity and self-esteem, poverty and ignorance, are some of the major problems afflicting these tribal populations. Their quality of life is not so enviable in any democratic set up to protect them from exploitation and pave way from their all-round development.

## Gandhian Thoughts and Tribal Development

Gandhiji repeatedly emphasized the need of social service to the poor and downtrodden communities including the Adivasis. He condemned the exploitation of poor and weaker sections by the dominant, rich and elite groups of our society. He mentioned that "when foreign invasion started in India, we abondoned the village industries one after another. Work for eradication of untouchability, uplift of Adivasis, equal rights for women, imparting training and bridging the gulf between the poor and rich and so on had never been taken up during colonial period" and emphasized the need of India's independence and fought for it and succeeded with the cooperation of all sections people including Adivasis. He stated the importance of communal unity and people's participation in freedom movement to achieve independence through non-violence.

Gandhi said that the execution of the constructive programme in its entirely means more than Swaraj. Such kind of programme has not initiated so far in the tribal areas even after India's independence, in order to alleviate poverty among the Adivasis. Such kind of programme is the need of the hour to improve the socio-economic conditions of the tribals. Gandhiji principles of 'Ahimsa' and non-violence are more appropriate to achieve harmonious life with integrity and solidarity. Integral effort needed for the progress and peace of whole community. According to Gandhiji "social order must be based on ahimsa, harmony service, duty, swadeshi, self restraint and self-sufficient autonomous local communities that emphasize non-possessiveness, equality, non-exploitation and decentralization of decision making". Gandhiji principle of non-exploitation definitely protect the tribals from outside agencies which pave way for their upliftment. Once the tribal communities were self-sufficient and self managing when the forests were intact and assured with food security. Tribals are very simple people and lead harmonious life within the natural environment of forests in which they live. Outsider's intrusion into the tribal areas creating unrest among them which resulting to revolts added with naxalite activities.

His concept of "Swadeshi" still persists in rural and tribal areas in some extent even today. Most of the environmentalists, social scientists, activists and scientists now realized the importance of Gandhian ideology of indigenous science and technology in order to protect, conserve and regeneration of natural resources and which pave way for the environmental sustainability and sustainable development of mankind. Tribal areas are considered to be potential for indigenous knowledge usage even in the era of industrialization and Globalization. His ideology is more appropriate to attain sustainable development among tribal communities who are marginalized and affected with impoverishment.

Gandhian thoughts of equity and equality were the guiding principles in framing the Indian constitution. The members of the Constituent Assembly were great men with vision and liberal outlook. They strived take care of the interests of all sections of the pluralistic Indian society marked with inequalities. The plight of the tribal populations received due attention while framing the Constitution. A policy of "positive discrimination" is incorporated in Publications, pursuance of the constitutional obligation. Certain Constitutional safeguards were provided to tribals for their upliftment and protection from exploitation.

The Constitution of India provides to all the citizens, social, economic and political justice and equality of status and opportunity. Article 46 specifically provides that the state shall promote with special care the educational and economic interests of the weaker sections of the people and in particular of the scheduled castes and scheduled tribes and shall protect them from social injustice and all forms of exploitation. For achieving these objectives, various safeguards relating to protection and development of weaker sections, particularly scheduled castes and scheduled tribes have been made under the constitution. The constitutional provisions relating to safeguards for protection and development of scheduled tribes are as follows:

> Safeguards relating to protection, which broadly classified into a) Social safeguards: Articles 17, 23, 24 and 25 (2); b) Educational and cultural safeguards: Articles 15(4), 29 and 46; c) Political safeguards: Articles 164. 320 (4), 332, 334, 243D, 243T, 371B, 371C, 371F, 371G, 371H and d) service safeguards: Articles 16(4), 335 and 338.

Safeguards relating to economic development are contained under Articles 275(1) and 339 (2) of the constitution. Although constitution has made elaborate provisions for safeguarding the interest of scheduled Tribes, the enforcement of the same has not been of desired level, provisions made under Articles 371 (A), 371 (B) and 371 (C). Provisions relating to economic development of Scheduled tribes, the article 275 (1) envisages for grants-in-aid for meeting the cost of such schemes of development as may be undertaken by a state with the approval of the government of India for the purpose of promoting the welfare of its Scheduled Tribes or raising the level of administration of the rest of the areas of the State. In pursuance of this Article,.provision of special Central assistance has been made to the States having Scheduled Tribe population. As per the provision, the grant is to be made against such specific schemes as are necessary for the welfare of scheduled tribes and are undertaken with the prior approval of the Union Government. But this is not done. The grants are released without specific schemes.

Article 339(2) goes still further and empowers the union executive issue directive to a State as to the drawing up and execution of schemes specified in the directive to be essential for the welfare of the Scheduled Tribes in the State. Despite poor performance by State Governments the powers wasted in these provisions have not been utilized so far and no directive has been issued. It is a fact that large majority of the tribals not aware of the constitutional provisions and Rights provided to them due to illiteracy, ignorance and innocence. They are exploited by the non-tribals in numerous ways, especially in the area of market.

Gandhiji's ideology 'non-exploitation' definitely gives scope for the upliftment of tribals.

The influence of Gandhiji on Pandit Jawaharlal Nehru was considered as origin of 'Panchsheel' approach of tribal development. As per this approach Nehru evolved five fundamental principles for tribal development, such as 1) People should develop along the lines of their own genius and we should avoid imposing anything on them. We should try to encourage in every way their own traditional arts and culture 2) Tribals rights in land and forests should be respected 3) We should try to train and build up a team of their own people to do the work of administration and development. Some technical personnel from outside will no doubt be needed, especially in the beginning. But we should avoid introducing to many outsiders into tribal territory. 4) We should not over-administer these areas or overwhelm them with a multiplicity of schemes. We should rather work through and not in rivalry to their own social and cultural institutions. 5) We should judge results, not by statistics or the amount of money spent, but by the quality of human characters that is evolved.

Gandhiji's social service approach was well received by Non-Government organizations (NGOs), Activists, Social Workers and Christian Missionaries, which are currently working in the tribal areas for the upliftment of Aboriginals in India. These organizations are trying hard to develop self confidence and capacity building among the tribal community. Christian missionaries are mostly concentrating on 'orphanage' and conversion of tribals into Christianity. A considerable number of Christian institutions are functioning in the tribal areas of Andhra Pradesh. The earlier tribal beneficiaries through missionaries mostly found in north-eastern hill regions of Assam, Meghalaya and Nagaland.

Voluntary social service agencies have done considerable humanitarian work in the tribal areas, but often their idealism and spirit of service have not been matched by their understanding of tribal organization, values and problems. They some times went into the tribal areas with an omnibus solution to the tribal problems for different tribal groups and even for sections of one tribe, were often different. Their motives were probably laudable in their own cultural frame of reference, but not so according to the tribal scheme of values. They failed to realize that their well intentioned 'reforms' may be injurious to the tribes in terms of their socio-cultural integration. Cultural factors of tribals to be taken into consideration in order to create the development programmes with social service approach.

## Adult Franchise

Gandhiji explained that "in order to end the exploitation of the masses, political freedom must include real economic freedom of the starving millions. Some of the points in the concept of Adult Franchise mentioned by Gandhiji in one of the Congress conventions (1931) were more relevant for the upliftment and development of tribal communities. Such points are 1) fundamental rights of the people, 2) adult suffrage, 3) free primary education, 4) a living wage for industrial workers limited hour of labour, healthy conditions of work, protection against the economic consequences of old age, sickness and unemployment, 5) labour to be freed from serfdom or conditions bordering on serfdom, 6) protection of women workers and especially adequate provisions for leave during maternity period, 7) prohibition against employment of children of school going age in factories, 8) Rights of labour to form unions to protect their interests with suitable machinery for settlement of disputes by arbitration, 9) substantial reduction in agricultural rent or revenue paid by the peasantry, and in case of uneconomic holdings exemption from rent for such period as may be necessary, 10) protection of indigenous cloth by exclusion of foreign cloth and foreign yarn from the country, 11) total prohibition by intoxicating drinks and drugs.

Certain views expressed by Gandhiji in regard to development, appeared in the millennium development goals such as 1) eradication of extreme poverty and hunger, 2) achieve universal primary education, 3) promote gender equality and empower women and 4) ensure environmental sustainability with the use of indigenous knowledge systems of local people.

## Tribal Development: Policies and Programmes

Gandhiji urged the upliftment of Adivasis, which was also considered by the Indian Government after Independence, in formulation of policies and programmes for tribal development. Two diametrically opposing views were expressed on the policy for the development of scheduled tribes. On one hand, it was suggested that the tribal identity and heritage should not be disturbed leaving them alone with minimal interventions (policy of segregation) and on the other it is suggested that they should be integrated into the mainstream of the national life (policy of integration / Assimilation). Verrier Elwin was the votary for the former approach and Ghurye for the later. Elwin pleaded for the protection of their cultural identity and heritage from the impact of change so that the tribal communities are not forced into a state of "loss of nerve".

Ultimately, a middle path has been adopted in consonance with the views expressed by Nehru (in Elwin: 1963), who observed that "we cannot allow matters to drift in the tribal areas. In the world of today that is not possible or desirable. At the same time we should avoid over administration in these areas ... it is between these two extreme positions that we have to function." He desired that people should be allowed to develop along with lives of their own genius. Pant (1950's) concurred with the views of Nehru and stated that "the tribes should develop their own culture and make their contribution to the cultural richness of the country. The present policy is to bring the tribals to mainstream and make them participate in the development process while making efforts for preserving their identity and heritage.

A number of commissions and committees were appointed to look into the problems of development in the tribal areas of the country. These have recommended several measures to remove the socio-economic imbalances and also to break down the age old psychological barriers of the tribal communities hindering their progress.

The inputs from the recommendations of these committees have formed the basis for periodical review in formulating and reformulating tribal development policy and programs. For example, the Debar Commission (1961) recommended an integrated approach based on the minimum essential needs such as food, drinking water, education, employment, health and village roads. The Task Force on Development of Tribal areas (1972) suggested that the ecological, occupational and social parameters of the tribal population should be properly assessed for formulation of the policy and its implementation, so that a steady flow of benefits could be assured. The Dube Committee (1978) tried to define a new strategy for tribal development defined at the national level and national efforts required for tackling it. It also suggested an integrated area development approach in consonance with the genius and aspirations of the tribal people.

As a result, strategies and approaches such as multi purpose Tribal Development Blocks, Modified Area Development Approach (MADA), Tribal Development Block, Girijan Development Agencies and Tribal Sub-Plan approach with a focus on Integrated Area Development have been adopted. Since India's Independence, in each five year plan periods certain amount was allocated for tribal development. But the development in tribal areas taking place in slow pace manner due to lack of commitment on the part of implementing authorities, pilferage, exploitation and less participation of tribals in the ongoing development process.

## Gandhiji's Needs and Rights based Approaches

According to Need based approach, the basic needs of the tribals should be fulfilled through welfare programs of government. Needs approach works toward outcome goals, which recognizes needs a valid claims. For that empowerment is not necessary to meet all needs. Accepts charity as the driving motivation for meeting needs, which emphasized Gandhiji. It focuses on manifestations of problems and immediate causes of problems and also focuses on the social context with little emphasis on policy.

Rights based approach to development is a conceptual framework for the process of human development that is normative based on international human rights standards and operationally directed to promoting and protecting human rights. Essentially, a rights based approach integrates the norms, standards and principles of the international human rights system into the plans, policies and processes of development. The norms and standards are those contained in the wealth of international treaties and declarations.

A rights based approach to development describes situations not simply in terms of human needs, or of development requirements but in terms of society's obligations to respond to the inalienable rights of individuals, empowers people to demand justice as right, not a charity, and gives communities a moral basis from which to claim government assistance when needed. As per the Human Rights based approach in the context of Tribal Development, tribal people should be allowed to exercise their rights in accordance with the constitutional provisions and safeguards as well as permit them to exploit the land, forest, water and mineral resources available in and around their habitats.

## Conclusions

Tribes in India still live in isolation and extreme poverty condition. Gandhiji's thought of upliftment of Adivasis is more appropriate strategy for Tribal Development. His social service approach definitely useful for the improvement of socio-economic conditions of tribals. The constructive programme, community involvement and people's participation ideas of Gandhi definitely helpful for participatory development among tribes. His concepts of Adult Franchise and non-exploitation provides opportunities to the tribals in order to elevate their socioeconomic status. His ideology also incorporated in the Indian Constitution in providing certain safeguards and provisions for the upliftment and development of tribal communities. However, still the tribals are encountered with the problems like poverty, illiteracy, food insecurity, indebtedness, land alienation, malnutrition, morbidity and early deaths, due to scanty of resources in their habitats.

The development among the tribal communities taking place in a slow pace manner due to lack of commitment on the part of development agencies and non-participation of the aboriginals in the ongoing development process. So far large majority of tribals are not fulfilled with the basic needs through the government initiated development programmes, moreover, they are denied to enjoy the rights over the land and forest resources of natural environment in which they inhabits. These are also considered to be root causes for the unrest among the tribals and a number of land and forest disputes arises in recent times. In this context Gandhian thought of need and right based approaches are much suitable for the development of tribal communities of our country in specific and other nations in general.

## REFERENCES

1. Address to the 1st annual meeting of the federation of international fellowships held at Sabarmati from January 13 to 15, 1928.

2. Avarkar, AV. The concept of universal religion; philosophy of religion (ed), KMP Verma, Clerical Publishing Co New Delhi, 1982.
3. Biswas SC (ed) *Gandhi, theory and Practice--Social Impact and Contemporary Relevance*; Indian institute of advanced study, Simla, 1969.
4. Gargi, J. *Morality and Religion – A Critical Study*; Anmol Publications, Pvt. Ltd., New Delhi, 2000.
5. Katar Singh: *Rural Development, Principals, Policies and Management*, Sage Publications, New Delhi, 1986.
6. Leighton, Joseph A: *The Individual and the Social Order: An Introduction to Ethics and Social Philosophy*; D Appleton and Company New York 1930

# 26

# Gandhi and Youth

*P. Kishore Kumar & A.B.S.V. Ranga Rao*

Globalisation as a phenomenon has been accepted world over though it has been highly praised and slammed in equal measure. It is applauded for opening world markets to developing world through increased movement of goods and services and enhancing capital flow to these countries. It is criticised for increasing the gap between the rich and the poor nations and also for helping the rich and marginalising the poor country. Developed countries are blamed for exploiting the economy of the developing world and increasing their dependency on them. The critics point out that the political fallout of globalisation developing countries are compelled to toe the political line of the rich nations. It is contended that even the international trade and. development-related agreements are also drawn in a manner that they favour the rich nations. Globalisation is not an inclusive phenomenon. To some extent, it has contributed to the alienation and marginalisation of youth belonging, to communities or ethnic groups that find it difficult to keep pace with rapid technological advancement and consequential economic and social changes. They are not partners in enjoying the full benefits of globalisation.

"Youth" are frequently a crucial point for discussion, as they are considered as highly emotional, high on risk taking behaviour, vulnerable, treated as power for future and "energy to be harnessed" as popularly politicians refer it. Young people, by and large, are known to be rebellious and devoid of sense of accepting the realities, living in their own world. Though the voting age is 18 years in

India, young people are still treated as less than full political subjects. In our country, youth are still perceived as actors in training, raw material, flexible, waiting to be given form through careful socialization by the members of the family, community, society and organized institutions like educational systems, community organizations, religious organizations, political parties and economic/financial institutions.

Young people are the ones intensely affected by globalisation and they are also influencing globalisation process. I am defining youth vis-a-vis globalisation both as an active category of bringing change as well as being influenced by this process of globalisation. I do not consider youth as passive receiver; I see youth involved in social movements for global change for peace, social justice, equity, and creating space for the mankind to live with dignity in diversity. I also see youth facing negative consequences of globalisation in employment, education, gender discrimination particularly for those who are living under vulnerable conditions in low income countries. (Gandhi)

In our country, the situation gets further aggravated because our policies and programmes are not geared for equitable and balanced development, especially, with regard to infrastructural facilities, foreign investment, capital formation and setting up of industrial ventures. Often, rural and tribal communities get a raw deal from planners and policy makers though there are promises galoring for the disaffected communities by our political leaders. As a result, youth groups belonging to these communities do not have equal access to the kind of inputs required to help them make optimum use of the benefits flowing from globalisation or face challenges of the modern world as their counterparts from urban areas.

Mahatma Gandhi, the most impressive contribution to the history of mankind by India in the present century, was a great visionary. His contribution is always evaluated in terms of Indian National Struggle towards independence, which was successfully led by him in the first half of this century. But it will be wrong to consider national movement led by him as a mere political movement. Rather, concepts and means of social transformation and reformation has taken precedence in Gandhi's mind before they are applied as a mass weapon to political ends against the

British. Community is the centre of ideals and concepts in Gandhism. Before going for any political demands, Gandhi always sought to bring about necessary changes in community and get his ideas and methods well accepted by the community. Gandhi tried to bring about major changes in the Indian society. Though he borrowed his concepts and ideas from traditional Indian philosophy, which included Buddhism, Jainism, Hindu and Islamic philosophy, if we go through his life work, we find that Gàndhi opposed and challenged each and every *status quo* in the society. He interpreted the Indian philosophy in his own way and then implemented those concepts, which some times contradicted the contemporary thinking in the society. So Gandhi was a revolutionary; influenced by the utilitarian philosophers like Mill, Benthum, Penn, Thoreau, largely convinced by the ideals of democracy and European institutions but still spirited by the diverse Indian civilization and her history, Gandhi had his unique ways of social transformation. He contributed all new methods and concepts to the wisdom of the world, most of which were never witnessed in the history of mankind. And all these methods and concepts, by and large, were addressed and envisaged to be activated through the youth of this country. Youth was the prime actor in the process of socio-political transformation from the undemocratic, irrational, fragmented, hierarchical structure to the democratic, rational, united structure based on equality which Gandhi envisaged for independent India.

Non-violence and truth is the essence of Gandhian philosophy. Not only in present days but in the days of Gandhi also the relevance of non-violence was largely questioned and condemned by many in the society. Bringing change in the violent exploitative society through non-violent and persuasive methods was never witnessed in the history. Wrong belief has taken possession of us that non-violence is preeminently a weapon for cowardice, but this is not the case. While comparing non-violent resistance with passive resistance is for cowardice or it is a preparation for armed resistance. He conceived it as weapon of courageous and devoted people to the particular cause. And Gandhi knew youth of this country as the most courageous and enthusiastic section of the society and Gandhiji's concepts and ideas attributable to the youth.

Satyagraha is Gandhi's method of non-violent social transformation. Satyagraha is not merely a pious appeal, not merely verbal persuasion, it asks for revolutionary action by the exploited to elicit a revolutionary change in the attitude of exploiter and to bring about the total paralysis and extinction of system of exploitation. Youth has been world over a medium of revolution. Gandhi also used youth as a propagator and activator of his ideas and concepts in the process of transformation. We can find many instances of youth as an integral part of Satyagraha campaign, whether for political or social purpose. Gandhi largely motivated and made use of youth in various movements from Champaran Satyagraha to Quit India movement.

Besides political movements Gandhi called the youth to participate in various works like community development, swadeshi, health and sanitation. Gandhi was very keen about villages and rural civilizations. He accepted many drawbacks which inherited in the community and tried to remove them with the help of participation of youth. He used to say, "I asked you (young man) to go to villages and bury yourself there, not as their masters or benefactors, but as their humble servant. Let them know what to do and how to change their modes of living from your daily conduct and way of life". In his lifetime Gandhi persuaded many youth to live a simple life in Ashramas and work constructively for the community around them. As evident from the above mentioned quotation Gandhi laid emphasis on daily conduct and way of living of his men. He preached for dignity of labour while working for a social cause. He asked especially youth to engage in physical work like working in fields, cleaning the streets, the toilets and doing their own things.

He addressed to youth, "No labour is too mean for one, who wants to earn an honest penny. The only thing is the readiness to use the hands and feet that God has given us... if the sense of shame that wrongly attaches to physical labour could be got rid of, there is enough work to spare for young men and women of average intelligence."[1]

Self-sufficient and non-exploitative society was the main aim of Gandhi's Philosophy. He sought them through non-violent methods. Gandhi saw that ideas of trusteeship is inherent in the idea of non-violent revolution. While seeking the economic self reliance, Gandhi never lost sight of drawbacks which were present in the rural civilization. So in order to remove the defects in society, Gandhi looked at youth of this country as an inevitable agent. To put in his own words he said, "We are inheritors of rural civilization. The vastness of our country, the vastness of population. the situation and the climate of the country have, in my opinion, destined it for a rural civilization. The defects are well known, but not one of them is irremediable. I can, therefore, suggest remedies on the assumption that we must perpetuate the present rural civilization and endeavour to rid it of its acknowledged defects. This can only be done if the youth of country will settle down to village life. And if they will do this they must reconstruct their life." This shows how Gandhi heavily relied upon youth of this country to perpetuate his concept and ideas to bring about desirable changes in society in concurrence with fast changing world's social milieu.

Gandhi was a great communicator. He used to communicate with people in their own common language about their common problems. He could persuade people from backward classes, Harijans, women and young people with the same efficacy. This is illustrated from the large scale participation of younger generation in various movements like Salt Satyagraha and Quit India movement. Gandhi used to communicate through heart and to heart. Gandhi used this to persuade younger generation to participate in various activities of common cause. Because of this many young people worked for Harijans Sangha, Charkha Sangha, Goseva Sangha and other various organizations. Gandhi made them to think over various social evils like Dowry system, prostitution, widow remarriage, which were the part of contemporary society. He came down heavily on dowry system and urged the young' men to discard the system. He was the first leader to propound women's participation in politics and social work, in the history of India. To conclude, the process of social transformation lies beneath the political turbulence, in the beginning of this century. Gandhi encouraged the youth to participate in the process of social transformation by urging the courageous and enthusiastic youth of his country to follow non violent, peaceful and truthful methods.

## Students and Power Politics

Students cannot afford to have party politics. They may hear all parties, as they read all sorts of books, but their business is to assimilate the truth of all and reject the balance. That is the only worthy attitude they can take. Power politics should be unknown to the student world. Immediately they dabble in that class of work, they cease to be students and will, therefore I fait to serve the country in its crisis.[2]

## Students Participation in Politics

The greatest obstacle in the way of the students participating in politics is fear of consequences mostly imaginary. The first lesson, therefore, that students have to learn is to shed fear. Freedom can never be won by those who are afraid of rustication, poverty and even death. The greatest fear for students of Government institutions is rustication. Let them realize that learning without courage is like a waxen statue beautiful to look at but bound to melt at the least touch of a hot substance.[3]

## Non-violence

Ahimsa in education must have an obvious bearing on the mutual relations of the students. Where the whole atmosphere is redolent with the pure fragrance of ahiṃsa, boys and girls studying together will live like brothers and sisters, in freedom and yet in self-imposed restraint; the students will be bound to the teachers in ties of filial love, mutual respect and mutual trust. This pure atmosphere will of itself be a continual object lesson in ahimsa. The students brought up in such an atmosphere will always distinguish themselves by their charity and breadth of view, and special talent for service. Social evils will cease to present any difficulty to them, the very intensity of their love being enough to burn out those evils.

The sun of ahimsa carries all the hosts of darkness such as hatred, anger and malice before itself. Ahimsa in education shines clear and far and can no more be hidden, even as the sun cannot be hidden by any means.[4]

## Strikes

A labour strike is bad enough, a students strike is worse, whether it is justly declared or unjustly. It is worse because of the consequences it entails in the end and because of the status of the parties. Unlike laborers, students are educated and can have no material interest to serve by means of strikes, and unlike employers, heads of educational institutions have no interest in conflict with that of the students. Students moreover are supposed to be embodiments of discipline. A strike of student therefore produces far-reaching consequences and can only be justified in extraordinary circumstances.'

## Character

Taking things as they are, we have to consider what is responsible for students to do and what more we can do in order to serve the country. The answer that has come to me and to many, who are eager to see that the students world gives a good account of itself, is that students have to search within and look after their personal character. The end of all knowledge must be building up of charcter.[5]

I have no doubt that your teachers repeatedly tell you that all this mental and literary training that you receive will be of no avail to you unless it is broad based on truth and love. Truth will make you brave and fearless men, able to give a good account of yourselves, wherever you go. Love will make life bearable for you, because love has a special quality of abundance of live in return[6]

Our is a temple not of book -learning of liberty. Building of character is the task before us. We shall be fit Swaraj to the extent that we are successful among our students. Work with students is the only instrument with which to fashjion Swaraj.[7]

## Bramhacharya

Celibacy is a narrow interpretation of Bramhacharya. The original meaning is the life or the state of a student. That means control of senses, but the whole period of study or equipment of knowledge by means of control of the senses, but the whole period of study or acquirement of knowledge by means of control of the senses came to be regarded as brahmacharya.

Without continence of man or woman is undone. To have no control over the senses is like sailing in a rudderless ship bound to break to pieces on coming in contact with the very first rock. Hence my constant insistence on continence.[8]

Purity of personal life is the one indispensable condition for building a sound education. And my meetings with thousands of students and the correspondence which I continuously have with students in which they pour out their innermost feelings and take me into their confidence show me quite clearly that that is much left to be desired.[9]

Gandhiji warned the students against the baneful poisonous literature from the west that was inundating the country and sought under the respectable and attractive garb of science to seduce them from the path of purity and self-restraint.[10]

Sacred sex is based on commitment, responsibility, celebration and joy (Kumar, S, 2000).

Brahamchraya means control of all the organs of sense. He who attempts to control only one organ, and allows all the others free play is bound to find his effort futile.[11]

To hear suggestive stories with the ears, to see suggestive sights with the eyes, to taste stimulating food with the tongue, to touch exciting things with the hands, and at the same time to expect to control the only remaining organ, is like putting one's hands in the fire and expecting to escape being hurt.[12]

## Sarvatra Bhayavarjana (Fearlessness)

Non-violence requires us to speak our truth and that requires courage; fear causes violence. Gandhi was not afraid of death. We can become fearless by seeing each situation as an opportunity for learning; and developing confidence that we will overcome difficulties.

Fearlessness should connote absence of all kinds of fear - fear of death, fear of bodily injury, fear of hunger, fear of insults, fear of public disapprobation, fear of ghosts and evil spirits, fear of anyone's anger. Freedom from all these and other such fears constitute fearlessness.[13] Fearlessness does not mean arrogance and aggressiveness. That in itself is a sign of fear. Fearlessness presupposes calmness and peace of mind. For that it is necessary to have a living faith in God.[14]

## Self-organisation or Self Rule (Swaraj)

Self-regulation means self-knowledge and taking responsibility. We need to start on a small scale, applying self--

organising first to our selves; then in our families; our village or community.

**The Need to follow Gandhi Today**

The name of Mahatma Gandhi, today, transcends the bounds of race, religion, and nation-states, and has emerged as the Prophetic Voice of the twenty-first century; Gandhi is remembered for his passionate adherence to the practice of Nonviolence and his supreme humanism After the Great Buddha and Jesus, he once again demonstrated that Non-violence could also be an effective instrument of social change.

Gandhi successfully demonstrated to a world, weary with wars and continuing destruction that adherence to Truth and Non-violence is not meant for individual behaviour alone but can be applied in global affairs too. The unshackling of the majestic personality of Black Power, destroying the enslaving apparatus of Apartheid in South Africa, was the culmination of Mohandas Karamchand Gandhi's non-violent fight against racial discrimination that he had launched on the cold wintry night, on the isolated railway platform of Petermaritzburg in faraway South Africa on June 7, 1893.

Had Gandhi been alive today he would have been the least surprised, at the new turn of events in South Africa, for this is only an affirmation of the implicit faith he had in his mission.Gandhi had relentless and unshakable optimism He remained an optimist till his last Gandhi would often say, "My optimism rests on my belief in the infinite possibilities of the individual to develop non-violence".

"Good" said Gandhi, "travels at a snail's pace" On another occasion, he wrote, "Non-violence is a plant of slow growth It grows imperceptibly but surely" The sheer power of these words and the impression they leave on our hearts, derives from the fact that they are the quiet expression of the credo of a man, whose beliefs and actions were in complete accord. Gandhi would have us work ceaselessly for the realisation of what the sociologists call "common human" values, for the triumph of the common human way of life.

Mahatma held up before all mankind the image of what every human being could be; he held up before us all a mirror reflecting the spiritual heights all of us could reach The world in which Gandhi was born, lived, worked and died, was beset by a number of problems, some peculiar to his age others recurrent in every age. He worked for universal human values His life is a sure guide to a meaningful existence; he embodied the Eternal Indian concept of the superior being-of the Mahatma Anyone can become a Mahatma if one makes a vocation of living the meaningful life-putting principle above expediency, duty above pleasure-service above self, as reflected in the life of the Buddha or several of our epic heroes. Gandhi had a dream for India Realizing this dream has become a nightmare Today, we are living in a constant adjustment to changing conditions, which require a different kind of discipline. Now it rests on our shoulders, yours and mine to see that the democratic values in our country remains intact and that social justice, equity, gender equality is achieved for all Rights should follow duties If we are able to achieve this, we shall be helping to reinstate Mahatma Gandhi's dream, I firmly believe it can be done. Gandhi's unfinished task is the biggest challenge before the youth After all it is their future' It is their world; Does not look like it Does it? But it is; Gandhi had great faith in the ultimate success of his mission, because he had infinite faith in the individual's capacity to change He firmly held that the human nature is capable of radical reorientation; all one needs is a will to explore his own true self This explains why Gandhi, all through his life was striving to take humanity on to the path of spiritual and moral growth The progress of civilization, as it has evolved through the ages, is proof that human nature is a developing entity, capable of change for the better.

Remember that the contemporary crisis demands not only a careful analysis of the roots of current social disorder and strategies of transition away from the current violent system but also demands a total rejection of some of our present narrow cherished beliefs, images, creeds , and above all, a drastic reorientation of our life style and restructuring our political, social and economic institutions on radical moral lines.

Can we face the challenge of Gandhi's ideals and ideas? They have not yet been fully utilized. The Revolutionary Gandhi, who was far ahead of his times, has not been fully understood by the younger generation Gandhi's thoughts need to be disseminated amongst our youth. It is the ideas, which have a stupendous role in taking the human society forward; towards the desired pacifist goal. It is said that it is not the conquerors but the long line of men and women of thought, individually powerless, who are ultimately the rulers of the world Mahatma Gandhi certainly belongs to this August Hall of Fame—His Life's message will lead a new humanity on to a new path of Universal love and Harmony. Today, Gandhi is the sign at the World's crossroads. Is it too late to retrace the steps and follow the non-violent path of recovery shown by Mahatma Gandhi? But is there a future for us at all, if we don't- is the moot question.

## REFERENCES

1. *Young India*, 7-11-1929.
2. *Harijan*, Jan, 26, 1941.
3. *Young India*, 12-7-28.
4. *Young India*, 6-9-28.
5. *Young India*, 8-6-27.
6. Gandhi in Ceylon, p. 150.
7. 15-11-20. Gandhi Inaugural addrees.
8. *Harijan*, 3-10-36.
9. *Young India*, 8-9-27.
10. *Young India*, 28-2-29.
11. Bapu's Letters to Mira, p. 257.
12. *Ibid.*
13. *Bapu - Ke Ashirwad. Nov* 26, 1944.
14. *Harijan, Nov.* 3, 1946.

SECTION - 4

GANDHI'S CONCEPT OF SWARAJ AND HOME RULE

# 27

# Hind Swaraj: Its Significance

*G. Vijayam*

Raghavan Iyer writes that Hind Swaraj is "the point of appni [the fulcrum] of Gandhi's moral and political thought." Iyer states that "the essential relevance of Hind Swaraj is perhaps even more poignant today owing to the deepening and spreading sense of alienation, especially among the young, from the beliefs and values of an acquisitive, if affluent, society."

Gandhi wrote *Hind Swaraj* on the return voyage from London to South Africa (November 13 to 22, 1909), aboard the RS Kildonan Castle. He travelled to London to place the Asian struggle in the Transact before the Imperial government and public.

This small book of about 30,000 words was written in Gujarati. He wrote it in 10 days, 40 of the 275 pages being written with left hand. As stated by Gandhi himself "I wrote the entire Hind Swaraj for my dear friend Dr. Pranjivan Mehta. All the argument in the book is reproduced almost as it took place with him" [*CWMG*, 71 238]. Hind swaraj is in the form of a dialogue between the "Reader" and "Editor". The latter was Gandhi and the former were Indian extremists who in 1905 came to prominence in London.

It was published in the *Indian Opinion* in Natal and was soon banned by Government in India because it contained 'matter declared to be seditious'. On that, Gandhi published the English translation from Natal to show the innocuous nature of its contents. The ban was finally lifted on 21 December 1938. James Hunt, an American scholar in Gandhi in London (1978) writes that Gandhi "had his most public encounter with ideology of terrorism," during a dinner to celebrate the Dussehra festival on October 24, 1909, at Nazmuddin's restaurant in Bayswater, London, and that as a consequence of this encounter Gandhi wrote *Hind Swaraj*.

Gandhi and V.D. Savarkar (1883-1966), a spokesman for Indian terrorists – who was transported for life in the conspiracy to murder the British Collector of Nasik, - spoke at this dinner Gandhi in "A Word of Explanation." *Young India*, January 1921, writes, " It [Hind Swaraj] was written in answer to the Indian school of violence. I came in contact with every known Indian anarchist in London. Their bravery impressed me, but I felt that their zeal was misguided." Gandhi's moral and principled argument with Savarkar was that violence was intrinsically evil and opposed to human value. Hence, its ends of purportedly gaining swaraj for India were immoral and abhorrent. Gandhi using polemics as a literary device in Hind Swaraj dialogued with the anarchists on various critical issues relevant to India and he concluded that, "violence was no remedy for India's ills". Instead, Gandhi called for "a gospel of love in place of hate ... replace violence with self-sacrifice ... pit soul force [Satyagraha] against brute force."

Vivek Pinto, in his article, "Icon of Nonviolence", (*the Hindu*, Oct. 1, 2005) stated: "Gandhi wanted an India where terrorism and violence weren't an option to resolve conflicts. Violence created more violence and was a downward spiral into doom, death, and destruction of the social fabric. Gandhi pleaded life-long for non-violence, dialogue, consensus-building, love and understanding of the opponent; religious tolerance; massive employment schemes to give productive employment for India's millions, especially its youth, rebuilding India's villages and creating ecumenical communities of are and concern; promotion of local handicrafts and sills; self-reliance in agriculture and industry, production and need-based basic goods and services; empowering communities to participate and create their own political structures from bottom-up; encouraging self-help projects for human development of all so that swaraj would not result in dependency, making basic education a priority, ensuring that all Indians irrespective of their religion, caste, class, colour, or education were equal and had equality of opportunity in every sphere of life; and that one's moral values would underpin every activity."

Thus Gandhi highlighted the need for ethical dimension in political and economic relations. Gandhi had written the Hind Swaraj in a particular background. The backdrop of struggle for human dignity and equality of all people, irrespective of race was the primary concern in his anti apartheid struggle in South Africa. He also reached the plateau in the South African struggle and it was the time when he was developing closer links with India. He was observing with keen interest the developments in the Congress and the Nationalist Movement. The partition of Bengal, which resulted in the growth of Swadesi movement and the boycott of foreign goods, created an indelible impression on the mind of Gandhi. He was also trying to understand the rift between the moderates and the extremists within the Congress and terrorist movement in some parts of India. In view of his long association with the West. Gandhi saw the strength and weaknesses of the Western Civilisation and compared it with the Indian. In contrast to the growing city life in the West and the breakdown of social relations and the family structure of the West. Gandhi could see the strong point of India, i.e., the village life.

Being a great strategist, who had mastery over the minds of the people, he wanted to infuse courage and confidence among Indians so that they would act in a decisive way by shedding the inferiority complex. In Hind-Swaraj, inadvertently, the lawyer in Gandhi came to the fore. He was arguing the case of the superiority of the East and, in particular of Indian Civilisation over the Western Civilisation. It was a calculated psychological effort on the part of Gandhi to make Indians realize their past glory and infuse in them their present responsibility in coming out of the shackles of the Imperialistic rule of the British. Gandhi was also a philosopher highlighting the oriental wisdom. He was a champion of contentment. He advocated simple living and high thinking which would be in contrast to the Western way of living and thinking.

Even though some of the statements of Gandhi were contextual and had no significance for present day society still some of his observations reflect his profound thinking. He was not afraid to be in the minority of the one and he was a valiant fighter to champion the cause of the superiority of the East over the West. His objection to Western Civilisation was very fundamental and he questioned the values of the Western society. He was in total disagreement with the course of events in the name of civilization. Even though he did not use the word culture in juxta position to civilization, he was in fact equating Indian civilization with good conduct.

Gandhi's main concern was change in the value system of the people. He was for strengthening the bonds of friendship between people by transcending the differences. That is why he was appealing to innate goodness of the people and the necessity to be closer to the nature. Gandhi anticipated the crisis of ecology and environment, as Western Civilization using up the natural resources. Gandhi was advocating simple living and high thinking and rejected anything that was artificial. The objections he raised to the Western civilization are valid even today.

Gandhi was convinced that it would be a doom for India if it forgets its strong points in the centuries of tradition and apes the west.It is important to know that in 1909 when Gandhi wrote this book. Gandhi did not oppose the British, but he was opposed to the British, but he was opposed to the British system. He made a distinction between the person and the system and he was ready to accommodate the British to continue in India, if they gave up their rule and domination over India. He made a fervent appeal to the goodness of human beings and urging them to rise above the narrow and parochial considerations.

In fact, Gandhi was trying to champion a new value system based on equality, justice and fair play Like Rousseau. Gandhi was also a critic of the Western civilization and was appealing to the people, to preserve the tradition of good neighbors. Even though he did not use the tem decentralization in the book, in effect, he was arguing for Gram swaraj or democratic decentralization.

In *Hind Swaraj*, we can see the seeds for his future struggles in India. As we witnessed, later on Gandhi championed the cause of agriculturists in Champaran and Bardoli and Kheda. He started the Civil Disobedience Movement, as well as boycott of foreign cloth. He appealed to doctors, lawyers and educationists to come out of courts, professions and schools and colleges in Hind Swaraj we find the seedings for the Quit India Movement and no tax campaign.

In Hind Swaraj, we can also perceive the positive and

constructive attitude of Gandhi for social service and national reconstruction. He equated nationalism and patriotism with the Hindu-Muslim unity and in resolving the conflicts without the outside intervention.

In this book, the flowering of the personality of Gandhi is quite visible. He was not dogmatic. He expressed his readiness to change his opinions, if need be. He was a seeker of truth. He was not afraid of having a lone furrow. Gandhi was a keeper of human conscience and the sentinel of the Indian nation. He was aware of the fact that he was swimming against the current of Western Civilisation and modernization. But, he was not afraid to be in the minority of one to forewarn others about the impending calamity that would take place in India, if we adopt the Western methods blindly.

What we attained in 1947 was mere political independence for the country. We have to still achieve Swaraj. In this age of globalization and international markets, the warning of Gandhi is like writing on the wall. His wisdom and deep understanding of the processes of the human progress will benefit those who pay attention to him. Some of the ideas expressed by Gandhi in Hind Swaraj act as sign-posts to the future generation to ward off themselves from impending dangers and pitfalls. He appeals to humanity to follow a path to peace and human prosperity.

It is not possible to deal with all significant aspects of Hind Swaraj in this small article. However, some aspects that have relevance to the development work can be mentioned briefly.

### *Gandhi's criticism of the party system and working of Parliamentary democracy*

Gandhi compared Parliament to a sterile woman. He regarded it a costly toy of the nation. The experience of post-Independence and the recent happenings reveal in unmistakable terms the dangers of partisan approach of political parties and the failure of the party system. Gandhi also visualized how the Prime Minister and the party in power is more concerned with safeguarding their power, than the welfare of the people. He regarded that people's awakening is a must for effective functioning of democracy. It is quite clear that partisan approach is the bane of Indian political system.

### Hindu-Muslim Unity

The issue is still very relevant in the Indian context. It is not only eligion, but also caste and sub-caste consciousness that are leading to disastrous consequences and parochialism. Hence, how best we safeguard the secular ramparts we guard is of paramount importance. It is the time to outgrow the narrow considerations of caste and religion and to think in terms of the nation and its unity.

### Ends and Means

For Gandhi ends and means are equally important. Openness of methods, truthfulness and honesty in dealings is a must for achieving the goals.

### The futility of violence

Gandhi was witness to an era of two World Wars and the nuclear holocaust as well as the great exodus of the people due to the partition of India. Peaceful resolution of conflicts through discussion and dialogue and peaceful struggle for social justice is a must for the unity and cohesion in society.

### Satyagraha

The greatest contribution of Gandhi to the modern world was his method of satyagraha. It needs to be explored further in resolving the political, social and economic problems of society.

### Emphasis on Rural Development

Production by the masses rather than mass production that would provide employment to the millions in the rural areas. Without generating employment in the rural areas, the migration of the people to the urban areas in search of livelihood cannot be contained. The growth of urban slums is the result ruination of social and economic aspects of village life.

### Strengthening the Panchayati Raj and Democratic Decentralization

Centralisation and corruption go together Decentralisation is the key to development.Emphasis on ecology and environment and on the renewable resources. The unbridled exploitation of natural resources would cause great harm to ecology and environment. The inter-dependency between man and nature must be recognized and harmony must be maintained.

## Need for a New Value System

A new value system based on equality, fraternity, justice are essential for the onward march of society.

## Conclusion

What Gandhi wrote in *Hind Swaraj* in 1909 reflects the core of his thinking. As a seeker of truth, Gandhi had grown in his thinking and action over the years. His life was his laboratory and he boldly conducted his experiments with truth. He was a great democrat and did not impose his views on others. Gandhi said that my life is my message. Generations to come people will examine Gandhi's thoughts and re-examine their own beliefs and values. When they go in search of their roots, they find that Gandhi was much more relevant to them than they had ever realized.

# 28

# Hind Swaraj: Its Political Aspect

*Ch. Mutyalayya Naidu*

Mahatma Gandhi wrote the book *Hind Swaraj* in 1908 while he was returning from London to India by ship. It was published in book form in Gujarati first and later was translated into English by Gandhiji himself. This was the only book he wrote in English while his autobiography was translated by his Secretary Mahadev Desai from Gujarati into English. The peculiarity is his Secretary mastered Gandhiji's language so much that it looks like it was written by Gandhiji himself. However Gandhiji's writings and speeches constitute a vast mass of volumes about 100 edited by K. Swaminatham but most of them were printed in journals. So he was more an outstanding journalist than the author of a serious work. Yet this small booklet, which runs about 100 pages, has so far been sold about 89,000 copies. It reveals his deep agony against the British rule though it is not so consistent and gave scope for criticism. The reason is he was more an idealist than a pragmatist and so the Bombay Government quickly bamed it. Even G.K. Gokhale his guru was also upset and though that if Gandhiji stayed in India for a year, he would have withdrawn this booklet.

The reason for Gokhale's chiding of Gandhiji was that the former was a moderate while the latter made frontal attack on the British Government, a sort of provocation. So Sophia Wadia also sent copies of this book to leading western thinkers like Prof. Soddy, G.D.H. Cole, John Middleton Murray. Some of them complimented while others said it was a kind of mental agony. In a sense he was nearer to Tilak than Gokhale his guru and moderate. John Middleton Murray said, "The efficacy of non-violence is quickly exhausted when used as a more technique of political pressure, when the question arises. 'Is the non-violence *faute de mieux* really non-violence at all?"

Anyway when Gandhiji wrote this small booklet, the Home Rule wave was going in the country for national independence. When A.O. Hume founded the National Congress, it was only a party. Gandhiji was happy that it was a national organization because it carried the word 'national' before Congress. Actually it was a party, small gathering of 79 delegates, all from upper and middle class under the leadership of Dadabhai Naoroji, the Grand Old Man of India, a Parsi, at Bombay Congress in 1885. Had not he prepared India for the movement, Gandhiji believed, young men could not have spoken about Home Rule. But there are other persons, who also worked behind, including some British officers like Wedderburn who got vexed with the British policies. Gandhiji felt that it was Wedderburn who gave his body, mind and money to the foundation of the Congress. Further, G.K. Gokhale, too, for the sake of the party lived for twenty years in poverty.

But gradually when it wanted representation in the Viceroy's Council or the separation of judiciary from the executive or the enhancement of age for ICS examination from 18 to 21, the Government denied them and so its character was changed from being friend to foe in five years. Thus the Congress brought together Indians from different parts of India and enthused them with the idea of nationalism. In a sense it gave a foretaste of what Home Rule was.

However this change was further influenced by the Government's puerile act of Partition of Bengal by Lord Curzon. This Act gave rise to Congress demand for Swaraj in 1906 at Calcutta along with other objectives Swadeshi and National Education. But what Swaraj was meant was not clear, whether it was complete independence or continuation of British rule. Moderates like Gokhale believed that it was continuation of British rule while extremists felt that the British Government should leave India with bag and baggage. It may be a split in the party but it was due to the Partition of Bengal and further as Curzon wanted to throw a wedge between Hindus and Muslims, the Partition of Bengal brought about a counter blow to the British regime. In this regard Gandhiji opined that better the British should retire from India so that with the army left, India could well govern herself. Gandhiji added, "Rising from sleep, we don't continue in a comatose state, but according to our ability, sooner or later, we are completely restored to our senses."

The main reason is why the British should withdraw was the growing impoverishment in the country. Everybody believed, as R.C.Dutt said, in the Economic History of India that the British were responsible for the economic decline in the country. As Gandhiji said, "They take away our money from year to year. The most important posts are reserved for themselves. We are kept in a state of slavery. They behave insolently towards us and disregard for our feelings." So he too felt dissatisfied with the British Government's policies and he did not like it should continue because the Government was just like a tiger with which Indians cannot associate with. As Gandhiji said, "When a tiger changes his nature, English men will change theirs. This is not possible, and to believe it to be possible as is contrary to human experience."

Hence in case the British Government granted self Government which actually Moderates wanted, Gandhiji still did not agree for it. He said, "We must own our navy, our army and we must have our own splendor and then India's voice ring through the world." It means he was prophetic and saintly. Since India had got a rich civilization and culture and attracted all the world over with her Vedas, Upanishads, Sanskrit language etc, she must have a government of her own based on her culture but in continuation of English arms. He added, "If the education we have received be of any use, if the works of Spencer, Mill and others be of any importance, and if the English Parliament be the Mother of Parliaments, I certainly think that, we should copy the English people and this to such an extent that, just as they don't allow others to obtain a footing in their country, so we don't allow them or others to obtain in ours."

But Gandhiji had no objection if the English stayed in India and become Indianised. He Felt that Indians could accommodate but if they thrust their civilization, there would be retaliation. His worry was, "We are day by day becoming weakened owing to the presence of the English. Our greatness is gone; our people look like terrified men. The English are in the country like a blight which we most remove it by every means." In this respect he compared Indian movement with Italian fight for independence and their leaders like Mazzini and Garibaldi. But the difference is Indians did not have arms like Italians. "English," in Gandhiji's words, "are splendidly armed; this does not frighten me, but is clear that, to it ourselves against them in arms, thousands of Indians must be armed." But at the same time he was against to get armed as this would create violence and the holy land of India would be unholy. So what he wanted was a sense of sacrifice. As he said, "It is a cowardly thought, that of killing others. Whom do you suppose to free by assassination? The millions of India don't desire it. These who are intoxicated by the wretched modern civilization think of those things. Those who will rise to power by murder will certainly not make the nation happy. Those who believe that India has gained Dhingra's act and other similar acts in India make a serious mistake. Dhingra was a patriot but his love was blind. He gave his body in a wrong way; its ultimate result can only be mischievous."

Thus by methods of Satyagraha, soul force ever physical force, passive resistance, the British must be made to quit the country. As Gandhiji states, "Everybody admits that sacrifice of self is infinitely superior to sacrifice of others. Moreover, if this kind of force is used in a cause that is unjust only the person using it suffers. He does not make others suffer for his mistakes. This is the key to the use of soul force."

Thus Gandhiji's ideas of Hind Swaraj were in a process of evolution towards the ultimate goal of complete independence. He started with self government, later demanded outright withdrawal of the British and finally Poorna Swaraj in 1929 at Lahore Congress. So what he experimented in 1921 with his Non-Cooperation was just like beginning of germination of seeds and by 1930 with Salt Satyagraha, his demand became complete and he emerged as an unquestionable leader in the sub-continent. His principle of non-violence is difficult to understand but behind it there was a ferment of nationalism. He said, "What western thinkers often lose sight of is that the fundamental condition of non-violence is love. and pure unselfish love is impossible without unqualified purity of mind and body."

## REFERENCES

1. M.K. Gandhi, *Hind Swaraj or Indian Home Rule*, Navajivan Publishing House, 2005, p.65.
2. p. 24.
3. p. 26.
4. *Ibid.*
5. *Ibid.*
6. pp. 26-27.
7. p. 57.
8. *Ibid.*
9. p. 60.
10. *Ibid.*
11. p. 69.
12. p. 7.

# 29

# Indian Home Rule and Medical Profession

*N. Srinivasa Rao*

I saw book on Indian Home Rule where father of the Nation Mahatma Gandhi felt that whole modern system is like Upas Tree. Its branches represented by parasitical professions including those of law and medicine with immorality the root. He feels that medical men have not occupied a very honorable status and he sometimes think quacks are better than highly qualified doctors. He says as an example "I have indulged in vice and contact disease, a doctor çures me. The odds are that I shall repeat the vice. Had the doctor not intervened, nature would have done its work and I would have acquired mastery over myself and would have been freed from vice and would have become happy". This observation I cannot agree with. For example if an individual due to vices contact syphilis and doctor won't cure nature will not cure and disease progresses fast involving all systems of the body resulting in Tabesdorsalis, Dementia, GPI, Aneurysms of Aorta making him miserable and suffer to die. If doctor cures him and he continue to have his vices it is his weakness and he needs proper counseling to convince him of the consequences so that he will not be tempted to repeat.

Mahatma also expressed that hospitals are institutions for propagating sin for the sake of mistaken care of human body they kill thousands of animals. It is not necessary to takes so many lives for the sake of our bodies. He is right as a philosopher with humanitarian touch but common man wants to be healthy and avoid becoming sick. I agree with Mahatma on humanitarian grounds and philosophically looking at the point. But if Jenner did not experiment on Horses probably smallpox might have saved the world from population explosion. Vaccination is protecting people not only from smallpox but from tetanus, polio, measles, pertussis, typhoid and so many other diseases. Though it is a pity that we have to take few lives to save millions.

He also felt that doctors induce to indulge and the result is that we have become deprived of self control and have become effeminate and to study European Medicine is to deepen our slavery. I am stunned by this statement. Knowledge which ever source its comes from should enlighten the whole world like a lamp lit in the darkness shatters darkness all around and shows a path to progress. Modern Medicine in my view originated from India and Greece. West learnt from us and developed it further. But for the effort and enthusiasm of scientists of yester years Pathology, Anatomy, Microbiology, Medicine and Surgery would not have developed to the present state. It has contributions from all over the world. Now we are achieving stunning results through organ transplantation, Gene Therapy curing incurable diseases increasing the longevity of many.

Mahatma also said that we become doctors so that we may obtain honors and riches.' Though I have to agree to some extent in regard to majority of people there are many who have chosen to be doctors to serve the people and save him from illnesses. There are dedicated people like Dr.Yellapragada Subbarao who dedicated all his life to scientific research and discovered several antibiotics, vitamins, essential enzyme in the body etc., but he neither became rich nor recognized so long he was alive. He was not conferred noble prize just because probably he is an Indian.

Dr. Bernard who was the pioneer in Open Heart Surgery and Cardiac Transplantation or Dr. Best and Banting who discovered Insulin and Dr. Jenner who introduced vaccination known so many others who are known for their work and many more silently working in their laboratories go unrecognized. They never expected to become rich or famous but their work made them famous but not rich.

I do not understand the situation in those days to make

Mahatma come to such conclusion, probably he is not totally wrong, but he is not totally correct also. Coming to present day doctors we must be impartial in analyzing the situation as it stands today. Understand how much strain and trouble each candidate who has no god father has to take to become a doctor. Today very few people are interested in going for Medical Studies Why?

I will not deny the fact that there is corruption among doctors too. I look at it from different angle,. It is the individual who is corrupt. If the individual becomes professor, judge, lawyer, engineer or politician he will get bad name for that profession. It is a pity that man craves for monkey and stoops down to earn it by hook or crook. Remember there are many doctors who are honest and dedicated as the care many professors, judges, lawyers, politicians. But their number is dwindling.

There is a gradual degeneration of morals in the society as a whole and it is reflecting on the medical profession also. World is full of spurious drugs and spurious doctors. There are number of people practicing as doctors without studying in medical colleges. They are acquiring graduate, post-graduate and super specialist degrees which are forged by throwing thousands of rupees. Such centres issuing false degrees are present all over the world. How can anybody expect better results from such people, how can these people follow ethics than are we justified in passing adverse comments on the profession as a whole.

There are spurious and substandard drugs all over the country and govt and concerned people know but there are no efforts to prevent these happening. If such drugs are taken by the patient and not cured he blames the doctor who is helpless and not responsible. Who is bothered about the manufacturers of spurious drugs? Who is controlling the Pharmaceutical Companies who has no standardization of the drugs? Powerful Politicians and rich landlords and influential big shots are hand in glove with Police, ACB, CBI and other investigative agencies also influencing the judiciary at times to get away from the crimes.

If the political corruption can be eradicated in our country, if criminals, ghoondas are prevented from becoming ministers and prime ministers and if honest people are encouraged and protected and if dishonest people in all walks of life are booked and punished by capital punishment then and then only a ay of hope will be seen. Then only our country will prosper and people will have peace and prosperity. I wish people should raise their voices, revolt against existing system, refuse to elect antisocial elements and elect only honest and dedicated people then and then only we march towards progress and prosperity till then people will have to suffer.

I pray God to awaken the slumbering souls of ignorant Indians and to raise the banner of revolt and bring glory to the nation for which Mahatma sacrificed his life patriotism as disappeared. If every child is taught about the struggle for independence and about the lives of Mahatma and others. Who awakened the masses and led a peaceful struggle... to give us independence and create sincere feeling for country among people, to see them committed for the prosperity of the nation, then. Then again I assure the dreams of Mahatma will come true. The division of people by the caste, creed, and religion I erased. If people join lands forgetting them. Cash Creed & Religion and work for progress, prosperty of the country as a whole. If we can eradicate corruption, poverty from the land then again Bapuji's soul will have peace.

Let us work for it.

# 30

# Home Rule: Its Relevance in the 21st Century

*Dr. T. Sobhasri & Dr. G.Sanjeevayya*

"I want sympathy in this battle of rights against might."
– *M.K. Gandhi*

## Introduction

Indian Home Rule (Hind Swaraj) is a dream project of Mahatma Gandhi. He wrote it within a span of 10 days, at the age of 40, and it was published in 1910. Most of the Gandhi's basic ideas and philosophies of life can be found in this beautiful work. This is the only work Gandhi had ever translated into English and hence was particularly useful to English readers. Between November 13th and 22nd, 1909 Gandhi produced his master piece with 275 pages in about 30,000 words. He wrote it on the return Voyage from London to South Africa.

In his opinion, it teaches the gospel of love in place of hatred. It replaces violence with self sacrifice and pit soul force (Satyagraha) against brute force. Therefore, it can be called a "Serman of Sea". Had India adopted the doctrine of love as an integral part of its religion and introduced it in its politics, Home Rule would have descended upon India from heaven. But he was also painfully aware that, "that event is far off as yet".

Gandhi dreamt and aspired for India which never opted for terrorism and violence to resolve its conflicts. It is to show that violence breeds violence, which results in death and destruction of the social structure. Gandhi believed in non-violence and he always laid stress on dialogue, consensus – building, religious tolerance, love and understanding of the opponent. He emphasized on massive employment schemes for the teeming millions in India, especially for the youth. He wanted the Indian villages to become centers of economic development of care and concern. He strived to make basic education a necessity and wanted to ensure all Indians equal opportunity in every sphere of life. He was against to see Swaraj being born because of dependency. Swaraj must ensure all Indians irrespective of their religion, caste, class, colour, or education and provide equal opportunity in every sphere of life. He wished that one's moral values would underpin every activity.

Implementation of ban on nuclear arms, controlling armaments and avoidance of war and violence are considered to be negative yardsticks. Hence peace should not be judged on the basis of the above mentioned elements. It is stupidity to derive satisfaction from the fact that the third world war has not taken place yet. Peace should be established in the world which has the potential to create conditions that are suitable to the development of the human personality in all aspects. Peaceful environment gives individuals an opportunity to lead fuller and richer lives. Development must take place in social, cultural, political and economic aspects. This lays stress on the balance of all aspects but not one dominating the other, which is obviously not conducive for peace to prevail among individuals, states, nations and the world at large. Such balance provides a good relationship between the individual and the social order which would permit and promote socio-economic changes peacefully. These changes should be consistent and must match with the aspirations of the people and the nation as a whole. Two important factors that must present in the individuals and groups are initiativeness and leadership. This type of order reduces any conflict among the individuals, small groups and nations. Even if some conflicts arise they may be resolved speedily by implementing peaceful methods.

This will require a fundamental restructuring of the existing socio-economic order. He draws attention to three major revolutions that we need today (1) revolution against unbridled consumerism (2) revolution against technology beyond human control; and (3) revolution to provide human motivations in our dealings with fellowmen. Gandhi had pointedly and repeatedly referred to these revolutions. Had India and other developing countries heeded his advice, the world community would have taken several steps closer to a peaceful world order.

## Gandhi-Civilization

He was a person, who condemned modern civilization. He felt that if India will discard 'modern civilization, it can only gain by doing so, but he would warn the people against thinking that he was aiming at the Home Rule, and his corporate activity is undoubtedly devoted to the attainment of parliamentary Home Rule in accordance with wishes of the people of India. And he was not aimed at destroying railways or hospitals, rather he would certainly welcome their natural destruction. Neither railways nor hospitals are a test of high and pure civilization, but those are necessary evils. Nor was he aiming at a permanent destruction of law courts, much as he regarded it as a 'consummation devoutly to be wished'. Still less was he trying to destroy all machinery and mills. It requires a higher simplicity and renunciation than the people are today, prepared for civilization seek to increase bodily comforts, and it fails miserably even in doing so.

This civilization is such that one only needs to be patient and it will be self-destroyed. According to the teaching of Mahammed, this would be considered a Satanic civilization. Hinduism calls it the Black Age. He cannot give us an adequate concept of it. Civilization is not an incurable disease, but it should never be forgotten that the English were at one time afflicted by it.

A nation that is desirous of securing Home Rule cannot afford to despise its ancestors. We shall become useless, if we lack respect towards our elders. Only men with mature thoughts are capable of ruling themselves and not the hasty tempered. We who seek justice will have to do justice to others. Great events always produce great results. Nations are not formed in a day, the formation requires ages.

According to Gandhi "Civilization in the real sense of the term, consists not in the multiplication but in the deliberate and voluntary reduction of wants. This alone promotes real happiness and contentment and increases the capacity to service". Civilization is that mode of conduct which points out to man the path of duty. Performance of duty and observance of morality are convertible terms. To observe morality is to attain mastery over our minds and passions. In doing so we come to know about ourselves. The Gujarati equivalent for civilization means "good conduct".

This nation had courts, lawyers and doctors, but they were all within bounds. Everybody knew that these professions were not particularly superior; moreover, these vakils and vaids did not rob people; they were considered people's dependents, not their masters. There were no touts to lure people into them. This evil, too, was noticeable only in and around the capitals. The common lived independently and followed their agricultural occupation. They enjoyed true Home Rule.

## The relevance of Gandhi in the 21st Century

In 1947 what we got was mere political freedom for the country. We should still achieve Home Rule. It is due to the fact that the whole world is caught up in the concept of liberalization, privatization, globalization and development – there seems to be no escaping it. In view of the current economic situation, there is a yawning gap between the Gandhian economics and the current globalization. However, the defence policy and foreign policy though seemingly in contrast to Gandhi's philosophy of non-violence were in agreement with aggressive nationalism of the initial phase of independence, which has the support of Gandhi.

Swadeshi will be the cardinal principle for the people in the world and man will keep the machine under thump and machine will not misbehave in the 21st century. In politics, the cardinal principles will be service to the humanity and Home Rule will replace Ramraj. Therefore, sovereignty of the people is based on pure moral authority. Growing atomic weapons, abject poverty, unemployment and consumerist culture requires Gandhian remedies because other remedies had already proved ineffective. The relevance of Gandhi in the 21st century will be on global level. Therefore, his framework cannot be understood in fragments. (Janardan Panday 1998).

In his opinion, we have used the term "Home Rule" without understanding its real significance. He has endeavoured to explain it as he understood it, and his conscience testifies that his life hence forth is dedicated to its attainment.

## Conclusion

It is Home Rule when we learn to rule ourselves without others' influence. The Home Rule that Gandhi wished to picture is such that, when we once realize it, we endeavor to the end of our life-time to persuade others to do so. For the above achievement, what we need to do is to sacrifice ourselves. If we do our duties, i.e., serve ourselves, we shall be able to serve others. Real Home Rule is self-rule or self-control. The way to it is passive resistance, that is soul force or love force. In order to exert this force, Home Rule in every sense is necessary. Therefore the values and practice of Gandhian ideology should be well understood as there is no alternative to this in the $21^{st}$ century.

## REFERENCES

1. *Encyclopedia of Social Work*, Vol.III, Ministry of Welfare, Government of India, New Delhi, 1987.
2. J.S. Mathur, *Gandhian Perspective on Technology, Peace and Justice,* Gandhi Centre, Visakhapatnam.
3. Janardam Pandey, (ed) *Gandhi and $21^{st}$ Century*, Concept Publishing Company, New Delhi, 1998.
4. M.K. Gandhi, *Hindi Swaraj or Indian Home Rule*, Navajeevan Publishing House, Ahmedabad, 1938.
5. Vivek Pinto, Icon of Non-violence, *The Hindu*, $1^{st}$ October, 2005.

# 31

# Gandhi's Concept of Swaraj and Social Democracy

*Dasarathi Bhuyan*

Mahatma Gandhi is considered to be one of the unrivalled leaders of all ages and all countries. His personality and philosophy have inspired millions of people of the whole world. He was treated as God-incarnate on earth. He was a man of action and discipline. He was the saint among the politicians and the politician among the saints. He depended on the great moral force of the self and liked ethical values more. For his outstanding contributions towards Indian nationalism, independence and value system, Mahatma Gandjhi is considered as the father of Indian nation.

Gandhiji is dead but Gandhism is alive today not only in India but also in the whole world. Gandhiji;s theories and principles like non-violence, Satyagraha, end-means relationship, Sarvodaya, education, social reforms, nationalism and internationalism and Swaraj are quite relevant to the modern man and the modern society. Gandhiji never advocated Gandhism as an ism or ideology; he practiced it as a way of life. Gandhism has been a great ideology of modern age. It can guide us to solve the political and social problems of our modern society on the basis of the traditional principles of our culture and social life which Gandhism represents. It follows a spiritual and moral view of social life. Gandhism can indeed provide answer to many of our day-to-day problems. It has been a great ideology of modern age. It presents the best arguments against the evils of inequality, untoachability, narrow nationalism and aggressive state. It incorporates the modern idea of civil society. It solidly supports a true philosophy of social welfarism.

Gandhi is dead but Gandhiism is alive, Mahatma Gandhi as a temporal person is dead now. But his philosophy is eternally alive even today. His idea of Swaraj and social democracy is of lasting importance. Gandhi's concept of non-violence and Sarvodaya are more relevant today, because, everywhere there is violence, disturbance, militancy, conflict and socio-political turmoil. Peaceful, constitutional and non-violent approaches are required more today for solving confrontational and quarrelsome issues. He was against untouchability and racial discrimination, because he had basic faith in human beings. He believed in natural equality among men. The world public opinion today is in favour of that. He was a true nationalist and also a true internationalist. He did not see any conflict between nationalism and internationalism. The modern world is more interested to reconcile nationalism with internationalism. Peace, not war is the crying need of the day. Premier international bodies like UNO and Non-Alignment Movement are working hard in this direction.

Gandhi strongly favoured decentralization of power and authority with autonomy to village republics. Nowadays the villages get utmost priority in Government plans and programmes. All modern states are more or less welfare states because the need of the day is welfarism. This is nothing but the other name of Gandhian Sarvodaya in one form or the other. His concept of Swaraj and democracy quite agree with the modern liberal ideas which are much in demand today. His concept of Swadeshi is gaining ground due to national consciousness, national self-reliance and national identity. He was strongly against dowry, the implication of which is felt more today. His advocacy of prohibition, disapproval of child marriage is also widely accepted in modern societies. In view of all these facts and figures Gandhism today is not only relevant to India but also to the whole world and humanity.

The UN General Assembly unanimously adopted a resolution on June 15, 2007 to declare October 2, the birthday of Mahatma Gandhi, as the International Day of Non-Violence in recognition of his role in promoting the message of 'peace through non-violence' around the world. The UN resolution to honour 'the apostle of humanity and peace' was unanimously sponsored by all the major countries of the world and the subcontinent of India, including Great Britain against whom Gandhi successfully led an agitation through non-violent Satyagraha for India's Independence. The resolution "stresses the need for non-violence, tolerance, full respect for human rights, fundamental freedom for all, democracy, development, mutual understanding and respect for diversity as reinforcement for peace and growth of mankind". The resolution is a reflection of the international community's collective yearning for peace and the recognition of the relevance of Gandhi's ideals and methods in today's world which is confronted with violence, terrorism, intolerance, discrimination and exclusiveness.

Referring to Gandhi's public life and activities Vincent Sheean, one of the noted biographers of Gandhi, wrote in 1954,

> "He had the unparalleled misfortune to become a public saint in the twentieth century, canonized alive in the glare of flashlights and the relentless gaze of cameras. Only the most resolute attention to his immediate task, toilsome and endless, enabled him to ignore the world's fantastic and keep going. ..... Yet the myth arose and was a true myth, changing the behaviour of whole population, altering the course of history and the fate of empire. There is no other case known to us in which every fact is known and yet their sum amounts to an unknown. We cannot satisfactorily explain the phenomenon of Gandhi."

Gandhi was indeed a phenonmena and those who lived and worked in tune with him can probably claim an understanding to the Gandhian ideas.

## Issues involved

By the time Gandhi's attention was focused on *Swaraj*, it was not a problem in a vacuum. Although British imperialism was political order of the day in the India of the early twentieth century, the political ideal desired and striven for the *swaraj*. Bal Gangadhar Tilak the leading extremist leader of the Indian National Congress had already raised *Swaraj* to the high pedestal of the nation's birthright by proclaiming aloud:" *Swaraj* is my birth right and I must have it".

If *Swaraj* is of such a high political value, then one must be clear about its meaning, both for the individual and the nation as a whole. The second important issue involved in the demand for Swaraj was: "Is Swaraj compatible with imperialism"? Gandhi answered these questions in the unique Gandhian way.

## Meaning of Swaraj

Gandhi did not consider Swaraj to be a mere political concept. For him it had a wider connotation. He did not believe in double standards of morality-one to be practised in day-to-day life and another for the governance of the country. He said , "I have therefore endeavored to show both in word and deed, that political self-government-that is self government for a large number of men and women-is no better than individual self-government, and therefore, it is to be attained by precisely the same means that are required for individual self-government self-rule. His approach integrated Swaraj at three levels, i.e., at the level of the individual, the State and the community. At the level of the individual, Swaraj to him means-controlling one self or Swaraj of the self. At the level of the state it meant national independence and at the level of Community, his dream was to establish Gram Swaraj and social democracy.

## Swaraj for Self

Like Salter's ethical Religion another book which deeply influenced Gandhi was Ruskin's Unto this Last. Gandhi had translated it into Gujrati as 'Sarvodaya'. He also published its paraphrase in English. In his concluding remarks in that paraphrase Gandhi defines his concept of Swaraj at the level of the individual. He observes "Swaraj really means self-control. Only he is capable of self control who observes the rules of morality, does not cheat or give up truth, and does his duty to his parents, wife and children, savants and neighbours. Such a man is in enjoyment of Swaraj, no matter where he lives. A state enjoys Swaraj if it can boast of a large number of such good to citizens" When a large number of such good citizens' constitute the population of a state the national character of that state is elevated. Gandhi held weakness in our national character to be the main cause of our slavery.

## Swaraj for Nation

To Gandhi imperialism is immoral. In Gandhi's view an imperialist ruling system cannot be regarded as a State proper, because imperialism is immoral and therefore an evil. No nation should subjugate another. From this point of view imperialism signifies greed of a nation to which some other nations become prey.

## Home Rule

Gandhi's concept of 'Hind Swaraj' or Home Rule was distinguished from 'Purna Swaraj' or 'complete Independence', adopted later in the Lahore Congress resolution of 1929. It is important to keep in mind the foregoing development in the national political scenario which formed the background of Gandhi's treatment of the national goal of "Hind Swaraj" or Home Rule" in his very original and pregnant booklet'-"Hind Swaraj' the chapter of which Gandhi wrote in 1908 during his return voyage from London to South Africa.

## Social Democracy and Swaraj

In respect of social democracy, it may be said that like J.S.Mill Gandhi was a reluctant democrat. This was for two reasons, the similarity of which one finds in the works of J.S.Mill was suspicious of the 'tyranny of the majority and therefore made a strong plea for allowing freedom of thought, freedom of speech and expression, and freedom of conduct for every individual citizen in a democracy and also proportional representation for the minorities in all representative bodies. Secondly, Mill advocated decentralization of power. Likewise Gandhi boldly expressed his opinion that man-made law even though passed and adopted by a majority in a 'representative legislature' should not be binding if they are considered unjust. There were many examples argued Gandhi, where acts of majority were found to be wrong and those of minority to be right. These laws can be repealed or rectified by the action of one or a group of passive resisters. Therefore, the majority must listen to the minority views, tolerate the minorities and accommodate their view in the law-making.

## Gram Swaraj

Gandhi was opposed to all forms of centralization, whether of political, economic or social power. His concept of true Swaraj, as Gandhi consistently, maintained till his death meant 'self rule' or self-government by the people. Gandhi used to say that:"India's soul lives in the villages', and therefore, the ideal basic unit of a democratic government was the Indian village where people lived as a face-to-face community.

## Conclusion

To Gandhi Swaraj is the rule of justice and is not to be monopolized by any group, section or community whatsoever. He also pleaded for personal and civil freedom and maintaining the diginity of the individual. To him, frredom of speech and opinion was of high importance for realization of the true democracy. Till he breathed his last, he carried this sincere conviction with him that "Government over self is the true Swaraj, it is synonymous with *Mokshya* or salvation.

# 32

# Revisiting Gandhi on Swaraj

*K. Bhima Kumar*

The concept of Swaraj was politically meaningful and socially rejuvenating. The word Swaraj derived from "Swa" means self and "raj" means rule. That means "Self-governance" or "home-rule". Swaraj was a unique experiment that stood not only as a philosophical concept but a concept that had magical over the masses in the beginning of the twentieth century. Gandhi was not the first one to introduce the term in the Indian political scene of freedom struggle. It was first used by Dadabhai Naoroji and later popularized by Tilak.

The term 'Swaraj' appeared in Gandhi's writings for the first time on November 3, 1905. Gandhi gave serious thought to the question of Swaraj in 1903, during his return voyage from London to South Africa. The concept of Swaraj for the first time was expressed by Gandhi in his Hind Swaraj. Gandhi was emphatic in his book *Hind Swaraj* (1909) that, Swaraj was "much more than simply wanting (systems of) English rule without the Englishmen, the tiger's nature but not the tiger". Swaraj for Gandhi had both a negative and a positive implication. Negatively speaking Swaraj meant freedom from alien rule and its influence on civilization. Positively Swaraj meant freedom for the whole people, the peasants, the workers, and the women, everyone included. Gandhi's call for Swaraj represents a genuine attempt to regain control of the 'Self' – our Self-respect, Self-responsibility, and capacities for Self-realization from institutions of dehumanization. Gandhi states that, "It is Swaraj when we learn to rule ourselves". The real goal of the freedom struggle was not only to secure political *azadi* (independence) from Britain, but rather to gain true Swaraj (liberation and self-rule). This paper aim at finding out the philosophical basis of the Gandhian concept of Swaraj and tries to highlight the novel features of the Gandhian theory of Swaraj. The paper does not aims at giving a detailed account of all the features of the Gandhian account of Swaraj but tries to reanalyze the constitutive concepts like swadeshi, khadi, trusteeship etc to establish the above mentioned aim.

## Nationalist View on Swaraj

The nationalist movements were trying to identify and highlight the distinctive features of the entire country to justify their claims for one nation. The concept of Swaraj provided the nationalist with a clearly defined socio-politico-economic vocabulary under this banner. The prudent nationalist leaders consciously preferred words like 'Swaraj' and 'Swadeshi' in a country where people were not united by a common bond of religion, language and culture but by the common historical memories of oppression. The emotionally loaded words like 'Swaraj' and 'Swadeshi' were very close to Indian psyche. Swaraj was a great leveller that could actually inspire the common people of a vast country who were not bound by the common ties of language, religion and culture.

Since the educated classes of India were deeply influenced by the western models of Democracy and Parliamentary government of the British model, the moderative wing of the nationalist movement demanded an autonomous status for India within the British Raj. They thought that Swaraj could be achieved through peaceful means articulated in the form of 'petition, prayer and protests'. Even one of the most militant moderate like Surendranath Banerjee preferred constitutional means to secure political rights for the Indians within the constitutional framework of the British India.

The extremists on the contrary did not want to care about the means that were to be adopted for the achievement of the desired goal; they were determined to free India from alien control at any cost. Tilak played a major role in popularizing the concept of Swaraj. Tilak interpreted 'Swaraj" with an agitation against alien rule, an agitation which he actively pursued in his writings and speeches in Marathi. This ultimately culminated in the active participation in the boycott and the Swadeshi movement that took place at the beginning of the twentieth century, expressed repeatedly in his famous slogan, 'Swaraj is my birth right and I will have it'. In spite of the difference among the nationalist leaders regarding the means to be adopted in achieving this goal they realized that the dream of an independent nation is futile without the freedom from an alien rule.

For Gandhi Swaraj was never conceptualized in it's narrow meaning of political independence, it was a holistic concept for him which included social, economic and moral dimensions apart from the political one. As he clearly declared,

> "Let there be no mistake about my conception of Swaraj. It is complete independence of alien control and complete economic independence. So at one end you have political independence, at the other the economic. It has two other ends. One of them is moral and social; the corresponding end is Dharma, i.e., religion in the highest sense of the term .... Let us call this the square of Swaraj, which will be out of shape if any of its angles is untrue."[1]

Gandhi's concept of Swaraj is with four dimensions. They are:

1) Political
2) Social
3) Economic
4) Moral facets.

## Political Understanding of Gandhian Swaraj

For Gandhi, the political aspect of Swaraj is mainly concerned with freedom from British Colonial domination and the transfer of political hegemony to Indians. But on the other hand Gandhi believed that, mere political Independence from the British may not solve the problem. He insisted that democratization in the manner of possession and the exercise of governmental authority "for the people" should be done, so that people would constitute the sovereign power. For Gandhi Swaraj meant "perfect democracy" wherein there is no place for any discrimination, based on possession, color, race, creed etc.

## Social Understanding of Gandhian Swaraj

Socially Gandhi's Swaraj believes in the existence where all social distinctions fade away. He said that, every community would be equal with every other under the constitution of Swaraj. This makes us to understand that, Gandhi had given equal importance to all sections of Society.

## Economic understanding of Gandhian Swaraj

Gandhi has given lot of significance to the economic factor and he believed that the economic aspect must precede the political one, for political independence can never guarantee improvement of the economic condition of the general masses. He realized that political independence without economic self sufficiency is meaningless. The reason is that British Colonialism had completely ruined the village economy of our country and as a result the entire rural population was without work. He realized that actual India was found in the villages and for any kind of constructive change one should focus on the improvement of the living conditions of the village population. The minimum requirement of any population is the need for food and shelter that can be achieved through availability of work for each and every individual [2]. Freedom from alien rule can hardly guarantee the satisfaction of the basic requirements without which Swaraj is a vacuous concept. In 1924 Gandhi writes,

> "Swaraj for me means freedom for the meanest of our countrymen. I am not interested in freeing India merely from English Yoke. I am bent upon freeing India from any yoke whatsoever. I have no desire to exchange 'king log for king stork"[3]

In 1925 he reiterates the same view. He writes,

> "I however feel that fundamentally the disease is the same in Europe as it is in India, in spite of the fact that in the former country the people enjoy political self government. No mere transference of political power will satisfy my ambition, even though I hold such transference to be a vital necessity of Indian national life. Asian and African races are exploited for their political benefit, and they on their part are being exploited by the ruling class or caste under the sacred name of democracy. At the root therefore the disease appears to be the same in India" [4]

Gandhi thus argued,

> "If we want to give these people a sense of freedom we shall have to provide them with work which they can easily do in their desolate homes. This can only be done by the spinning wheel. And when they become self reliant and are able to support themselves, we are in a position to talk to them about freedom, about (the) Congress (party) etc. Those therefore who bring them work and means of getting a crust of bread will be their deliverers and also be the people who will make them hunger for liberty. [5]

Gandhi's opinion on the economic front is really commendable. In order to be politically stronger a country needs to be economically well equipped and self sufficient. He thus declares:

> "The Swaraj of my dream is the poor man's Swaraj. The necessaries of life should be enjoyed by you in common with those enjoyed by the princes and the moneyed men.... You ought to get all the ordinary amenities of life that a rich man enjoys. I have not the slightest doubt that Swaraj is not the poorna Swaraj until these amenities are guaranteed to you under it"[6]

In the Gandhian context theory and practice are inseparable. Gandhi connected his view of Swaraj with his principle of Swadeshi

## Moral Understanding of Gandhian Swaraj

Self-restraint and self-rule remained significant features of Gandhi's moral dimension of Swaraj. He also laid stress on performance of duty. To Gandhi performance of duty and observance of morality were two important terms. In the words of Wilfred Wellock, the basis of Gandhian Swaraj is the small community such as the village and the small market town. In such society politics are local and vital since they have to do with the organization of local economic life. In that circumstances there can be real political, economic freedom and full personal responsibility.

## Swadeshi

According to Gandhi Swadeshi means 'Unity'. The word Swadeshi is derived from 'Swa' which means one's own and 'desh' means the total cultural and natural environment of which one is an inseparable part. The spirit of Swadeshi in guiding man's economic decisions induces him to support the local farmers, to prefer the local products. It was Gandhi's firm conviction that the breach of the sacred law of Swadeshi caused unemployment, poverty that resulted in the general degradation of the economic life of India. In an address at a missionary conference held in Madras Gandhi Said, "Much of the deep poverty of (the) masses is due to the ruinous departure from Swadeshi in the economic and the industrial life. If not an article of commerce had been brought from outside India, she should be today a land flowing with milk and honey".

One might argue that the above mentioned attitude is inconsistent with Gandhi's principle of non-violence, with which Gandhi has never compromised throughout his life. Swadeshi apparently expresses an attitude of jingoism. But it would be a misunderstanding to think that the principle of Swadeshi encourages unhealthy competition and a bias towards indigenous products. Actually the principle of Swadeshi was a conscious step taken by Gandhi to revive the dying rural economy of the British India. Swadeshi certainly opposes the intervention of foreign capital, technical know-how and entrepreneurship. This principle actually encourages the best possible use of the local raw material, manpower to promote occupational equilibrium. Producers on their part must have a co-operative attitude towards the poor customers. The co-operation between the consumers and the producers will lead to a downward shift of the cost curve making the essential commodities available to each and every customer.

## Swadeshi as expressed through the Principle of Khadi

In the economic sphere the principle of Swadeshi was actually expressed through the principle of Khadi. The philosophy of Khadi played a significant role in Gandhi's plan of economic regeneration of the poverty ridden village India.

Gandhi's plan was that every family in India's half a million villages should take part in the khadi movement through spinning or weaving. Most of the villagers were out of work throughout the year and by means of the actual implementation of the khadi movement. Gandhi succeeded in developing the sense of self respect and the feeling of worth and dignity among millions of Indians. Khadi was an effective instrument with both political and economic underpinnings. Gandhi confidently argued that the wheel can become universal and can replace arms provided if the millions of

Indians cooperate in spinning the Charka for the sake of their economic liberation. The resulting effect will give them an invincible power to achieve political liberation.[7]

Gandhi writes in this context, "Khadi must be taken with all its implications. It means a wholesale Swadeshi mentality, a determination to find all the necessaries of life in India and that too through the labor and intellect of the villagers. In other words a reversal of the existing process, that is to say that, instead of half a dozen cities of India and Great Britain living on the exploitation and the ruin of the 7,00,000 villages of India, the latter will be largely self contained, and will voluntarily serve the cities of India and even the outside world in so far as it benefits both the parties.[8]

The question that arises in this context is that what is the special feature/features about Charaka that makes it so special? He could have proposed some alternative programme related to handwork or the indigenous crafts related to the different cultures of India. Buddhadeva Bhattacharya in his book *Evolution of the political philosophy of Gandhi* has pointed out the reasons that might have played an important role for preferring the charaka. The reasons pointed out by Buddhadeve Bhattacharya are the following:

1) The spinning wheel actually supplied occupation to the millions of unemployed underutilized youths of India.
2) It was cheap, easily available and almost known to everyone.
3) Gandhi must have realized that the philosophy of khadi can be effectively used for generating awe-feeling throughout India irrespective of the religious beliefs and other class and caste distinctions.
4) Khadi movement had the potentiality to prevent the drain of wealth that is used for purchasing the foreign cloth.[9]

Khadi actually stood for a particular philosophy that aimed at reversing the existing order. The philosophy of Khadi symbolized a 'new system' that stood as an alternative culture to the over – centralized factory civilization. As Gandhi writes in this context, "The science of khadi requires decentralization of production and consumption"[10]

Whether Khadi was a valid proposal for the economic development of India in the days when Gandhi launched this programme or whether it bears any relevance today in the economic growth of modern India is a separate issue altogether.[11] At least one must appreciate that his experiments with Truth ware actually applied at the time when India was going through a difficult phase. Gandhi was not simply a dreamer but he could show the world that he actually meant what he said by applying his economic programmes of self sufficiency into practice with effective results. Khadi was an extremely innovative non-violent method which could elevate the masses to a sense of dignity and could empower the toiling masses to stand up against any abuse of power by the authority.

***Trusteeship***

As a part of the owner of property, Gandhi proposed the theory of Trusteeship, and an economic extension of his philosophical concept of man as a trusty of all his powers, capacities, energy and time. This theory was propounded in order to avoid evils and combine the advantages of both capitalism and communalism and to socialize property without nationalizing it. Capitalism encourages maximization of wants and perpetuates exploitation. Communism though free from these evils insists on a kind of uniformity and moreover it is not hesitant to achieve its goal through the path of violence. In contrast to communism Gandhi in his endeavor to bring a stage of economic equality proposed the theory of Trusteeship, another innovative procedure where the rich men are expected to possess their wealth for social benefit and social purpose. Gandhi in this context argued that since human beings are products of nature and they owe a lot to their social environment, all their properties and talents must be sued by the society for public welfare just as nature is a collective human heritage. According to the same logic any product of human labor is a product of social cooperation and naturally no individual can have an exclusive claim over it.

It is interesting to note that Gandhi was sometimes unrealistically optimistic regarding the essential moral goodness of human nature, who would ultimately realize 'the truth'. The use of violence according to Gandhi actually denies the possibility of the different fragmented vision of 'truth'. Trusteeship was thus a unique proposal conceptualized by Gandhi to minimize the inequalities prevalent in the society through a non-violent method.

## The Satisfaction for the Basic Necessities

In the Gandhian theory of Swaraj the economic aspect is most fundamental because unless and until the basic necessities are available to the common masses the concept of non-violence, non-cooperation, civil disobedience and many other similar concepts would appear alien to them. The concepts of individual freedom, social freedom, spiritual emancipation can sound reasonable after one is equipped with the basic necessities of life and are relatively free, if not completely free from the evils of exploitation. According to Gandhi there are three criteria of judging whether a community is free from the evils of exploitation. They are as follows:

1) The availability of the basic necessities of life ( food, clothing and shelter)
2) The ability to enjoy the fruits of one's labour.
3) The opportunity for the physical and the spiritual development of an individual.

The community must ensure that each and every individual gets a job so that one can lead a dignified life. Industrialization must be planned in accordance with the supply of labor power. According to Gandhi we should not follow the west blindly as far industrialization is concerned since in the underdeveloped countries the basic ratios between the capital at hand and the existing supply of labor are far more unfavorable than they are in the industrially developed countries. The economists are of opinion that the poor countries must evolve methods of production suited to their resource endowments. Again the rate of population growth must also be considered before introducing large scale industry. Gandhi would allow industry in his scheme provided it does not act as an obstacle to his ultimate goals. In his framework the use of machinery is constrained by certain principles. They are:

1) The introduction of machines should not create more unemployment
2) It should not destroy village crafts.
3) It should not be used as a weapon for exploitation and perpetuate economic inequality.

Gandhi consistently insisted that industries should be supporting the decentralized local production, and large scale industries would be allowed only in case of vital necessities. Production will be for use and not for profit according to Gandhi, So that the highest priority would be on the availability of maximum number of jobs for the local people. Gandhi was convinced that economic self sufficiency would enable the toiling masses to develop a sense of dignity and self respect that would ultimately inspire them to participate in the political activities. As far as the political aspect of Swaraj is concerned, Gandhi was again innovative in his approach.

Unlike the pre-Gandhian nationalists who understood 'freedom' in a negative way, as an absence of the colonial rule, Gandhi used 'freedom' as a weapon to acquire 'freedom'. Gandhi showed his creativity in interpreting the concept of 'right'. His articulation of 'Satyagraha' was probably one of the most novel conceptualization regarding the method to be used in securing rights and freedom. As he writes in this context,

> "I contemplate a mental and therefore a moral opposition to the immoralities. I seek entirely to blunt the edge of the tyrant's sword, not by putting up against it a sharper edged weapon, but by disappointing his expectation that I would be offering physical resistance. The resistance of the soul that I should offer instead would elude him. It would at first dazzle him and at last compel recognition from him, which recognition would not humiliate him but would uplift him."[12]

Satyagraha was not mere passive resistance; on the contrary it denoted intense activity involving large masses of people. Gandhi clearly articulates that "Satyagraha differs from passive resistance as the North pole from the South. The latter has been conceived as a weapon of the weak and does not exclude the use of physical force or violence for the purpose of gaining one's end, whereas the former (Satyagraha) has been conceived as a weapon of the strongest and excludes the use of violence in any shape or form."[13]

In South Africa, Gandhi realized that in an imperial context rights directly serve the interests of the ruling power. The fact that rights and freedom are tied up together largely depends on the context in which they are politically designed. Again those rights are bestowed upon everyone, once the nation is politically free can hardly be realistic in a hierarchical and divisive Indian context. This observation probably played an important role in reinterpreting the concept of 'right' in the form of Satyagraha.

Gandhi like many other thinkers related rights with Duties. In his framework 'rights' are meaningless if they are not organically connected with 'duties'. 'Dharma' is an instinctive code of conduct which Mahatma called 'soul force'. Thus he maintains,

> "Dharma does not mean any particular creed or dogma. Nor does it mean reading or learning by rote books known as Shastras (traditional sculptures) or believing all that they say. Dharma is the quality of the soul and is present, visibly, or invisibly, in every human being. Through it we know our duty in human life and our true relation with other souls. It is evident that we cannot do so till we have known the self in us. Hence Dharma is the means by which we can know ourselves" [14]

Thus truth seeking and non-violence constitutes the basis of an immutable soul force, an essential component of Satyagraha. [15] Satyagraha endowed with highest moral values was a weapon to fight all forms of injustice with the canon of non-violence. Gandhi was right in realizing the limits of rational discussion and also the dangers of violence and thus explored new forms of political praxis that broke through the narrow straight jacket of reason-violence dichotomy. Satyagraha actually highlighted the value of moral persuasion. It aimed at building deeper emotional bonds with a firmer foundation so that future conflicts can be minimized. Although Satyagraha was indeed a novel way of resolving conflicts one cannot ignore the fact that it overlooks the stark reality that tells us that a good number of conflicts can never be sorted out in spite of sincere efforts simply because societies have different views regarding what constitutes,

1) a moral gesture
2) what is right in a particular situation?
3) what is ultimately good for a society or for an individual?

This possibility follows from the fundamental premise of Gandhian Thought that we as limited beings possess a partial vision of Truth and because of our ontological status we are inherently incapable of knowing the whole truth. Thus the possibility of disagreements cannot be ruled out and there is no reason to think that they can be resolved by the method of moral persuasion. However the uniqueness of his proposal has to be appreciated.

We can see how the economic, political, religious aspects and the final stage of self rule are intertwined together in Gandhian Scheme. So much so that it becomes difficult to compartmentalize them. Swaraj is thus a complex concept necessarily involving other concepts and if any of them are improper the square of Swaraj will be out of shape according to Gandhi. As far as economic and political dimensions are concerned no one would disagree with Gandhi that they were indispensable for attaining Swaraj.

Thus in the present scenario an understanding of the Gandhian principles mentioned above plays a significant role. In our day to day life we may face many problems. In this context Gandhi's ideas may not provide a direct answer but definitely they indicate a direction to solve the problems. Hence Gandhi's preaching's were most noble and good for mankind. Today people all over the world agree and admire many of his thoughts.

## NOTES

1. *The Harijan*, 2.1.37.p.374
2. Vivekananda also emphasized on this aspect.
3. *Young India*, 12.6.24.p.195
4. *Young India*, 3.9.25., p.304.
5. *Arne Naess*, p.176.
6. *Young India*, 26.3.31. pp. 78-79.
7. *Harijan*, 06.04.40.
8. M.K. Gandhi, Constructive Programme, p. 111.
9. Buddhadeva Bhattacharyya, *Evolution of the political philosophy of Gandhi*, pp. 278-279.
10. *Harijan*, 2.11.35. p. 300 + BDG p. 279.
11. The relevance of Khadi has not been dealt in this paper.
12. *Young India*, 8.10.25. p. 346.
13. *Young India*, 14.1.20., p. 5.
14. Bidyut Chakraborty, p. 38.
15. Truth and non-violence are considered to be the two aspects of one activity.

## REFERENCES

Bhattacharya, Buddhadeva. *Evolution of Political Philosophy of Gandhi.* Calcutta. Calcutta Book House, 1989.

________. "Gandhi's Political Thought". In Krishna Roy. *(ed) Political Philosophy East and West.* New Delhi; Jadavpur University Calcutta in collaboration with Allied Publishers limited, 2003.

________. *"Gandhi's concept of freedom: People's Swaraj."* In S.C. Biswas (ed) *Gandhi Theory and Practice Social Impact and Contemporary Relevance.* Indian Institute of advanced study. Along with K.P. Bagchi and Company, 1969.

________. "Ramrajya". In S.C.Biswas (ed). *Gandhi Theory and Practice Social Impact and Contemporary Relevance,* Indian Institute of Advanced Study. Along with K.P.Bagchi and Company, 1969.

Chakraborty, Bidyut. *Social and Political Thought of Mahatma Gandhi.* New York. Routledge Publication, 2006.

Gandhi.M.K.*Hind Swaraj or Indian Home Rule.* Ahmedabad Navjivan Publishing House, 1938.

Naess, Arne. "Can violence lead to Non-Violence? Gandhi's Point of View". In Sibnarayan Ray (ed.) *Gandhi Gandhism and Our times,* Calcutta, Renaissance Publication, 2003.

Narayan, Shriman. (ed.) *The Selected Works of Mahatma Gandhi.* Ahmedabad: Navjivan Publishing House, 1968.

Parekh, Bikhu. *Gandhi: A Very Short Introduction.* Oxford University Press, 1997.

# Index

□□□